W9-DJN-590

TELEVISION—RADIO—FILM
FOR   CHURCHMEN

TELEVISION—RADIO—FILM FOR CHURCHMEN

B. F. JACKSON, JR., EDITOR

VOLUME 2

COMMUNICATION FOR CHURCHMEN SERIES

WITHDRAWN
by Unity Library

UNITY SCHOOL LIBRARY
Unity Village
Lee's Summit, Missouri 64063

ABINGDON PRESS
NASHVILLE & NEW YORK

TELEVISION—RADIO—FILM FOR CHURCHMEN

Copyright © 1969 by Abingdon Press

All rights in this book are reserved.
No part of the book may be reproduced in any
manner whatsoever without written permission of
the publishers except brief quotations embodied in
critical articles or reviews. For information address
Abingdon Press, Nashville, Tennessee.

Standard Book Number: 687-42694-4

Library of Congress Catalog Card Number: 68-28826

Parts of Chapter I, Part III, "Introduction to the
Medium of Film," by John M. Culkin are from his
article, "The Name of the Game Is Excitement."
© 1967 by The New York Times Company. Reprinted by permission.

Parts of Chapter II, Part III, "Notes on McLuhan,"
by John M. Culkin, are from his article "A School-
man's Guide to Marshall McLuhan," from the March
18, 1967, issue of *Saturday Review*. Copyright 1967
Saturday Review, Inc.

Chapter V, Part III, "Perspectives on War: A
Teaching Unit of Films," is reprinted from *Media
and Methods,* December, 1967. Copyright 1967
Media and Methods Institute.

The quotation from "The Incarnate One" by Edwin Muir is used by permission of Oxford University Press, publishers of *Collected Poems* by Edwin Muir, and Faber and Faber, publishers of
Collected Poems 1921-1958 by Edwin Muir.

SET UP, PRINTED, AND BOUND BY THE
PARTHENON PRESS, AT NASHVILLE,
TENNESSEE, UNITED STATES OF AMERICA

BV
4319
.J3
T4
1969

TO DICK AND STEVE

INTRODUCTION

Communication and learning are recognized as subjects of importance to a growing number of churchmen. Many employed and volunteer leaders in the three major faiths in the United States believe the future of the church depends on its ability and willingness to make a better use of the processes of communication and learning.

To churchmen interested in these subjects there are a number of kinds of questions which arise.

What is communication and how does it take place? What is learning and how is it achieved? What is the place of the media such as print, film, television, radio, audio tape, and video tape? In what way is oral communication different from written communication? And what about nonverbal communication?

How can the most appropriate medium or combination of media be chosen for a particular task? What resource is best for achieving maximum learning in a given area?

What place do facilities have in learning and communication? What kinds of rooms and buildings are needed to provide the climate in which effective learning and communication take place? What audiovisual equipment and other electronic facilities are desirable for the church?

What are the technological revolution, the communication revolution, and the revolution in instructional technology? Are all these part of the same revolution? Do these movements have significance for the church?

How can churchmen better understand the secular media? Is dialogue with film and television programs something for the church to consider? Is there a need for serious study of film as an art form?

What are the theological implications of all of these considerations?

The general view of the series is that no single communication medium or learning resource is better than another. Rather, all communication media and learning resources have value; and, if the unique capabilities of each are understood, the value will be even greater. A renewed stress on individual differences in people calls attention to the desirability of having a variety of learning resources and communication media with which to reach these quite different persons.

The books in this series are written for the churchmen who desire to make a serious study of communication and learning with the hope that a better understanding of these processes will be of help to them and their church.

The writers for the four volumes have had extensive training and experience in the fields of communication and learning. Five of the group are laymen and eight are clergymen. An editorial committee of three have given continuous assistance to the editor. Appreciation is expressed to Donald P. Ely, William F. Fore, and Walter N. Vernon for this help.

B. F. JACKSON, JR.

CONTENTS

PART THREE FILM AND THE CHURCH
JOHN M. CULKIN, S.J.

PART I

TELEVISION
AND
THE CHURCH

PETER A. H. MEGGS

INTRODUCTION

Late in the summer of 1968, some twenty years after network television began to change the face of America more radically than any of us have been able to assess, a television critic wrote these words in a mass-circulation magazine:

Back when TV was just starting out, the churches did a lot of talking about how they were going to use the new medium to reach new millions in new ways. It was all talk. I do not count the little "message" playlets shown just after dawn on Sunday or the local sustaining telecasts of local matins. And aside from these there is nothing. Organized religion has left us to get our notions of moral anguish from newscasters, our best understanding of courage from Czech citizens and the mothers of black school children in New Orleans, our best examples of passionate selflessness from the secretaries-general of the U.N., our clearest images of grace in pain from the widows of assassins' victims and our ideas of ethical rigor from Dr. Spock. As for The Word itself. . . . Well, here is Billy Graham, with $1,000,000 to spend (he hopes to recover it from sales of a booklet called *Billy Graham Answers Your Questions,* a reputation as a showman, and the courage of his convictions).[1]

[1] Barbara Moon in her column "Of Late," *Toronto Star Weekly Magazine,* September 14, 1968.

Courtesy of the Canadian
Broadcasting Corporation

Peter Meggs

Anyone who has labored over the past few years in the name of Jesus Christ in the television medium—that most potent of primary mission areas for the church in our age—would be tempted to speak or write for days on every phrase of that statement. Indeed it would make an excellent springboard for a conference of Christian communicators. Mercifully it is not possible to undertake such a task in the pages of this section, but it may be useful to examine a few of the questions raised by the columnist. Questions like: Why was such a column considered worthwhile in the first place? How does the columnist see the role and impact of television within our society? Why should the church be interested in an "entertainment" medium? And how? What is meant by "religious television"?

Is a Billy Graham rally a valid expression of the gospel on television, or does the medium change the old-time message? Is theology (a *word* about *God*) present in a secular newscast, a documentary, or a situation comedy?

These and related questions will form the basis of our discussion in what follows. And since the very act of committing words to paper represents a process of selection, it is perhaps only fair to mention at the outset the context in which they are written.

They express the point of view of a Canadian who, because the natural lines of communication in North America run north and south, bringing the blessing and curse of American television to every Canadian hearth, cannot really be considered an outsider. Still there is such a thing as Canadian television, which has distinguished itself from time to time in the world scene, and no excuse will be attempted for bringing into the discussion such light as may be found in it. Canadian television networks carry material from other countries as well, and the experience of other parts of the world in coping with the medium must be considered, particularly as it applies to Christian communication.

It must be remembered too that television is moving at high speed into the age of space communications and the global village. If you

14

read these pages in 1975, global television may be as common as short-wave radio. But obsolescence in the mass media cannot be helped. And if we anticipate it, we may be able to reduce it a little with a few predictions.

Two further comments are in order before we turn to the task at hand. These pages are written out of an ecumenical experience in broadcasting. They represent a conviction that denominational broadcasting is as wasteful and self-defeating as denominationalism itself in our time. And they represent not a catalog of the entire religious television scene but a selection of those experiments which appear to the writer to reflect most clearly the new theological understanding of television which shows most promise in claiming the medium for Christ.

I.   THE WORLD AND TELEVISION

It was the best of times, it was the worst of times, it was the age of wisdom, it was the age of foolishness, it was the epoch of belief, it was the epoch of incredulity, it was the season of Light, it was the season of Darkness, it was the spring of hope, it was the winter of despair, we had everything before us, we had nothing before us, we were all going direct to Heaven, we were all going direct the other way.[1]

Why   should a newspaper columnist be concerned with religious television? Why should there be such a thing as religious television with which to be concerned? If the religious exercise is about God and the world in which we live, then Christians who hold such a belief can perhaps only understand the answers to such questions by taking stock of the kind of God they worship and serve in the context of the world which shapes their destiny. And that world includes and is largely formed by the mass media, particularly television. Television has been with us for a quarter-century. But religious television, according to our columnist, is still not airborne. The columnist is not clear about the term religious television. Neither are the churches, if one glances at the program schedules of our networks and local

[1] Charles Dickens, *A Tale of Two Cities*.

17

stations, where religion seems to mean many different things. And if either the columnist or the churches had made their peace with the words "religious" and "secular," another dimension would be injected into the discussion; one could then consider whether or not a good number of what we have called secular programs are not profoundly religious in their communication. The same criteria could then be applied to so-called religious programs to see whether indeed they convey in any sense an element of growth for the spirit of man. Religious television, however listed in the papers, should say something about the world and its Creator. And it would seem logical early in this discussion to look briefly at our understanding of God and his relationship to a world which sees itself most frequently and extensively through a screen in the home.

God as Communicator

In the earliest pages of Genesis, God appears as a communicating being. He has something urgent to say to his people. He has given them freedom and power—freedom to respond to him or not and power over all living creatures. Almost never does he communicate with his children verbally; he withdraws and leaves them responsible for their own actions. He is a hidden God anxious to be found but never imposing his presence upon his world. His communication is usually visual and frequently so obvious and commonplace that his children need assistance in even "hearing" him. When he calls Abraham out of the security of Ur, he speaks through ordinary men whom, because of their message, Abraham describes as angels. To Jeremiah the truth about God and his world is revealed in such everyday objects as an almond branch and a boiling pot. For Amos it is a basket of summer fruit. For Ezekiel it is more difficult; he has to wade through a storm cloud, the figure of four strange creatures with wheels beside them, the likeness of a firmament above their heads and the outline of a throne above the firmament, and finally the human form seated upon the throne. And even then there is some doubt in Ezekiel's mind because of the surrounding glory as to whether this was really just a rainbow. The best description he can give it is "the appearance of the likeness of the glory of the Lord." And the question God puts to his prophets as he speaks to them in an everyday context is, "What do you see?" To see, for the Hebrew, was to believe, to have some intelligible view of the world and the import of world events and to see within this context a caring God.

If we look further into the New Testament, we find Paul puzzled by the same brightness that overwhelmed Ezekiel, not able to see God except through the command to change the direction of his life. On Calvary itself the crowd stood silent in expectation when the cry went up from the cross; they listened for a verbal response from God to his dying Son. And there was silence on Calvary as God refused to speak. Still, in retrospect the disciples were able to see in every movement and action that day outside Jerusalem the mighty hand of God, not giving instructions verbally but communicating through even the most debased matter of his creation.

The Old Testament picture of God is of a creator who cares and communicates his care not *in* the world but *through* it. In the Incarnation itself we see the ultimate in God's communication as he immerses himself bodily in human affairs. And for the Hebrew this intervention in the unexpected corners of life meant that there was always more to life than met the eye. Life revealed God if the heart were tuned to his voice. Centuries later God did not speak out of a thunderclap to Abraham Lincoln about slaves; he showed him one being sold.

The hiddenness of God itself says something about him. It speaks of his care for man's freedom. A God who hovered constantly over man would rob him of his independence and his ability not to return God's love. As Bishop Simon Phipps has put it: "The ability to say 'I will' is the ultimate expression of freedom; it can only be said by someone who can also say 'I won't.' And the latter can never be said by a slave." [2] Yet while he remains hidden to preserve man's freedom, he speaks nonverbally through the world he has created. And he speaks reconciliation. In calling Abraham out of security he demonstrated not only that he was a God to be trusted but that he was a God of change. Time and again he insists that his children move forward into the unknown without any institutional supports. Time and again it is in order that his children may bring about reconciliation between man and man. So the word "God," which was never spoken or written by the early Hebrews, becomes synonymous with function; God is discovered in what he does. Any Jewish child asking his mother about God in pre-Christian days, as today, would be told that he led the people of Israel out of captivity.

[2] *God on Monday* (London: Hodder & Stoughton, 1966), p. 13.

What comes through the pages of the Bible is a God who communicates his will while remaining hidden, giving his children the opportunity to accept or reject his proposals, whose message is one of reconciliation not between his people and the rest of the world but among all men equally. And this reconciliation is necessary because within one world we live in a number of individual worlds shaped by culture, language, belief, vocation, race, economic status, and so on. Recognizing the consummate difficulties encountered in reconciling the "subworlds," God becomes man himself to show us how to live authentically in all our worlds together. He does so in the life of Jesus, which transcends structures, institutions, and all the man-made worlds and reestablishes communication among men. The lesson of the entire Jesus episode in history is that greater love flowing out of better communication really is possible among men.

The World—God's Communication Medium

Thus to understand God, man must understand the world he created and creates. Perhaps one of the clearest outlines of man's comprehension of the world he inhabits is that traced by the Dutch sociologist and lay theologian, C. A. van Peursen and quoted by Harvey Cox in *The Secular City*.[3]

According to van Peursen the question of our age seems to be whether or not the concept of God works, whether God himself is at work, rather than whether he merely exists. Gone is the God of fear, the God of the gaps called in to explain the inexplicable, the *deus ex machina* with all the answers, the God who lived in one compartment after another of life down through the ages until twentieth-century Christians attempted to box him in on Sundays. Gone are all these Gods who have crept into our churches only to be rejected by maturing teen-agers. What remains is the God who cared enough that he sent his Son to live and teach and die and rise again, to live so successfully that he belonged to all the world and not to any one part alone.

All biblical evidence points to one world, not two. Nowhere do we find God's people called to withdraw from the world; they are saved in it, not from it. And the separation of spiritual and secular, church and world or church and state, is as artificial as the attempt to separate soul and body. It has produced, among other things, the Sunday-

---

[3] (New York: Macmillan, 1965), pp. 64-66.

morning ghetto for religious television simply because we have been willing to see it that way. The story told of Horst Symanowski, the great industrial chaplain in Germany, illustrates the twisted, unbiblical theology we have been content to live with in this century. Symanowski was entertaining a young American clergyman also associated with industrial missions. When Symanowski inquired just what it was the young clergyman did, he replied, "I am taking God into industry."

"Oh," replied Symanowski, "how very interesting for him. And tell me, where will you be taking him next?"

Churches that insist it is their task to take God into his own world via religious television will continue to inherit the early hours of Sunday to do so. They deserve no better. Churches that imply by their theology that they have a monopoly on God and must introduce him to his own world perpetuate the two-world theory. To sum up, then, the biblical view of the world, we turn again to Simon Phipps:

> The biblical outline of the world shows it as man's means of freedom, God's means of communication, and man's means of response. The Christian detail, filling in the outline, shows us man being free in order to love, shows us God communicating to him the call to love, and in Jesus, the Nature of Love, the cost of Love and the triumph of Love, so that man may dare to make his response of Love. And it all happens in one secular world, in Hebrew history, under Pontius Pilate, in countless Christian lives and in countless Christian decisions, between the "In" tray and the "Out" tray, day by day.[4]

The World Today—New Factors

But there are characteristics of the twentieth century which must be added to our biblical outline of the world. The most obvious for us in our age is that of rapid change. For the medieval church the world was relatively static. Today the rate of change increases with each dramatic new development, as we shall see more graphically when we come to look at one aspect of that change, the communications revolution.

Another characteristic of the secular world as we experience it is the factor of power structures. The secular world behaves collectively in our time, giving each man at least one dominant set of loyalties during his life, probably to his employer. And employers are now collective entities. And whereas the churches in England attempted to make Christians of industrial men, they failed entirely to make Christianity

[4] Phipps, God on Monday, p. 35.

industrial. In other words, the churches failed to recognize that power structures were emerging which would eventually command so much of an individual's time that there would be none left for the church, and the church as a power structure would dissolve. The mass media represent just such a modern power structure. They cannot be claimed for Christ, summed up in Christ, to use Paul's phrase, as long as the churches fail to respond to the opportunity to indicate the presence of the holy within them. The mood for the church in our time must not be the imperative "thou shalt," hurled at the world as a tablet of stone; instead, the mood, particularly in all efforts within the mass media, must be the indicative. We are not called to introduce a forgotten God; we must indicate the presence of a living God of change who is in the vanguard of all world change "making all things new."

Perhaps the most relevant insight of the New Testament for our age is Jesus' own involvement with power structures. The pattern he applies to them is one which is reviving the dialogue between Christian and nonbeliever in the freedom movements throughout the world. That insight is servanthood. Throughout his ministry Jesus is concerned as much with the proper use of collective power as he is with infusing the individual with new life. The final struggle of his life is with the religious and political power structures of his time.

On the cross he shows up the power structures for the paper tigers they really are and overpowers power itself with gentleness, forgiveness, and love. His intent is not to destroy them but to rob them of their power and make them servants of man again. The restless movement of men today out of one power structure and into another, the organized protest movement, the struggle on our campuses, all may be manifestations of the human desire to return structures to their proper role as servants. For whenever a structure—including the church—moves from a position of service to one of domination, then its very power becomes a kind of god, and a movement begins to return it to servanthood once more.

Change has become revolution in almost every sphere of life. But the outcome hardly looks like bliss. The Secretary-General of the United Nations has reminded the Western nations of their one great development of the past few decades: the ability to create their own resources. It is this factor that threatens to widen the gulf each year between the wealthy nations and those who depend upon them. The "have" nations find themselves with an economy based on what Robert Theobald has called "compulsive consumption." In order to keep our economy

22

healthy we must market our resources. And we assist this enterprise partly through communication. An advertising executive, writing recently in *Broadcasting* magazine, said:

> I anticipate a considerable increase in advertising in the next ten years in quantity and quality. And commercial television will play the leading role because the public needs it and wants it. The next ten years in broadcasting will include a growing-up of the communications industry with liberalization of archaic censorships and puritanic restrictions. Telstar and the newer satellites [will bring] our world closer together. Network radio or television will have rate-cards with special rate extensions for spot commercial or program coverage in South America, Europe, Africa.[5]

Again the former norms are shattered as new responsibilities fight for recognition, new moral values try to emerge. At the Fourth Assembly of the World Council of Churches in Uppsala, British economist Barbara Ward warned that because "we live in a physical and material planetary society which has been created by economic and political drives and not by moral purposes, and the consequences of this economic and material unity confront us with the necessity of devising the moral policies for the rest of the century and beyond, I take it to be the central problem that we are united, but not yet in a neighbourhood." [6]

Or is it the other way around; are we tied by the new media into a neighborhood without unity? In what has become known as the "revolution of rising expectations" we have all looked in on our own affluence. Our affluence can now be seen by those who do not share it. And they expect their share, one way or another, now. With the median age dropping in most parts of the world, the present state of uneasiness is likely to extend over the next several decades.

The Communications Revolution

Behind and informing all revolutionary developments in our time is the communications revolution, a revolution that is itself paradoxical. For while it informs us immediately of each development in our world as it happens, it also deprives us of the thinking time we used to enjoy. This is particularly true in the area of value judgments. When the Pope issued his *Humanae Vitae* encyclical on July 29, 1968,

[5] Ben Bliss, "The Next Decade: An Era of Innovation and Giant Steps Forward," *Broadcasting*, May 2, 1966.

[6] *The Rich Nations and the Poor Nations* (New York: W. W. Norton, 1962).

he was moved to comment within the text of the document itself that the new teaching would be hard to accept because of "voices contrary to the voice of the Church which are amplified by the modern means of propaganda." Within twenty-four hours the news media had provided him with massive and disquieting feedback. The Gallup Poll later revealed that more people were aware of the Pope's encyclical than had known about any other issue discussed in a survey by the company. Several weeks later Cardinal O'Boyle of Washington took to television to announce his unswerving support for the encyclical and penalties for clergy who did not conform. Once again the media provided instant global coverage, and instant reaction. There can be little doubt that the media themselves in this instance influenced the decisions of Catholic bishops in other countries who made much more liberal statements following the television appearance of Cardinal O'Boyle. Half a century ago there was time for church teaching to filter down and become interpreted over a long period. With global television that luxury is gone, not only for the church but for all of society. We are indeed in the midst of what Marshall McLuhan has termed an "all-at-once world." Dramatic developments in every sphere of life are pressing in and demanding decision all at once and being reported to us all at once. And television, in informing us about them, is also forming us. In order to assess the impact of television upon us and explore its role in bringing about the kind of human communication which will contribute to communion among men as the Christian understands it, we must look at its rapid development and present structural status. But first let us get a fix once more on the Christian understanding of communication.

We have seen that God's purpose in communicating is to establish a loving community on earth, free to grasp the opportunity to serve and love one another and to enjoy Him forever. God's communication technique is nonverbal. Through God's communication man finds self-awareness. He discovers that he is a being in the world, a bodily person with individual rights and freedom to choose. The Hebrew contribution restores man's worldliness; the separation of soul and body is a later Greek concept. The Old Testament also reveals man as a "being-with-others"; Adam is completed in community with Eve. Society is seen not as a group of individuals but as a people with a common purpose, responsible for one another and for the maintenance and development of the group. The group is not static. Abraham is called out with his people to begin a pilgrimage of change

24

with no immediate destination, a pilgrimage toward a wider community and mutual responsibility and interdependence. The pilgrimage is toward a promise, not a fixed geographic or mental state. Throughout this pilgrimage God's communication sustains man and makes possible all human communication. It is always an enabling communication: Jesus on the Emmaus road begins the dialogue by listening, by asking a simple question about current events in the world. He then attempts to place these events in the context of the pilgrimage of man. When words fail, he turns to a visual act, a common secular act, the breaking of bread; and recognition and communication take place. Finally we discover ourselves as beings-in-responsibility. Just as God handed over creation to Adam to name and care for, so Jesus promises his disciples they will perform greater acts than he. Man is to assume responsibility in God's world. The entire Jesus episode indicates the possibility of greater communication; his final act in the Upper Room indicates that the end of the pilgrimage is the kind of communication which sees and cares for all men as brothers. Thus the end of communication is the receiver; by concentrating on him and his need we shall be able to encode our love for him in terms that all men can recognize.

Postbiblical insights into the quest for human communication must take into account the development of God's communicating gifts to man and man's response to them. In considering them we can only touch them in a cursory way and only as a backdrop for a better understanding of television and the church today.

Television—A Return to the Visual

For many young people it is impossible to recall a time when television was not. For such people, involved as they are in the production of films in school, linked to the world of reality en route to and from school by the ubiquitous transistor radio, and participating in popular culture through records, tape recorders and video tape recorders, television is simply another part of their environment. As McLuhan says, they "wear it," spending more time in front of the screen than at any other occupation apart from eating and sleeping. As long ago as 1964, U.S. television households averaged six hours and four minutes of television viewing per day. John M. Culkin has pointed out that

by the time the average American student graduates from high school today, he has watched more than 15,000 hours of television and seen more than 500 films. . . . During this same period, this average student has attended school

25

five hours a day, 180 days a year, for 12 years, to produce a total of 10,800 hours of school time. Only sleeping surpasses television as the top time-consumer. . . . [Thus the need for] the development of habits of perception, analysis, judgment, and selectivity that are capable of processing the relentless input of such data.[7]

In North America today there are more radios than people, more television sets than bathtubs. In Japan fewer than 10 percent of the homes have flush sanitation and only 35 percent have running water, but 75 percent of all Japanese homes have television sets, and some 98 percent of the Japanese people have television available to them. Five years ago there was no television in Africa. Two years later thirteen African countries had their own television systems, and the number had risen beyond twenty the following year. A recent survey by churches in the Philippines revealed that 90 percent of the college graduates interviewed listened to the radio daily; only 30 percent had read anything beyond what was required by their work during the same period. The reading figure declined in direct ratio to the educational level of those interviewed, but in no instance did the survey discover anyone who had not listened regularly to radio.

Africa and the Philippines and many other areas which contain portions of the world's 700 million illiterates may overleap the scribal or print era. It is now commonplace for a world event via satellite to enjoy an audience around the globe in excess of one billion viewers. And the world is rapidly approaching saturation coverage by television similar to that of shortwave radio, with the same choice and availability. More people than ever before receive the majority of their images of the world through mass media, and that communication is constant. It is not like church attendance—once a week; it is continuous. And it is a conditioning experience.

Communication in the Church

With such an explosive development in a mere quarter-century it is difficult to place television in the context of an evolving pattern of communication in the world. For historical reasons it has been particularly hard for the church to assimilate the electronic revolution. In the early days of Christianity flexibility of communication was natural in the church's approach to the world. When monologue preaching failed for Paul in Ephesus, he simply hired a hall and

[7] "Great Movies Go to School," *Saturday Review*, July 16, 1966, p. 52.

brought smaller groups into dialogue. "This went on for two years, with the result that the whole population of the province of Asia, both Jews and pagans, heard the word of the Lord." [8] Preaching for Paul and his colleagues meant argument, discussion, feedback. They were conscious, with the writer of Hebrews, that "at various times in the past and in *various different ways,* God spoke to our ancestors." [9] That meant that the setting for proclamation could and did become the secular world, and any means at all was open to them for communicating the good news. When the common language of the world was Greek, the church used it. Later the Fathers of the church used Latin for the same reason. The Mass was never rigid in the early centuries of the church because people were not literate; they couldn't follow prayer books. The nonverbal action of the Mass itself communicated its message. In the Middle Ages, as illiteracy persisted, traveling miracle and mystery plays depicted the salvation story. Palestrina adapted drinking songs to bring the music of the common man into the church. Stone carvings and wall paintings in the medieval cathedrals and parish churches combined with words and music to provide a multimedia experience of the gospel truth.

With the invention of movable type, the church, still in a position of power in the world, adapted easily. The first book to use the new invention was a psalter published in Mainz in 1475; papal documents began to appear in print in the next few years. So committed was the church to this new form of communication that it eventually became a form of idolatry. There is a certain permanence about the printed word which has a natural and unique importance in the total mass media pattern. But print had a steady and permeating growth for almost 500 years before the beginning of the electronic revolution—long enough for the church to fall victim to its permanence. Once committed to paper, the words of Cranmer's first Anglican prayer book in 1549 changed very slightly throughout the Anglican Communion, even to the present day.

Edwin Muir sums up the church's slavish adherence to the printed word in the second stanza of his poem "The Incarnate One":

> The Word made flesh here is made word again,
> A word made word in flourish and arrogant crook.
> See there King Calvin with iron pen,
> And God three angry letters in a book,

[8] Acts 19:10, NEB.
[9] Heb. 1:1, Jerusalem Bible (italics mine).

> And there the logical hook
> On which the Mystery is impaled and bent
> Into an ideological instrument.[10]

More serious for the church, however, was its devotion to the cult of literacy which attached itself to the development of the print medium. The Reformation emphasis on the printed word and the expunging from church life of all forms of art and music dealt Christian communication a blow from which it is only now beginning to recover. Too often the gospel became an intellectual exercise, as the exclusive use of print and words spoken from print moved it into the realm of literacy. In the eighteenth century when Robert Raikes in England began his Sunday schools, his concern was to help children become literate in order that they might have intelligible access to the Scriptures.

In light of this long and pervasive development of print within the church it is understandable that Christians scarcely noticed the promise of that faint signal which reached Cornwall, England, from Marconi in Newfoundland on December 12, 1901, and which heralded the age of broadcasting.[11] Still and moving photography were under development by this time, and the stage was set for their collaboration in what was later to be known as television. Baird's experiments with television in England in the 1920s are regarded as the first serious attempts to explore the possibilities of moving visual images across great distances. Just as World War I interrupted the development of network radio, World War II delayed the wide application of the television principle. It was only after the second war that television became a reality in America.

Two observations can be made regarding this very cursory review of mass-media development. The first is that the sudden appearance of film and broadcasting on the world scene almost simultaneously within the present century produced an integration of the arts unparalleled since the medieval synthesis of sculpture, architecture, painting, and music that gave Europe its Gothic cathedrals. The electronic revolution has produced the multimedia environment in which we live, move, and have our being today. Second, this revolution arrived at a period when the church was no longer the power structure it had

---

[10] *Collected Poems* (2nd ed.; New York: Oxford University Press, 1965).

[11] In 1894 Robert S. Hyer, at Southwestern University, Georgetown, Texas, transmitted messages for over one mile; Marconi accomplished the same in 1895. (Raytt Brown, *The Man I Knew* [Salado, Tex.: Anson Jones Press, 1957], p. 37.)

been at the time of the print revolution, and the church was unable to fully use its potential.

The church's relationship with the new media is discussed elsewhere in these pages. It would be well to note at this point, however, that the church has had its visionaries in this as in other fields. It is now more than a decade since Hans-Ruedi Weber of the World Council of Churches returned from missionary work in Indonesia and urged upon the churches the priority of audiovisual resources in Christian education. His small book *Communication of the Gospel to Illiterates*

Courtesy of the Broadcasting and Film Commission
Bishop John A. T. Robinson joins the panel on *Lamp unto My Feet*

anticipates many of the later prophecies of Marshall McLuhan regarding audiovisual impact. And Bishop John A. T. Robinson, of *Honest to God* fame, has long berated the churches for their slavish adherence to monologue preaching which is "six feet above contradiction."

The Immediate Future

The most significant insight of the church's few prophets of the new media is that no one medium should be studied in isolation since they all complement one another. But there can be no doubt that television holds a key spot in the future of media generally, a fact which predictions about television seem to confirm. Television may soon be the nerve center of many other activities besides viewing television programs. It will be capable of video-recording programs automatically and playing tapes at home from video-tape libraries, e.g. a home instruction course on video tape. (Does such a development say anything to churches that continue to provide Christian education only to those willing to attend church? Could a series on Christian ethics be produced for viewing by families in the home?)

So significant is the worldwide potential of television that it is given space of its own in these pages. Perhaps, however, it is apparent that the electronic revolution is far from over and its impact on society is merely beginning. As it develops, so will the revolution in paperback books (of all books ever published 75 percent have been published in the past ten years) ; in radio (which has settled into a new role) ; in film (376 million people around the world see a film each week) ; in the press, the poster, and the audiovisual tools for education. Can the churches see what the author of Hebrews said about the various different times and ways of God's communication as having meaning in the communications revolution? Dare the churches overlook the possibility that God has chosen these new ways for his communicating purpose? If they do so, it will be at their own peril, according to Marshall McLuhan, because the environments set up by different media are not just "containers" for people; they are processes which shape people. Such influence is deterministic only if ignored.

What's Happening to Us

We have looked at what television can and probably will do *for* us. What can be said at this stage of its development about what it is doing *to* us? Unfortunately opinions swing from one extreme to another. S. I. Hayakawa of San Francisco State College told the American Psychological Association at its meeting in 1968 that television is a powerful sorcerer that can bewitch children into becoming alienated and rebellious dropouts or even drug addicts. Not only do the programs shape values for young people; the commercials also have their effect: "There is a simple, instant solution to all problems. Acid indigestion can be relieved with Alka-Seltzer; unpopularity can be overcome by buying a new Mustang, which will transform you into an instant Casanova." [12] Hayakawa extends his criticism as far as the documentary, which he says offers neat wrap-ups of complex events. But his real quarrel is with the inability of television to speak of a world of reality: "The world makes all sorts of demands the television set never told you about, such as study, patience, hard work, and a long apprenticeship in a trade or profession, before you may enjoy what the world has to offer." [13] He contends that young people, deprived of their childhood television "trips," begin to turn-on in other ways, hoping for the same kind of escape. Not willing to condemn television outright, Hayakawa points out that we are all "simply victims of the unforeseen circumstances of a technological revolution." [14]

Until recently few counterbalancing viewpoints to this opinion of Hayakawa's were available. One study, based on considerable research almost a decade ago in the United States and Britain, argued that there was little evidence that television shaped values and opinions; rather it tended to reinforce those already present. It wisely recognized that television was not an isolated factor in human communication but that viewers brought to the screen a set of values informed by experience, culture, and a host of other factors including other communications media.

One can assume that since television is a talked-about medium it works some kind of collective influence. People do share their television experiences. And there is probably a link between the Chinese Communist posters which depict Americans toting six-guns and wearing stetsons and the exposure of *Bonanza* to 350 million viewers around the world every week. NBC markets its programs (many of which are westerns) in seventy countries. While there is a growing body of research concerning viewing habits among social and economic groups, there is very little evidence as yet as to the impact of television on a whole culture or people. And there is a need, which should be brought out by the churches, for more competent and widespread investigation into the effects of television. In the United States the Broadcasting and Film Commission of the National Council of Churches has stressed the urgency of establishing communications research units in American

[12] *Time*, September 13, 1968, p. 96.
[13] *Ibid.*
[14] *Ibid.*

31

universities, and Canadian churches have pressed the government in resolutions for the same kind of action. Much more needs to be done. Research into individual viewing habits is growing and should be made known throughout the churches. Events of the past few years in the United States are raising the issue of television content as never before. Three assassinations, race riots, student unrest, and political conventions have all given the American people a sense of sickness and despair. And they are becoming aware that their understanding of these events comes to them through television. The President's Commission on Civil Disorders has included a study of the role of television in the entire violent American scene. Concern for television, then, has increased in the light of concern for the bewildering sociological picture in the United States.

Prominent among the many concerns about television is the credibility gap; can television really be believed? The former governor of Alabama was not considered a serious threat in the 1968 presidential race until television, unable to consider the other candidates colorful enough for sustained coverage, turned its attention to George Wallace. And George Wallace was ready. He encouraged the cameras to pick up the hecklers and protesters as part of his campaign. Cameramen themselves had learned techniques which told a story without words. (A camera focused on a vocal group singing "America" suddenly notices a burly state trooper out of focus in the background. A slight zoom in and the hostile-looking trooper is caught fullface in the lens with the strains of "America" in the background. Not a word of commentary is spoken, or needed.)

In an article in the *Wall Street Journal* David R. Boldt takes us beyond the editorial capacity of the lens itself to the actual manipulation of the lens:

Frank McGee of NBC was covering the 1964 Republican Convention when he spotted a civil rights demonstrator who had prostrated herself on the convention floor. He told the control-room director, who replied it would be a few minutes before they could put him on the air. Mr. McGee then asked the woman how long she planned to lie there. She raised her head slightly and asked, "How long would you like?" [15]

In a recent investigation of television's impact on crowds, Sophie Burnham in *New York* magazine recorded the account of a fire in

[15] *Wall Street Journal,* December 20, 1967, p. 16.

32

Washington following the death of Martin Luther King, Jr. This is how Philip Geyelin of the *Washington Post* reported the event as he saw it:

It was not a racial thing; it was more like an event, or a curiosity, and the tension was in wondering whether the cascades of water could shield the nearby houses.

Then it happened. Abruptly from a group of fire-watchers perched on an embankment there was a flurry of fist-shaking and a cacophany of angry cries —"Honky" and "You killed Martin Luther King" and "You killed our soul brother." And every bit of it was aimed at the funnel-shaped snout of a television camera; the medium had moved in. As the cameraman panned across the crowd, it was as if some unseen director was calling out cues. It was Instant Showbiz. . . . If somewhere, in somebody's living room that evening a few feet of film showed a small group of Negroes shouting racist epithets in defiance of Whitey and in deference to Dr. King, then the Medium *was* indeed the message. And the message was not the way it was.[16]

Between 1964 and 1968 the power of television had been recognized by the average man, particularly the young. Stories turned up in the press of protesters telephoning the television station before arranging the time of a march in order to make certain of coverage by the medium. It is interesting to note in this regard that it is the young (under thirty-five) who have seen the power of direct involvement in television. In 1966 the major news item for Canadians was the threat that the management of the Canadian Broadcasting Corporation would remove from the air an enormously popular and adventurous public affairs program called *This Hour Has Seven Days*. The controversy centered around the inclusion by the producers of certain material which the CBC management thought unsuitable. The young producers stated their case bluntly, on television. Their elders on the management side replied solemnly on each occasion in the press. The producers received over 7,000 letters of support in two weeks; the management received 272 letters, many of them supporting the producers. It is worth considering the impact for the future of the discovery by large numbers of people that change can be effected through television. When corn farmers advanced in tractors on Parliament Hill in Ottawa in October, 1968, their cause was hopeless. But they received full television treatment; and their spokesman expressed himself in an interview as totally satisfied: "We made our point."

Television at present is selective. The type of programming is it-

[16] *Washington Post*, September 16, 1968.

self selective. The producers and cameramen select the shots, making yet another editorial decision. Viewers watch in conditions of interruption, and the chance of distortion grows. A growing number of people with a variety of motives are learning how to manipulate the medium by "arranging" demonstrations. Producers have more than once been accused of "arranging" events themselves in order to have the jump on competing stations and networks. And none of these factors can be resolved by legislation alone; indeed legislation is not likely to help very much.

In addition to a particular slant that might be taken in an individual event there is a feeling among many observers that the media have developed a general approach to all news which is best described by Beland H. Honderich, publisher of the *Toronto Star:*

Is not the concept of news too narrowly confined to these four C's: conflict, controversy, contradiction, and condemnation? We are zealous to report nearly everything that is going wrong in our society, in our country and in the world—and we should, because it is only by exposure and public debate that ills and injustices can be corrected. But we are not nearly so keen to discover and report the things that are going right. We should remember that people are at least as inclined to follow good examples as they are to be warned by bad ones.[17]

Honderich extended his criticism of the press to radio and television, which he said were "falling even farther short of their best potentialities in news and public affairs broadcasting. They have subordinated program content and scheduling to the selling of goods." [18]

The effective control in mass media, particularly television, rests not with the publisher or program management. In the last analysis it resides with the producer and performer. Standards of production can be laid down by the management, but they can never fully cover the situation. It remains for the producer to select what the viewer will receive. And broadcasting, in America, like the press, has yet to decide what constitutes a well-trained producer in the context of the new technology. Much of the training of current television personnel has been either on the job or in how-to courses. And despite the large number of communications schools in the United States, too few are yet concentrating on the "why" of broadcasting, the place of television within the whole social structure.

[17] *Toronto Star,* August 24, 1968.
[18] *Ibid.*

Since there is a tendency in television for staff to work under pressure without relation, often, to other groups in society, they run the danger of becoming superficial. With television's commitment to short material which must be intelligible to a broad spectrum of people, the danger of oversimplifying issues grows. Working conditions within the medium do not often promote an open dialogue between management and producers on common goals.

Joseph Kraft, in an article from Washington, adds another dimension to the problem. He points out that most personnel within the communications media come from white, middle-class America, whose work naturally shows a bias in favor of young people, minority groups, and political candidates who appeal to them and show up well on television. They tend, as well, he contends, to favor celebrities above ordinary people: "There is no . . . press interest in ordinary things done by ordinary Americans." [19]

Kraft agrees that producers' interest in Negroes and young people is natural, not merely because these groups create much of the news these days but because their sympathies lie with such groups as a result of their own background and age. He concludes that "the press is not the public. Between the news media and middle America there is an imperfect relation, a lack of touch, a disharmony";[20] the media should try to regain contact with all Americans.

In those examples, and they are too few, where churches have organized conferences between television producers and church representatives to discuss the difficult areas of responsibility, bias, and what Honderich calls "the things that are going right," the industry has responded positively. It must be remembered that little attention has been given within the television industry to such discussion between production crews and their seniors. Churches are able to provide facilities removed from the pressures of the studio where producers, management, and church communicators can relax and explore the questions that beset television. It is a catalytic role for the church which is usually welcomed by the industry. It must be done in complete openness with the churches assuming their proper role of listening and not preaching. It should be a learning experience for the churches as well as for the industry and can provide a vital facility which until now has not been present.

[19] *Toronto Star,* September 4, 1968.
[20] *Ibid.*

Children and Violence

It would be misleading to infer from what has just been said that all knowledge of television and its impact lies in the future. Far more information is available to us than is being applied in program decisions. A pioneer in the study of television's effect on children, Hilde Himmelweit of the University of London discovered almost a decade ago that "it is not so much the program content but the camera play that causes fear. The moment you show children close-ups of emotional expressions of anxiety and tension . . . then the child responds to this rather than to the number of people dead or injured." [21] In 1962 Dr. Himmelweit revisited the scene of her earlier research to test changes in television effects after the medium had become established in England. She discovered that children's viewing hours had grown, but television occupied no more central a place in their lives than it had five years previously. She found again a direct relationship between viewing habits and intelligence. The more able the child, the less he viewed, the brighter ones reaching saturation earlier. Heavier viewers tended to be less selective.

Taking up Dr. Himmelweit's work and other research, J. D. Halloran of the Centre for Mass Communication Research at Leicester University reported in 1965:

We know that children of high levels of aggression are especially attracted to violent programs on television. If television now feeds, rather than reduces children's aggressive tendencies and if it gives them hints as to how to take out aggression with fists, knives or guns, then an opportunity may come to use those weapons at a moment when they are angry. We assume that this does not happen often because social norms teach them not to behave in such a way. But certainly there is little to make us believe that violent programs on television *reduce* the likelihood of violence in real life.[22]

Kenneth Cox of the Federal Communications Commission voices the same warning in *Variety:*

There are no doubt many causes for the increasing violence which seems to characterize our national life. But unless and until it can be demonstrated that television's continual depiction of violence does not contribute materially

---

[21] "The Effects of Television on Children," a report delivered to the Academy of Television Arts and Sciences, 1959.

[22] *The Effects of Mass Communication with Special Reference to Television* (Leicester: Leicester University Press, 1964), p. 24.

to this problem it seems to me that responsible broadcasters will want to take whatever steps they can to minimize risks in this sensitive area.[23]

Halloran is insistent that television must only be considered in the wider context of the social communication process. He stresses that wherever the relevant areas of development (social, moral, spiritual, cultural, etc.) have been adequately covered in a child's experience by such forces as family, school, church, and community, the influence of television is lessened. Where values have not been instilled through these other facets of the socialization process, television will play a more significant role. Thus competent study of the television medium must take into account the insights of other disciplines concerned with human development. He warns against studies of school television that do not first consider the role of the school in society, and against studying television's impact on young people without first studying young people and how they perceive reality.

Television research has revealed that the visual medium has rearranged rather than replaced other activities. Books are still read as before but different kinds of books. Taking his stories from the new medium, the child seeks out other kinds of books that add to his inventory of information rather than provide a story line. Studies show that children tend to watch the same shows as their parents and stay up later to do so. But young people have their own favorites as well, according to a survey conducted by the Home Testing Institute in the United States which indicated that viewers in the 12-34 age group identified with a group of television stars quite different from their elders. The young people accepted newer performers and Negro stars far more readily than did their parents. The generation gap showed in the fact that there was almost no overlap in preferences of the younger and older viewers.

Given the choice, children seem to prefer fantasy rather than reality in their television fare. But since less than 10 percent of television programming is oriented toward real-life situations, it is difficult to measure the possible effects of reality programs.

Thus we can begin to distinguish some of the impact of television on the young. The effects will vary with age, sex, intelligence, parents' attitudes and viewing habits, the amount and kind of viewing available, competing interests and activities, other media, and social and emotional characteristics of individual children. Since all these factors

[23] September 11, 1968.

of development are interrelated, churches cannot overlook the effects of television on growth any more than they can ignore slums, race, family unity, and similar concerns which are traditionally considered areas of concern and ministry.

There can be little doubt, from research that is available, that television is shaping the way we live and interact in the world. Its effects are cumulative and should be studied over a long period of time in conjunction with other areas of socialization. Television research needs to be thorough and far more widespread than at present and its results made available to program producers regularly. Churches have a responsibility to support such research just as they undergird other projects in social improvement.

Theology in Entertainment

But there are other opportunities for the churches. Writing in *Children and TV*, Ralph Garry outlines the role of television in the home and concludes with some thoughts for parents:

If they take the time to view and discuss programs with children; make their beliefs and attitudes clear in words and deeds; and maintain healthy emotional relationships with children, any disturbing or damaging effects of television on children, by and large, are likely to be minimized. . . . In its present form, television appears to have little positive impact. Where it has negative impact, it represents a default also of particular parents.[24]

It is difficult to agree entirely with the statement that "in its present form, television appears to have little positive impact" unless it is considered as a reminder that television has yet to realize its real potential. Each of us could quote examples of the positive values of television from his own experience. One that has meaning in the writer's experience concerns our second boy, who is very much a child of television. Some years ago, when he was six, we were living in a particularly cold part of Canada. It was January and his pet hamster, which had been a Christmas gift, expired suddenly. While he went through his brief period of mourning, his parents wrestled with the problem of a decent burial for a hamster at a time when there was a thick covering of snow on the ground. Eventually our son emerged from his room with a report that the heavy snow of that winter had driven snowy owls down from the north in search of food in the larger

[24] (Washington: Association for Childhood Education International, 1967).

centers. He had learned this from a newscast on television. From a television program for children he had learned that owls feed on rodents; it was part of a natural cycle. And since the hamster was a rodent it was a shame to waste him in burial. Instead we all went out, at his instructions, and placed the small body on the limb of an elm tree for the next snow owl that happened by. There were several lessons in all this. Television had given the child accurate and helpful information. This information had helped him to distinguish between the death of an animal and that of a human; his mourning was real, but it was in perspective. It would be inaccurate to suggest that he had applied values learned only from television; but television had enabled him to work out a situation in concert with information learned in the home and elsewhere.

If parents will study television with their children and if churches will assist and encourage them in doing so, they will find a new and valuable experience. Not only will they find in secular programming an oportunity to add to their knowledge; they will find much of what they watch to have profound theological content. They will find, for example, that a program like *Star Trek* is not as fanciful as it first appears. The universe explored by the heroic Captain Kirk, the enigmatic Vulcan named Spock, and the resourceful Dr. McCoy, is filled with "spiritual influences." The basic theme of each program is the battle between good and evil and the growth of the characters as they distinguish between these forces. Those who prosper are those who love and create. War is deplored because it denies life. Frequent references are made to man's bloody history on earth, how close he has often come to self-annihilation, and how long it has taken to begin to discover the governing power of love and creativity.

Each episode of *Get Smart* gives food for theological thought. The war here is even more explicit in contemporary terms; it is between Control and Kaos. Smart himself is the personification of all of us as we rather stupidly attempt to cope with technological society. Even the much-maligned *Beverly Hillbillies* is a weekly study in frustrated communication. Each plot derives its comedy from a misunderstanding born of inadequate communication. Television commercials provide the stuff of sermons and discussion as well as raising, day in and day out, the question of real versus phony values. And since television enjoys the most faithful attention of any medium in our midst, its entire schedule becomes identifiable to almost everyone and provides unparalleled opportunities for Christian consideration.

One further comment only can be selected from the many aspects of television's hold over our age. It is the element of enjoyment. Television has provided the individual with a choice that is unique in his experience. In his working life he responds to the demands of institutions; with the dial of his television set he is free to make choices that are entirely his own. In a fascinating study of this aspect of television William Stephenson distinguishes between two principles at work in society.[25] The first he calls *social control* and indicates its operation in our inner beliefs and values. It gives us our religious belief, political bias, and status in life. People who live in a certain area are likely to have the same religion, customs, cultures, and system of government. Social control is something we embrace as a means of conserving things the way we have known them through common agreement. His second principle, called *convergent selectivity,* operates quite differently. It introduces new ways of doing things, new customs, new ways of pleasing ourselves and freeing ourselves from social control. It is characterized by excitement, individuality, and wishes and wants. Advertising, according to Stephenson, like the mass media themselves, represents the principle of convergent selectivity since each of us is free to try out a certain toothpaste, like a certain program, change an attitude into something innovative, and so on. Convergent selectivity is seen to be at odds with social control since the choice is wide and changing daily and since each man decides for himself.

In Stephenson's distinction of principles we can discern the generation gap, the tension in the churches and in society generally. It may also help us to see television as a dominant force on the side of convergent selectivity. It is a principle that must be recognized. In our discussion of the future of television we touch on space communications satellites and the possibility of an open society. The hope for such a global village concept through television is not determined by the hardware alone; it grows out of the possibility opened up in our imagination by television itself. It must be remembered in all our thinking about television that people watch it because they like it.

T. S. Eliot has called it "a medium of entertainment which permits millions of people to listen to the same joke at the same time, and yet remain lonesome."

[25] *The Play Theory of Mass Communication* (Chicago: University of Chicago Press, 1967).

We will certainly want to encourage television producers to provide people with the opportunity to want something better than they now experience. But television is enjoyment. We may try to ridicule it with epithets like "idiot box," "boob tube," and "animated wallpaper"; we may even be senseless enough not to watch it. But the churches which have only begun to see television as something more than an entertainment appended to the real life of man, must understand television as a serious gift from God to his children. And they must learn to admit that the sheer joy television affords God's children in a world of trial and fear is part of his will for those he loves.

II.   THE CHURCH AND THE MEDIA

Recently William F. Fore, executive director of the Broadcasting and Film Commission of the National Council of Churches, said, "Our job is to provide, through communication, a voice for the voiceless, a sensitizing agent for the insensible, a picture of the real world for the escapist, a view of God at work within His World and His Church."

Having touched upon a biblical concept of Christian communication and the nature of television today, we may find it useful to examine the changing understanding within the churches themselves of the role of media within society. Perhaps this will assist us in projecting the relationship between church and media in the dramatic developments which confront television in the immediate future. Since that relationship began with the invasion of the churches by the media themselves, we turn now to the question of the initial extension of the gospel through broadcast church services.

One of the continuing debates among church communicators concerns the question of the validity and effect of broadcast church services. One can trace its history clearly through forty-five years of religious broadcasting, and still it persists unresolved. And while very few of today's champions of the broadcast of church services would wish

Courtesy of the Broadcasting and Film Commission
Newsman Ed Newman (left) consults with guest Ashley Montague (right) and co-workers for a filming of *Frontiers of Faith*

to settle for the exclusive use of the air-waves in this way, a large number would give it primary consideration. The arguments pro and con for church services as primary vehicles for broadcasting the gospel are well illustrated by two recent documents.

The first is an article by Clarence W. Jones entitled "Television Airwaves—Evangelism's Frontier" [1] in which the author enthusiastically reports the impact of the Billy Graham 1967 All-Britain Crusade which originated from Earl's Court stadium in London. Here was a gigantic church service piped out of London to twenty-five other cities by television. The entire TV technical facilities of the British post office system plus all the Eidophore cameras in Europe were mobilized for what Jones calls "evangelism-in-width." Two and

[1] *Christianity Today*, September 13, 1968, p. 3.

one-half times as many people attended the crusade via the relay system as attended the stadium service itself. Follow-up surveys indicated that 24,163 inquiries made decisions via TV meetings compared with 9,830 at Earl's Court.

In the case of the Billy Graham crusades, as with most Protestant services on the air, the presentation relies heavily on preaching. And the preaching, even though it frequently shows itself familiar with camera technique, is identical with in-church preaching. In other words, it is an extension of the church sanctuary, a televised church service in which the audience is permitted to drop in and observe the proceedings and hopefully to participate. There is very little in the way of competent research to support Jones's claim (about the Graham crusade): "Across the nation, viewers felt themselves a part of the crusade." Most of the decisions came out of the "television meetings" in which people gathered together around a giant screen, an experience which provided at least an element of live fellowship. As to the impact on the ordinary viewer alone in his living room, little is known.

The other side of the church-service telecast question is put by Albert van den Heuvel, director of communications for the World Council of Churches. In an address to the Saint Paul University School of Communications in Ottawa, to which we shall return, van den Heuvel expresses his doubt about the efficacy of such broadcasts: "I do not think that ubiquity implies necessarily the blessing of the Holy Spirit." [2] Van den Heuvel supports in general the position of Hans-Jurgen Schultz, director of religious broadcasting for Suddeutcher Rundfunk in West Germany, who told a group of Christian broadcasters recently:

The church walls hermetically separate the two worlds (sacred and secular) from each other. When the church walls become transparent (by means of the camera and the microphone), this is bound to change what goes on inside them. The language of the church service must either stay inside the walls or be completely changed. To broadcast it into homes, schools or cars is not mission but enlarged self-assertion.

Television, a new medium with new possibilities, a truly biblical medium, has returned the potential of the visual into our midst as never before. Most early television was essentially visual radio; it

[2] "Is It Proper for Churches to Broadcast Their Liturgy?" *Christian Communications*, April, 1968, p. 2.

merely added a picture to existing production patterns. But the arts moved in rapidly with drama, dance, movement.

It was at this point that the church was most helpless. Drama, dance, and movement had long ago been banished from the church. Church worship, particularly among Protestants, had become static, tied to the printed word and its proclamation from a fixed and remote point. Hardly the stuff of television. Furthermore the new medium, as it introduced all the visual arts, became suddenly extremely complex. And the churches which had relied down through the years on clerics to handle their radio programs faced another dilemma. Some clergy had managed to master the art of the microphone with some degree of competence. Very few were free to concentrate on radio apart from other pastoral duties. But the complexities of television demanded full-time training and application.

The churches had little alternative but to invite cameras into churches as they had done with radio. Occasionally a cleric can still be seen sitting rigidly before a single camera with closing prayers and comments at the sign-off of a television station. But generally the churches retreated within their own walls. The costs of television were terrifying, the time for preparation impossible. Above all, the churches had surrendered the medium to the secular world with a sense of relief; after all it was show business.

It must be noted in passing that the early years of television coincided with the beginnings of theological ferment within the churches, and the church service represented the one kind of television for the church which assured protection from curious outsiders who in other forms of broadcasting would be tempted to open up with church leaders issues they were not often prepared to discuss.

So the evolution of the telecast church service has been a natural one. Why should theologians like Albert van den Heuvel and Hans-Jurgen Schultz now denounce such Christian broadcasting as a hindrance to the proclamation of the gospel in our time? The answer must be found in the development of both the media and the churches.

A Secular Medium

The first reason critics of church telecasts give for their opposition is a theological one. If God "so loved the world," not just the church, then what right does the church have to monopolize time on public airwaves for the dissemination of the church's point of view? By their very nature the mass media are public media; they are for all men, and anyone can tune in at any time and hope to find relaxation, enlighten-ment, or a sharing of public concerns. By their very nature the mass media are popular; the average man can hope to tune in and partici-pate in what is going on. What right does a particular group have to time on the air to promote what appears to many as "enlarged self-assertion"?

In response it is often argued that Christian communicators are correct to assume that the Christian portion of the audience has a right to be served, just as the medium serves other minorities like sports enthusiasts, opera fans, and so on. Still the agnostic may argue that the Christian enterprise on the air excludes him by its in-group approach; that he is not antagonistic to what is being presented but he just can't "get aboard." This is probably the reason he rejects church services—the language and behavior are just too specialized. And if the Christian purpose is to communicate the good news, then surely the needs and the position of the agnostic viewer must be con-sidered. Otherwise television is simply used to undergird the faith rather than to reach out in mission to those who do not share Christian convictions. One could also question whether, indeed, it even under-girds the faith if Christian viewers who have experienced the live fellowship of the worshiping community must settle for the role of spectator through television.

The first argument against church telecasts, then, springs from a concern for the non-Christian. Christian communicators might well consider the recent difficulties in the Netherlands which saw atheists and agnostics protesting vigorously the special status given to Chris-tian worship on their TV screens every Sunday morning. An excerpt from one letter to a Dutch paper will illustrate the feeling of many:

I was sick and tired of being spoken about as a man who is lost because I don't accept Christian gods; to hear that my life is meaningless, without hope, and that I am judged and am on my way to eternal perdition. I do not want my children to be designated as non-Christians, as if they are non-entities. This arrogant mixture of quasi-moral judgment and self-centred claims of excellence ought to be banned from public life lest we, who do not believe, lose our friendship for our Christian fellowmen and our respect for a tradition which has been influential in the history of our country.[3]

This letter is reminiscent of a remark by a teen-ager on a BBC

[3] From *Christian Communications,* April, 1965.

television panel: "I wouldn't say I don't believe in the existence of a Supreme Being . . . but I don't know how people can really believe that a Being that made this universe so intricate, so unbelievable, . . . sent down a child who was crucified and then rose from the dead and went up to heaven on a cloud—you know, this is so crummy, isn't it?"

The crisis of belief in our midst is too broad a subject for these pages. But it is worth noting, in passing, a few key phrases in the above quotes. Phrases like "friendship for our Christian fellowmen," "influential in the history of our country." Here is a meeting point for believer and unbeliever, a mutual respect. It is surely what God intends through his mass media, the development of the dialogue of mutual concern. And to place obstacles in the way of such development is a matter which should give Christians pause. The Christian, above anyone else, should respect the rules of communication. And the first of these is to examine honestly the needs of the receiver,

Courtesy of the Broadcasting and Film Commission
Paul Deats, Jr., D. Williams McClurken, and Ralph Nader discuss environmental pollution on *Frontiers of Faith*

who in the case of Christian broadcasting must be the nonbeliever as well as the believer. And a further consideration might well be the facility for the nonbeliever to "turn off" the church and the good news it should bear to all men.

While there is little in the way of serious research to indicate the kinds of religious topics viewers prefer, Christian producers are beginning to discern a growing interest in Christian ethics which would parallel the theological emphasis on involvement. In February, 1968, the BFC of the National Council of Churches began distributing scripts of its NBC *Frontier of Faith* series. The response was light until the program began a series under the title *Moral Implications of the Future*. From a dozen or so requests a week the demand grew to almost a thousand. One program in the series, on "Crisis in the Nation," with James Baldwin, brought 5,000 requests. Through television both Christian and non-Christian look for a Christian response to secular issues. The opportunities for the churches lie not only in their own productions but in the context of secular interview and panel shows as well.

So far we have considered the atheist and agnostic viewer only in the Western context. Some Asian countries have excluded Christian worship from the air rather than discriminate against other groups. And even in Western countries the Sunday worship telecast is being gradually excluded except in cases where it means considerable income for the station. The reason given by most broadcasters is that the church service deals a heavy blow to ratings and affects programs on either side of the Christian broadcast. Instead the time is being sold for light-entertainment spot-carriers.

Viewing Conditions

Christian broadcasters should consider, too, the conditions under which their service is viewed. In recent years, as the TV set has gone underground into the family room or upstairs into the bedroom, family viewing has become more exceptional than in the past. The new locations for the set have in some cases resulted in greater concentration for smaller groupings. But in all cases the set is still in the midst of the busyness of family activity with conversation in the room competing with the message on the screen. Some feel that television's inability to dominate completely in the home can be attributed to screen size. A 23-inch Billy Graham is just not big enough to command

Courtesy of the Broadcasting and Film Commission
Alva I. Cox interviews Chief S. O. Adebo, ambassador from Nigeria to the UN, on *Frontiers of Faith*

attention. He is smaller than life, and a different communication re-sults from this exposure than results from his exposure live in the stadium or life-size on a large screen. The Vatican Council's Consti-tution on the Liturgy implies concern for this point: "The broad-casting and televising of sacred rites must be done with discretion and dignity, under the guidance the responsibility of a suitable per-son appointed for this office by the bishops. This is especially im-portant when the service in question is the Mass." [4]

We will return to the question of discretion and dignity in the origination of the service telecast. But the question of dignity and discretion in the viewing area should not be overlooked. If we are concerned by the possibility that the telecast be received in the home as it would be in a church, then we are back to the dilemma the Dean

[4] *Ibid.*

49

of Westminster faced in 1923 concerning a church service being received in pubs by men wearing hats. It is well to remember that we have no control over the viewing conditions and to program accordingly.

Standards of Presentation

Tied to the questions of our intended audience and the viewing conditions is the quality of the presentation itself. Put briefly, the question is simply whether or not it is well done. Most programs on television, regardless of their content, generally display the American genius for superb techniques in production. In secular programs the

Courtesy of Washington Cathedral
Rehearsal for a Christmas program in Washington Cathedral

participants are usually carefully selected for their ability to communicate, their competence in their own field, and are rehearsed until the entire production is cohesive and commanding. It is at this very point that Christian services tend to fall down, either on or off the air.

Roman Catholic Masses are still mumbled in an almost unintelligible garble. Protestant ministers still read very badly. Choirs tend to be underrehearsed. And the entire service tends to be a series of isolated elements rather than a moving unity. It becomes the familiar "hymn sandwich." It would be interesting to conduct surveys among those who have given up churchgoing in the past five years. It may well be that as many have left as a result of boring services as have rejected the church over theological issues.

Liturgical renewal in all churches raises the question of what is being communicated and how. Even Christians, apparently, are not sure what the traditional service is supposed to communicate and are beginning to ask questions. New forms of the liturgy and church services which have a better chance of communicating with the outsider

Courtesy of Washington Cathedral
Cameras focus on the sanctuary of Washington Cathedral during a Christmas telecast

generally are emerging. And the outsider, incidentally, is not merely the nonbeliever but anyone outside the particular denomination being telecast. Who, outside the Roman Catholic, Lutheran, or Episcopal traditions, would grasp the meaning of the priest's gestures at the

51

Mass? It is doubtful if many outside the Protestant tradition would be interested in a twenty-minute television address based on a Bible which is seldom read.

The Problem of Language

The matter of standards relates directly to that of language. If a nonbeliever or a Christian of another denomination cannot cope with the language of a telecast, he will feel excluded and tune himself out. Traditional versions of the Bible simply do not communicate meaning to many people in the twentieth century. Furthermore, they deny the infinite care with which Jesus himself communicated meaning to his audiences. So great was his concern for the receiver that he chose the most common tongue of his society. Sixteenth-century English belonged quite naturally in sixteenth-century England. But the change even in that language can be seen in the span of Shakespeare's plays. Only in the church did the language of this period become ossified. Today in many parts of the church there is a kind of idolatry attached to Elizabethan English, and we find it hard to imagine that it never had the sanction of the man Jesus, who never heard it spoken. The writer has experienced difficulties with theological students on this point. One student in a seminar could accept the phrase "great with child" but could not bring himself to read aloud the synonym "pregnant" as it appears in the New English Bible. "Great with child" had about it an aura of sanctity through its association with the mother of Jesus, whereas "pregnant" was a secular word which contained for him none of the mystery of the Elizabethan term. It is easy to see just how difficult it is to shape a contemporary theology when the sense of mystery cannot be found in modern language.

Since language is a vehicle for meaning, it must be accepted that meaning can change as the language takes a different shape. What meaning can be assumed for the modern teen-ager who hears the following words:

If the ministration of death, written and engraven in stones, was glorious, so that the children of Israel could not stedfastly behold the face of Moses for the glory of his countenance; which glory was to be done away: how shall not the ministration of the spirit be rather glorious? For if the ministration of condemnation be glory, much more doth the ministration of righteousness exceed in glory.[5]

[5] II Cor. 3:7-9, KJV.

Here the biblical passage is not only heavy with phrases like "minis-tration of condemnation" and "ministration of righteousness" which are unfamiliar in today's everyday vocabulary, but the entire passage demands an understanding of the early pilgrimage of the people of Israel. It is common for Christians to employ such words as redemp-tion, atonement, oblation, and memorial as though everyone under-stood their meaning when in fact they carry concepts which need translation and interpretation before they can begin to convey mean-ing even within the church. To use them on the public airwaves is to imply to the average viewer that the church really does not care whether or not he understands.

The story is told of missionaries in Madagascar who preached the concept of the Christ as the Lamb of God, a phrase which assumes an understanding of ancient Hebrew sacrifice. When the natives in-sisted that a hatred of sheep was inbred in their culture and asked per-mission to translate the phrase "O Calf of God," the missionaries re-fused on the assumption that with patience the biblical phrase could be accepted. Twenty-five years later they were depressed about the apparent failure of their mission.

Visual Language

Language is important. And it is equally important to understand that a new visual language is possible in television which would have delighted the heart of the teacher from Nazareth who employed the visual wherever possible. Parables are word pictures. Jesus took the ordinary events of life and drew pictures which would so involve his audience that the individual could find in them his own meaning. Such is the power of the visual that Jesus refused to attach his own meaning to the story. The visual speaks for itself, and its message is found in freedom by each person in the audience. The visual language of television is seldom exploited by church broadcasters, who prefer instead to depend upon the power of the words and actions of the service. Jesus said very little about the lilies of the field or the tribute money with Caesar's image; he focused attention on the visual and let it assist his intention.

A recent experiment with a televised church service on a Canadian network demonstrated the potential of the visual. Behind the altar three screens carried film and slides. Two additional slide projectors played images on four more screens near the chancel steps. Through-

Courtesy of the Canadian Broadcasting Corporation
The liturgy in a multimedia telecast from St. Thomas' Anglican Church, Toronto

out the service images of the world in all its agony and joy followed one another on all screens simultaneously. The television cameras followed the action on the screens as much as the action of the liturgy itself, using the words of the service to complement the action on the screens. Prayers were selected to strengthen the visual elements of the telecast. The sermon was a twelve-minute missionary film showing poverty in Asia. The entire telecast was directed at the viewing audience rather than the congregation in the church. The congregation found themselves caught up in the meaning and impact of the liturgy in a new way. The critical decision about target audience was carefully considered in this telecast; clergy and producers *had* looked at the possibility of communicating to over 300,000 viewers and gave this audience priority over the congregation in the church. They had also considered the needs of that viewing audience and had shaped language and action and pictures in a way that would speak to that audience.

The problem of the visual becomes most acute in the reformed tradition, which depends so heavily on the spoken word and a minimum of artistic or architectural embellishment. Perhaps the best indication of the problem is seen in the camera almost desperately panning up and down a stained glass window during the sermon or a long prayer. When a telecast ceases to be visually attractive, it loses its impact and its audience. This should not rule out the possibility of telecasting the less-liturgical services. Most producers are more than willing to cooperate in the selection of still photographs, graphics, and film to illustrate points in a sermon and give it a new dimension for the church congregation as well as the viewer at home.

Exposing Theology

Whenever the television camera is brought into the setting of church worship, it is as critical of the action as it is in any form of broadcasting. We have mentioned the need for updated language, a high standard of performance, a critical analysis of the intended audience and how to speak to it. Having considered all these factors, we find that the most important remains. It is the power of television to expose an outdated theology. Between the funeral of the late President John F. Kennedy and that of his brother Robert, a good deal of change took place in the language and liturgy of the Roman Catholic Church. In the case of each funeral an excellent commentary was provided with the picture. But in the case of Senator Kennedy's funeral the updated language served to lay bare before us a theology which still contained the medieval emphasis on death rather than the hope of resurrection. In all our broadcast services we shall be made increasingly aware of the overriding need to speak clearly of a God of love and forgiveness. Television in a church service setting will reveal, as no other medium can, the inadequacies of our theology for today. It is a one-way communication in this context, and the need to be clear about our God-language is acute.

How, then, do we respond to the insistence by some theologians that church worship should not be telecast? We have tried to contend that no church telecast should be directed only at a minority of Christians, even a minority of "shut-in" Christians. Formerly a case might have been made for preserving church services intact as an opportunity for worship for the shut-in, even in the face of such an experience's being devoid of true Christian involvement and fellowship. But with the development of the tape recorder, and more recently the domestic video tape recorder at a reasonable price, broadcasters may well be justified in suggesting that groups of Christians from a congregation should take recorded services from their church to homes and institutions. This would release broadcast time for other purposes and maintain a vital link between the shut-in and his worshiping community.

Perhaps it is too early to agree entirely with the communications theologians who would banish worship services from the air. The promise of a revised liturgy and a greater concern for the medium itself may hold out the possibility of demonstrating worship in a way that is helpful even to the outsider in relating this activity of the spirit to everyday life and concerns. If television forces us to look at our worship as the outsider does as we put his interests ahead of all others, the exercise could be extremely beneficial to the churches. And the broadcasters may be willing to cooperate if we demonstrate a concern for their audience. Nevertheless, the broadcaster himself will probably introduce one more factor which will put the churches to the test in this whole question.

The Ecumenical Dimension

That factor is the ecumenical dimension. As we have said, broadcasting is in essence ecumenical: it is for the world. In denominational broadcasting the churches do not appear to share that concern for the world. And it is on the level of worship itself that the churches have been most reluctant to express their unity. Whatever may have been the success of denominational efforts in television in the past, the future for religious television lies in ecumenical approaches to the medium. This does not suggest that individual denominations may not find it efficient to devote their attention to a particular area of work. But the project must bear the support and approval of a number of churches if we hope to have it taken seriously by the broadcaster.

The real answer to the church telecast resides, in the last analysis, beyond the sphere of the liturgical. Perhaps the best criterion which can be applied is that of the most effective use of broadcast time. There can be little doubt that church services of community and national significance, such as the Kennedy funerals and the funeral of Martin Luther King, Jr., will always be carried voluntarily by television. These are occasions in which the viewer outside the church can find identification and, hopefully, strength from Christian worship. And the churches must stand ready in these troubled times to speak the hope of the gospel to the hearts of Americans who cannot always cope with Christian language and imagery of death and resurrection. These are supreme opportunities for the church, not to project an image but to be God's servant to his people in binding up wounds and bringing hope where only despair seems to reign.

It is not unreasonable to suggest that churches should survey seriously the kinds of services they may be called upon to provide in times of national crisis and to have personnel and resources available to secular broadcasters just as secular broadcasters themselves make such preparations. But having said and done all these things, the churches must become honest with themselves regarding the most effective use of air time now existing.

Priorities in Christian Broadcasting

Having in mind what was said earlier about television's capacity to provide the viewer with a wider choice than ever before, we must reexamine our motives for religious telecasting. Do we wish to win converts to a particular point of view? Do we wish to stem the exodus from our churches and encourage people, through television, to fill our pews again? Do we wish to project an image of the church as a group of individuals committed to prayer and worship? The broadcast advertiser is clear about his motives. And he constantly checks his success with competent research. The churches, on the other hand, have never seen the need to assign the comparatively large sums of money required to assess the impact of religious television. Too often they program on the basis of what they think is good for people.

But the gospel itself is a choice. The Christian communicator's task is to present the good news within the hearing of modern man in such a way that it becomes intelligible to him in its implications. In order for it to become intelligible it must be clear to him in terms of the secular world in which he works out his destiny and salvation. The choice must then be left with the viewer. The Christian communicator must resist at all costs the temptation to indulge in special pleading or "hard sell"; the critically honest camera will reveal the shallowness of such panic evangelism.

During a rehearsal break in a television studio recently, the writer

57

encountered a stagehand whose dilemma illustrates the need for Christian broadcasters to assess the potential of television for expressing to modern man the insights of Christianity. The man admitted that his daughter never attended church because it bored her. He and his wife avoided Sunday worship for the same reason. But he was aware that his family needed direction in interpreting and dealing with the problems of daily living. He was also conscious that there was a Christian view of the world and of man's purpose within it. His question was how to discover and possess a continuing Christian commentary and understanding of the world—which he could weigh and either accept or reject—without going to church. And his dilemma may well be the church's opportunity in the days ahead—to reach out through television to God's people where they are with the choice of the gospel.

The question, then, in religious television is not does it preach or persuade but does it provide a living option in a dying world. Does the program inform in an open-ended way, or does it insist on the acceptance of its point of view? Is there within the program a recognizable healing and reconciling element? As long as we are unwilling to come to grips within the church with the relationship between worship practices and the daily work situation of the average person, we should be just as reluctant to involve the viewer in our confusion. The writer recalls being present as a lay broadcaster a few years ago at the opening of a television repeater station in the Upper Ottawa Valley. It was interesting to watch the officiating priest, in those pre-Vatican II days, feverishly attempting to translate into Latin such technical terms as transistors and resistors. The area was largely French-speaking, and this was to be the first French-language service available from the CBC French network in Quebec. It was an exciting occasion for the whole community. In the midst of blessing the room and its equipment, an operation which was extended unduly by the difficult Latin, the relentless second hand reached the top of the clock and the new network service burst into the room. The priest's voice was swamped by the spontaneous cheers and even tears of the little group of civic dignitaries who, for the first time, were linked with their own people in the province of Quebec by television. It was embarrassing to see the irrelevant liturgical practice of the church overwhelmed by the secular, and yet it was theologically sound. The church had totally misunderstood the occasion and in applying to it the only language the church could muster had missed the real joy of the presence of Christ in the event itself. The cheers of the group in that small room celebrated Christ's presence in a way that escaped the church entirely.

Liturgy in the Secular

Space does not permit an adequate exploration of the secular setting of worship practices. This is a task the churches themselves must undertake if worship is to be meaningful even to the most devout of Christians in our age. But it is surely time to recognize the presence of the liturgical in the heart of secular movements in the world. A significant proportion of modern pop music is liturgical, and some churches are recognizing its application to church worship as Palestrina adapted drinking songs to the Mass in his day. There is nothing in life which is worthwhile that does not take on a liturgical form. A mother talking to her child, children playing games in the street, the complexities of a business conference, all are liturgical acts. The civil rights movement in the United States with its chants, processions, hymns, leaders, responses, repetition, and storytelling, is a profoundly liturgical movement. Modern drama is liturgical: the tramps in *Waiting for Godot* express their anxieties and huddle together in a modern version of the handshake of peace as they await their salvation. In the closing scenes of *Who's Afraid of Virginia Woolf* the dawn begins to illuminate the room of despair where the principal characters have lived out their hell during the night. Significantly they do not walk out into the sunlight of the campus but turn together back into the room itself where forgiveness and redemption must begin. Their action is liturgical; it is totally concerned with sin and redemption, the very staff of liturgy. The parish priest who laments the fact that his people turn out in far greater numbers to the parish barbecue than to receive "spiritual food" on Sundays fails to recognize the eucharistic quality of the barbecue itself.

Until this truth about liturgy and worship becomes clear in the churches we should be careful about televising our current understanding of worship. Otherwise we shall continue to promote the separation of religion and life in the Sunday morning ghetto. Albert van den Heuvel's point should be taken seriously, whether or not the churches can at present agree with him:

Within the media there is much worship because man is a worshipping animal. He may worship the wrong things. He may worship in the wrong way.

59

But he worships. The task of the Christian church is not to insist all the time that he says the Lord's prayer or that he repeats the Apostles' Creed, but to order and guide and help the world celebrate through its proper medium. . . . That is the essential educating task in the world—the church being, in her missionary task, a teacher. In that sense, it seems to me that we would learn a liturgical language for the media which would be a new form of communicating the Gospel and would be infinitely more appropriate and exciting than taking our family worship Sunday after Sunday and prostituting it in a thousand living rooms where my children have no chance to behave as the Second Vatican Council wants them to behave—fully active, fully participating, and with dignity.[6]

And here the matter must rest with the churches themselves. If a new liturgical language is to be learned, it must take into account the new language of television itself. And that requires an approach by the churches to the broadcasters themselves, an approach in humility with its purpose a listening dialogue and its goal a new expression through television of the healing news. In many areas that dialogue has already begun, and we turn now to a survey of a variety of existing formats for religious television which look seriously at what is possible for the churches in the new medium.

New Approaches to Religious Television

There are 5,500,000 people living on the Japanese island of Hokkaido and a television network to serve them. There are also 245 Christian churches on the island with sufficient insight not only to recognize the value of a television ministry but to integrate their TV efforts into a total multimedia expression of the gospel. In 1967 they formed HOREMCO (Hokkaido Radio Evangelism and Mass Communication) and began broadcasting a thirty-minute weekly telecast on the STV network. The program format varies: sometimes a musical group, sometimes a drama or interview, sometimes an examination of a local or world issue in Christian perspective. The Christian dimension is central to the entire multimedia project. It is clear to the viewer that the program's understanding of the world is that of something called the New Testament. At the end of each program viewers are invited to write in for a free copy of the New Testament which has been donated by a Christian living on the island. The Christian's name and address are inscribed in the front of the book, and the inquirer is invited to contact the Christian donor if he wishes

---

[6] "Is It Proper for Churches to Broadcast Their Liturgy?" p. 4.

clarification about any passage or further information about the community of Christians. The initiative rests entirely with the recipient of the New Testament. HOREMCO also has an audiovisual bus which tours the island arranging meetings and introducing people to the gospel through films, filmstrips and slides. Thus the telecast becomes part of a wider thrust, and several media complement one another. Viewers who write in for a New Testament can also enroll in a course in Christian education, and they can become associated with

Courtesy of HOREMCO

With over a million television sets on the island of Hokkaido, there is a set for every five people. The average Japanese family spends about 3½ hours a day watching television.

HOREMCO Friendship Clubs throughout the island. Two Japanese pastors, two missionaries, and six office workers devote full time to the HOREMCO operation, and eight local pastors from five denominations serve part-time in followup counseling through correspondence. A five-minute daily radio broadcast maintains continuity of the HOREMCO purpose throughout the week.

Although mail response increased fivefold in the first year of its mass media operation and 3,000 New Testaments were distributed among the 13,379 correspondents, HOREMCO does not speak of "success" in its reports. Instead it hopes to extend its opportunities for open dialogue with the people of Hokkaido, offering simply the choice of the gospel.

In Quito, Ecuador, some 50,000 viewers each night tune in HCJB-TV the "Window of the Andes," which provides a regular service in cultural, public service, and religious programs. The station is operated by the World Radio Missionary Fellowship. Its viewers are mainly professional and business people who can afford sets and those who view through publicly installed receivers. HCJB-TV's religious programs reflect a strong evangelistic stance. Dialogue is encouraged through open-line sessions with the audience following the evangelist's remarks. Inquirers are encouraged to visit the station for further discussion and free literature. Other cities have asked HCJB-TV to set up repeater stations in their areas, and the Ecuadorian government is reported anxious to collaborate with the station in extending service to the northern parts of the country.

Courtesy of HOREMCO
Timothy Ishikawa of HOREMCO interviews novelist Miura and her husband, both Christians, for a local television production

In the small lumbering town of Terrance in the mountains of northern British Columbia, a group of churches gather at the local TV station to prepare a series of telecasts on issues of local importance.

They have been able to bring labor and management groups together on television when immediate contact seemed impossible. Youth problems in the community have been discussed, as have national and international affairs. The local ministerial group encourages Christian businessmen in the area to provide funds for the series, and when the money runs out so does the series. The format of the program insists on very short opening statements by the participants (who are non-clerical and often non-Christian), and the main portion of each program is given over directly to open-line dialogue.

In Sweden, where a religious telecast will attract 10 percent of the viewing audience (about 600,000 persons), a religious alphabet is presented in word and picture (B is for Babylon, belief, Benjamin, blessing, blood, body, book, bread, etc.). At other times drama will illustrate the lives of national and international personages who are Christian. Programs of community singing command an audience of up to 30 percent. The Swedish Broadcasting Corporation says: "It is part of our policy not to let religion be confined to certain hours. Debates as well as religious news of general interest are handled by the ordinary news service or other appropriate department. We avoid treating religion as something apart from general broadcasting."

In Pittsburgh the Broadcasting Commission of the Greater Pittsburgh Council of Churches video-tapes significant religious and secular telecasts on the new one-inch domestic tape for replay and discussion among study groups throughout the city.

In New York the Broadcasting and Film Commission is at work planning dialogue sessions with prime-time commercial television producers and writers to develop an understanding of the Christian purpose in mass media and a mutual development of responsible broadcasting.

On the shores of Hudson Bay a clergyman attacks the government for its inability to accommodate Indian children in schools near their homes. A church broadcasting officer 600 miles away in a large center places a long-distance call to the clergyman and records a statement on tape for a secular radio newscast later the same day. He then sends the same report to the television network with still photos from church files of the area under discussion as visual backup for the clergyman's voice report.

In Toronto, Canada's most famous atheist is invited to a television studio to discuss his views with an articulate theologian, and the exchange is the coffee-time topic in offices and plants for days.

In Scotland viewers have a choice between hymns from a church or a simulated press conference with the apostle Paul.

In Kansas City a businessman turns on the evening sports, waits through two commercials and then finds that the TV stationbreak is preceded by yet another one-minute message. It is an impressive spot in full color. A sea gull floats overhead, and waves roll in on a beach. Slowly the camera discovers a bottle drifting on the sea with a note inside it. As the lens closes in on the bottle, the message becomes briefly discernible: Keep in circulation the rumor that God is alive. It is one of a series of spots on the same theme produced by the United Presbyterian Church and distributed through the National Council of Churches.

New Discoveries

Such random examples scarcely scratch the surface of the churches' growing involvement with television, but they indicate to some degree the scope and nature of that involvement. Tired of the Sunday ghetto, churches have ventured out into secular broadcasting itself and made a number of interesting discoveries. They have found a welcome they didn't expect in the midst of secular programming. They have learned that the TV schedule is not always filled with commercial spots and that public-service spots produced by churches can find nationwide circulation.

They have seen that involvement in the prime time periods demands of them the same caliber of production as the secular material surrounding their efforts. The churches' social activities in the world have found a place in regular newscasts; no longer is religion a separate compartment of life. In experiments like the Hokkaido telecasts television is seen to be a strong partner in a much wider and more integrated use of a number of media. The language of television begins to be explored as a new and powerful tool in Christian education. Such discoveries, the result of the churches' serious appraisal of the new electronic technology, are developing a partnership between broadcasters and the church which will have far-reaching consequences in the future of the media. In short, it would appear that American churches are beginning to explore the implications of words addressed to them by the General Board of the National Council of Churches as far back as 1960:

The General Board realizes that religious organizations and individual religious broadcasters have been guilty of not using television and radio solely for the public good. There have been occasions when religious groups have put their institutional interests above the public interest. They frequently have failed to give serious attention to their broadcasting opportunities or to allocate sufficient resources to their programs to maintain the standards that, as critics, they demand of secular broadcasters.

The churches should look upon participation in mass communication in much broader terms than they do now. They should take cognizance of the influence the mass media of communication exert upon current issues whose resolution will determine the future of mankind. While the Christian churches of the world have remained committed to face-to-face or printed communication, whole nations, including our own, have made radio and television the dominant means for disseminating information, opinion, and standards of taste. Now the influence of these mass media is being extended to international affairs through rapidly growing interchanges of television and radio programs between nations and by the imminence of world-wide broadcasting by means of satellites.[7]

Courtesy of the Broadcasting and Film Commission

A CBS special from the triennial meeting of the National Council of Churches featuring a discussion with Hubert Humphrey

[7] *The Church and Television and Radio Broadcasting,* a report adopted June 8, 1963.

The New Demands

If the warning of the BFC seems to be heeded in the new involvement of churches with the mass media, there is still no sign of a coordinated strategy among churches in the use of these media. Such a strategy must take into account a number of urgent factors. First, a church's involvement with the media must be seen as a primary area of mission, and a priority must be set upon the potential of this mission. This will mean a realignment of resources, including financial, to meet the high costs of such involvement.

Second, the costs should not be seen merely in terms of production. The need for the future will be for trained personnel. In the past it has been possible to assign church productions to free-lance agencies. Now the media are looking to the churches for consultants. They need specialists in such fields as Christian ethics who are familiar enough with the broadcast media to make almost instant comment on significant newsbreaks. Pressures within the secular media are such that they will depend on church film crews to shoot professional footage of important church activities in the world. And they will need such help on the local as well as the national level.

Third, the churches must respond with competently trained personnel. There are hundreds of American colleges offering academic and technical training in television. Organizations like the BFC and the Roman Catholic NCORT are in a position to advise on the most suitable courses available. Church personnel, both clerical and lay, possessing a theological sensitivity must be freed from other duties to undertake study in mass media. Theological colleges and seminaries must themselves begin to build an understanding of the social impact of mass media into their curricula. At present there are very few seminaries in the United States with such foresight.

Fourth, the churches must assess the kind of training needed by their personnel. A course currently being prepared for clergy-retraining by a number of churches has three main sections: an introduction to consideration of the impact of culture on media and media on culture; a workshop period on radio, TV, and film, in which participants will actually express an aspect of the Christian faith through an original production of their own in one of the media; and lectures on the analysis and utilization of media. No one medium can be studied out of context of the media spectrum. Since secular communications courses do not stress the Christian dimension and application, it will be necessary for churches to develop personnel who can include Christian communication insights into courses for clergy and laity.

Fifth, opportunities must be made frequently for lay conferences on local and regional levels in which mass media are studied as instruments of social formation. The Roman Catholic experiments in many parts of the United States with cine clubs are a promising beginning. Lay people must be trained to explore and discuss the theological dimensions, good and bad, of the constant communications reaching them through media. Young people and children must be shown how to "read" television. Church groups must turn from less relevant activities to regular television viewing followed by Christian discussion of what they see.

Sixth, the churches must press for better criticism of the media by the media themselves. It is traditional for the press to seek out experts to review books and plays in the daily and weekly papers. The television column, on the other hand, if it exists at all in the daily press, is often given to the junior reporter. The number of competent television critics in the United States is infinitesimal compared with the social importance of the medium. Churches should not be content with such a situation; they should confront the media with the need for greatly improved self-analysis.

In order to encourage and advance the question of television criticism awards of excellence might be established in the area of secular programming. At present the Broadcasting and Film Commission grants annual awards for secular films, and the Catholic Association of Broadcasters awards "Gabriels" for excellence in specifically religious broadcasting. The two groups could well consider a joint award for secular television programming. Those who denigrate awards as publicity stunts for churches should study their constructive value. Television awards afford the churches an opportunity to indicate the theological dimension of a series like *The Defenders* or *Star Trek* and other individual programs which assist man in his quest for self-awareness.

Researching the World

Constructive criticism of a medium like television cannot be divorced from the churches' responsibility to establish adequate research facilities to assess man's growth in the present world-situation and to project this assessment into the future. For the most part churches have not developed research units which function for all de-

67

partments of church life together. Television will have just as profound an effect in the future in foreign mission fields as it does in North America. Television research should be available to mission departments of the churches as much as to the social action units at home. Its educational capacities should be known to all whose task it is to shape a strategy for Christian education. And because television is constantly changing and opening up new possibilities for the churches, it will be necessary for those entrusted with television research to develop means of internal communication which will keep other areas of church life aware of its potential.

Failure to provide and maintain such research will simply extend what the BFC Board of Managers described as placing the churches' institutional interests above the public interest. The Stan Freberg radio spots of a few years ago illustrated this problem. Because the churches saw television as merely a sales vehicle rather than a social medium they fell for the Madison Avenue approach and simply attempted to define the product. If the product was salvation, then how did one get the product to the people, how was it to be marketed? And the only answer acceptable to the institution was "by going to church." The communicators themselves were less sure about the validity of this market information and hung all kinds of attractive words around the central message in order to "get . . . people thinking about God." What most people apparently heard was the bit about going to church. In effect the churches had misunderstood the medium; they had sold it short and settled for the electronic billboard.

Freedom and the Institution

The Freberg spots pointed up the churches' basic unwillingness to admit that evangelism was possible outside the church building. They also showed, as have later radio and television spots produced by churches, that Christian vocabulary (which is really jargon to the outsider) is abandoned only slowly and reluctantly by the church. It is well known that the word "rumor" in the United Presbyterian "Keep in circulation the rumor that God is alive" spots caused some anxieties within the institution. It suggested to some within the church that there might be some doubt about a living God. The Freberg spots tested, and found wanting, the churches' confidence to speak about God without mentioning his name, to speak of salvation without insisting on the church as its only vehicle. And the suggestion in some of the spots that the world might end in a nuclear holocaust was heard by many listeners as a kind of threat to drive them back to the church.

It is worth noting here that when such fears are projected in radio and television, they show up clearly for what they are. In the book of Esther the characters are clearly motivated by an understanding that this is God's world and he is in control, yet the word "God" never appears throughout the entire story. In the New Testament accounts of Jesus' healing events, Jesus himself waits until the wonder and mystery of the event have struck home before he adds that the glory must be given to God. Without a real grasp of the event itself the word "God" would have remained meaningless to his audience. The dual temptation to sustain and project the image of the church and preserve credit for it, coupled with the failure to see the media as anything more than bearers of sales messages, has hampered the churches in becoming meaningfully involved with radio and television. Given the openness and choice of both the gospel and the television medium, the words of Roy McKay, former head of Religious Broadcasting for the BBC, are worth the attention of church communicators:

I believe that Christianity—the grace of our Lord Jesus Christ and the love of God and the fellowship of the Holy Spirit—can meet the needs of all men at all times. I also believe that those who stand outside the Christian tradition, or think they stand outside it, can only be won for the Christian faith because they recognize that it meets their needs and hopes in the world in which they live and love and work and play. Moreover, it must persuade them of this by the power of its own inherent truth. There are now no external motives to persuade them to believe. If Christians are to speak to this situation their first and last need is for humility and compassion. Without these they will communicate nothing. It is in humility that we are prepared to receive the grace of God and it is in compassion that we learn to share it with our fellow-man.[8]

It is time for the churches to express humility toward the television medium, time for them to repent of the sin of distributing in mission fields "fix-tuned" radio sets which exclude all but Christian transmissions, and to encourage actively the exploration of the potential of television medium for dialogue in a world where human communication problems threaten to terminate our earthly pilgrimage.

[8] Roy McKay, *Take Care of the Sense* (London: SCM Press, 1964), p. 123.

Re-creating Human Dialogue

Earlier in this section we gave examples of new attempts by the churches to explore the capacities of television in a new way. It would be impossible to list all the formats being developed by the new partnership of church communicator and secular producer. But it is encouraging to note, both in radio and television, the probing of the media possibilities in freeing people to communicate better in their daily lives. The *Night Call* series produced by the United Methodists on a network of American radio stations shows the potential of the mass media to re-create dialogue in society. Its Negro host, Del Shields, encourages conversation among his guests in various parts of the United States by a special live hookup and then opens the line to anyone who wishes to call.

Another such example is the *Concern* program on the Canadian radio network in which the series is based entirely on the concerns listeners express in their letters and on the occasional open-line program within the series. In each case churches are directly involved in the production, but an attempt is made to reach listeners for whom Christian jargon would be an offense and a stumbling block. One *Concern* program, which featured a young girl telling in detail of her abortion, prompted a letter from another teen-ager in a small town. Her name was Susan; she was pregnant and couldn't communicate with her parents. Her community was so close-knit that she felt unable to communicate with anyone including her pastor. She wrote to *Concern* for help. As a result of several letters she was placed in a Christian home in another part of the country where she was accepted by the Christian community. Next the father of the child wrote to the program for counsel, and letters were exchanged to help him in his dilemma. After the birth of her baby, Susan returned home to a new job and a new start. As a result of the experience her "second family" started proceedings to encourage their church to replace their institution for unwed mothers with a program of placing such girls in Christian homes.

The point of the *Concern* example is an important one for the churches and for the media. The media will remain one-way, impersonal means of communication as long as we fail to see their potential in enabling people to communicate freely. Susan had considered an abortion until she heard the explicit description on the program. Without this option she was desperate and out of communication entirely. Her initial letter began "Dear anybody." And her letter led her to rediscover the healing power of human communication. Radio and television have the power to re-create personal dialogue.

In one Canadian center the adoption agency was experiencing extreme difficulty in placing babies in homes. They had publicized their plight in print media without significant success. The host of a religious interview program recognized this community problem and decided to bring it into the sphere of television. One day each week for fourteen weeks he asked a social worker to bring a different baby to the studio. They were adopted in each case within a few hours of the end of the program.

Television is a new gift from God to his people. It belongs to them. And apart from all its other benefits it has the power to unite. With the limited resources at their disposal the churches should examine their formats in the light of this potential. Communication among men is the critical issue of our age; our survival depends upon it. The development of television's power to unite and reconcile should be the principal concern of all churches in all their programming.

III. NEW INVOLVEMENT WITH TELEVISION

Interest, Convenience, and Necessity

One of the most controversial sections of the Fourth Assembly of the World Council of Churches at Uppsala in 1968 was that dealing with *A New Style of Living for the Christian.* Under the pressure of such world events as the war in Vietnam and the Nigeria-Biafra crisis, and the demand for Christian social action by the youth participants, the document produced by the section indicated that the New Testament was indeed the *Now* Testament, that the theological emphasis for our age was to be one of social involvement rather than merely personal piety. Christians were encouraged to act collectively to bring Christian values and insights into the heart of the world's powerful social structures. Just as Paul had spent his lifetime intent on reaching Rome, where decisions were made, so the Christian of this age was to seek fulfillment by influencing change within the structures where change was needed and possible.

For the Christian broadcaster this has profound significance. We have touched on the continuing attempt of the churches to develop religious programs which reflect a Christian view of life. But if the Christian vocation is to be intimately tied to the structure of television itself, it may be useful to look briefly at the framework of that struc-

CBS and the BBC cover the closing press conference, Lambeth 1968

ture in America. In doing so, we shall look first at the secular medium and two new Christian responses to the secular framework. We shall then look at options and extensions to the present system.

In the Communications Act of 1934 Congress declared that broadcasting frequencies must be used "in the public interest, convenience, or necessity," that the airwaves belonged to the American people and their needs and interest took precedence over all others. Indeed, to this day it is necessary for a radio or television license applicant to demonstrate to the Federal Communications Commission that he has consulted his public regarding their needs before being granted a license, and every renewal of a license carries the understanding that such consultation is continuing.

For Americans accustomed to greeting each new television season as a further extension of the "wasteland" described by former FCC chairman Newton Minow, the concept of public interest must seem remote indeed. And waning public confidence in the Federal Communications Commission, the organization charged with representing the public interest in broadcasting, has deepened the sense of public helplessness and apathy. California congressman John Moss has described station license renewals as "nearly as perfunctory as library-

73

card renewals." *Time* magazine summarized the dilemma of the FCC, and thus of the public:

> The FCC is strapped . . . for the funds to hire an adequate staff. It is smothered in routine business and has little time for policing the industry— even if it wanted to. Moreover, the commission is subject to pressure from the President, who appoints its members, and from Congress, which appropriates its budget. Both the Administration and the Congressmen have many friends in the broadcasting business. Some members of Congress are in it themselves.[1]

The United States is the only major country in the world whose broadcasting system resides entirely in private, commercial hands. Constant efforts have been made to preserve the free enterprise system in American broadcasting and avoid any suggestion of a government-controlled or even publicly owned system. Thus the stated interests of congressmen in broadcasting can do little to relieve the depression Americans feel about their broadcasting system, if indeed they think about it at all. Perhaps FCC Commissioner Nicholas Johnson speaks for many Americans when he says, "We haven't got any plan, we have no goal, we have no idea where American communications will be in twenty years."[2] Chapter II, "Radio and the Public Interest," in Part Two of this book is a careful consideration of the above subject. See pages 124-36.

It is interesting, though not surprising, in the light of the churches' changing theological outlook toward broadcasting, that the initiative for reclaiming the broadcast media for the people should come from American churches. Recognizing broadcasting as the most influential of twentieth-century power structures and the need for Christian responsibility to be immersed in such a structure in order to effect change, American churches have launched significant projects aimed at developing dialogue between broadcasters and their audiences.

Local councils of churches have been active for some time in encouraging discussion of the importance of broadcasting in society. But special mention must be made of two major thrusts by national church bodies, both of which take into account the need for reliable information and some adequate form of strategy.

---

[1] "Static in Broadcasting," *Time*, September 27, 1968, p. 58.
[2] *Ibid.*

Television Valuation Month

In April, 1967, the national office of TRAFCO—the Television, Radio, and Film Commission of The United Methodist Church— circulated among its members a plan for involving each Methodist in America in a positive evaluation of the television programs appearing on the air in the United States during the following October, which was designated Television Valuation Month. Its purpose was to encourage the average person to become aware of the cultural and moral influence of television on him, his children, and the society in which he lives; to assist the viewer in critically evaluating TV fare; to provide opportunity for him to voice his opinion about what he had seen; to impress upon the local congregation the place and impact every day of television programming; and to open up the dialogue between broadcaster and viewer which many Americans had assumed was not possible in a commercial system.

The Methodists had a strategy involving several media in stressing the seriousness of their project. In May every congregation received a poster announcing the October evaluation. The same month pastors and church leaders were sent a plan book outlining resource materials and possible programs for each congregation. Local congregations were encouraged to form lay committees for publicizing the event, arrange meetings which could be addressed by local station managers, enlist youth groups to participate, provide time for "minute-man" addresses in church on Sundays, and share the experience ecumenically wherever possible. In July a filmstrip on the project was issued, together with the TV Valuation booklet, a viewer's guide to be used in every Methodist home. The guide was designed to help the average viewer understand his role in shaping present television programming and how that role could be changed in order to influence the medium in fulfilling its potential usefulness in modern society. Each viewer's guide contained evaluation postcards on which comments on programs could be recorded and sent to local and network broadcasters. Some 5,000 completed cards were later received by New York CBS network headquarters alone.

Throughout the campaign, emphasis was placed on constructive action. Initial publicity stressed that "TV Valuation Month is designed not to 'knock' TV, not just to complain, but to offer constructive comment to local television stations and the networks and to help individuals evaluate their own viewing habits, bringing to

75

bear the Christian ethic, suggesting that care and thought be exercised concerning the influence of TV in our lives, leading ultimately to changing the viewing habits of the American public." During the summer of 1967 more than 900 television stations were advised of the project. And more than 2,500,000 Methodist kits were issued throughout the country. Through councils of churches in at least four states, every pastor of every denomination received copies of the material.

Positive Criteria

This campaign by the Methodists stands as perhaps the most significant effort on the part of any of the churches to expose the question of what constitutes good broadcasting. Mention has already been made of the tension regarding the Christian dimension of church-produced programming. The Methodists' intention in their Valuation Month was to enable Christian viewers to evaluate the content of so-called secular television, to seek out the presence of God in the history of our time as it is recorded visually every day in American homes. Programs of pure escape were acknowledged as helpful at times to all men in a pressurized society. Television could fill the gaps of loneliness, provide information which stretched the mind and helped us to cope with a technological age, and delight the heart with professional entertainment. All of this was good. But did it represent the full potential for the most powerful communications medium ever devised?

What was the motive of the broadcast producer in presenting a program? What was the need of the individual viewer as he watched it? Did it reflect or degrade what the Christian understands as a viable doctrine of man? How did the program deal with problems; were they resolved by exploitation of another person or recourse to violence? Did the program contribute to a real understanding and knowledge of the world? Did it present inferior values? Did it reconcile or alienate? How was the viewer affected by the program? Did it leave him with a better grasp of the value of all people as the people of God?

By raising such questions in the home of each Methodist, TRAFCO attempted to bring for the first time to the American public an understanding of the role of television in their lives and a sense of participation in the medium itself. No longer was it being seen, as the church has been guilty of seeing television, as merely home entertainment unconnected to the fabric of life. The same message was brought home to broadcasters as well, who welcomed the project as a first effort in a public understanding of the pressures and difficulties they face.

What were the results? TRAFCO wisely resisted any detailed tabulation of results. Indeed, viewers were discouraged from sending cards and comments to the church itself. Television Valuation Month was to stimulate critical thought about the medium, not to produce protest or vigilante groups. By deliberately directing church members' attention away from specifically religious programming on television, it encouraged a theological view of all television. Despite the national office's best efforts to discourage cards being sent to New York, a

Courtesy of TRAFCO

One of the features of *Breakthru,* a TV series distributed by The United Methodist Church, is a discussion of a dramatic sketch devoted to a pre-teen problem. Here the Rev. Gene Atkins chats with children from different parts of the country.

sufficient number arrived to enable TRAFCO to draw a few conclusions. They discovered that a substantial number of congregations did in fact invite local broadcasters to speak in churches, thus opening up a dialogue which continues within communities between the broadcaster and concerned viewers. Television stations held open houses in many parts of the country and welcomed citizens into their studios for further understanding and discussion. Families found a sense of purpose together in assessing programs in the light of the Christian gospel. Above all, television, in hundreds of communities across the land, became a topic of social relevance.

The Methodist project was deliberately a one-occasion event. By using attractive, professionally produced materials, serious attention was focused on it. It represented careful strategy for a single event without tying its members to an ongoing organization with indefinite goals. It made its point and dissolved. While leftover materials from the campaign were picked up by some local councils in 1968 in order to repeat the project on a smaller scale in a few areas, TRAFCO considered its task, for the present at least, complete at the end of October, 1967.

A New Strategy

In Television Valuation Month the Methodists demonstrated what is becoming a new strategy arising out of a new theological understanding of public needs in society. Their motive was profoundly Christian. Their promotional materials, professionally produced to the level of the best secular design, stressed the importance of the campaign. By carefully eliminating "religious" language and ecclesiastical jargon they were able to make clear their Christian intention in a secular situation. By urging their members, in writing to stations, to be fair, positive, helpful, and courteous, they removed the sting of religious "watchdogging" which has so long been the official stance of the Christian toward the media. In short they demonstrated that the Christian should be the first to recognize the rules of real dialogue. They gave concrete help by listing the addresses of network headquarters to which comments could be sent. And they left their members with these words: "Don't stop writing when October ends. Broadcasters will continue to need your help as long as programs are being produced."

TRAFCO left no doubt that broadcasting is a power structure and that Christian responsibility does not reside merely in pious individualism but in collective and constructive action brought to bear on the power structures of the world. Television can be the greatest of all modern change agents. It does in fact change us as individuals and as a nation every day. TRAFCO indicated that change could go in many directions, not all of them good, and the average viewer could play a part in that change. If he were a Christian viewer, he must.

If the TRAFCO experiment was a first, it was also a landmark in Christian involvement in the media. If the dialogue continues, television can never be the same again. Broadcasters will no longer be dealing with pastors who threaten them with their "right" to be on the air with devotional programs alone. Instead they will find a new freedom to consult with Christians on a variety of issues in secular programs apart from the pressure-group atmosphere. If God cannot be contained in the church building box, he can no more be confined to what we have been content to call religious programming. He is the God of all creation, including secular televsion programming.

Courtesy of TRAFCO
The *Breakthru* series includes courtroom conversations on such topics as cheating, lying, prejudice, injustice, and death. The Rev. Ernest Dixon helps focus ideas.

It is possible to see as well in this experiment a new freedom for Christians within the broadcast media who for so long have felt the tension between their own vocation and the disapproval of their church for all forms of show business. And if the dialogue can continue in an unstructured and informal manner, the results will be profound and lasting. In Canada the owner of a number of broadcast outlets has set as an objective for 1969 the opening of informal discussions with community leaders on the purpose of television and the needs of the community. A Christian himself, he has sought the assistance of Canadian churches in selecting people to engage in these conversations. It is hoped that the churches throughout North America will respond openly to such opportunities, operating as responsible Christians in dispersion rather than holding the church as a power structure over against the power structures of the world.

Involvement with power structures demands openness and strategy. It also holds up the possibility of sacrifice and conflict when the Christian doctrine of man is flaunted. To examine the ramifications of Christian involvement in media power structures we now turn to the actions of another major American church, the United Church of Christ.

The United Church of·Christ vs. WLBT

One of the significant developments in ecumenical broadcasting co-operation in America over the past few years is the ability of individual denominations to concentrate alone in a single area of Christian media involvement while sharing and extending their experiences through the Broadcasting and Film Commission of the National Council of Churches. We have seen how the Methodists were able to launch a program of TV evaluation and extend it through councils of churches. This allows for efficient deployment of staff within the denomination, preserves church identity, and yet provides opportunity for broader thrusts through the BFC. The preoccupation of one BFC member, the United Church of Christ, has for several years been in the field of broadcast legislation. In 1964, before the race issue had reached the crisis proportions it has since assumed, the United Church of Christ encouraged viewers in Jackson, Mississippi, to monitor the program-ming of television station WLBT. As a result of this regular monitor-ing the church's Office of Communication, under its director Everett C. Parker (a co-author of this volume), presented evidence to the FCC that the station "had not served the needs, tastes, and interests of the substantial Negro population in its service area and had, in its programming dealing with the racial issue, presented only the segre-gationist viewpoint." [3] The church's brief claimed that the station has never presented a Negro child in its children's programming al-though thousands of white children had appeared, and that Negroes had never been permitted to participate in local programs during the

[3] *Saturday Review*, August 24, 1968. For the latest report on this see *Time*, July 11, 1969, pp. 68-69.

period when the station was charged with failure to serve adequately its Negro audience. The Negro population of Jackson is 47 percent of the total. The station's license was up for renewal at the time of the church's action, and the church was pressing for denial of renewal. Its management had been accused of discrimination since 1955 by Negro citizens in the community.

In its first effort to bring the matter before the FCC, the church was overruled and denied "standing" on the grounds that the public has no standing before the commission except in cases in which it is economically involved. The UCC appealed to a U.S. Court of Appeals and received the encouraging response that the public does have a legitimate interest in broadcast policies and does have a standing before the FCC regardless of whether or not it is financially involved. This was not merely a victory for the church; it was a victory for the public. It also served to bring into the open the whole question of FCC jurisdiction and power.

Although the FCC had renewed the station's license conditionally for a year, the court ordered a public hearing in Jackson. An FCC examiner conducted the hearing and recommended the renewal of the license for a full three-year term. The commission was, however, split on the decision, a majority of five of the seven commissioners recommending for renewal on June 28, 1968. By mid-July the two dissenting commissioners, Kenneth Cox and Nicholas Johnson, filed a seventy-page minority dissent which called the majority decision "a classic caricature of the FCC at its worst." The case has, at the time of writing, returned automatically to the circuit court in Washington.

The church is pressing for another hearing in Jackson. It contends that the FCC hearing did not deny that no Negro had ever appeared on most of the station's regular local programs, that Negro organizations received almost no public service announcements. Further, the church argues that the hearing officer refused to admit evidence of "the operation of a right-wing, anti-civil rights bookstore on the station premises and the broadcast of thousands of promotional announcements for such bookstore without opportunity for reply; the licensees' response to these proceedings by eliminating most local programs for youth, rather than integrate them, and by sharply curtailing local programs dealing with controversial issues, rather than present both sides." [4] Dr. Parker, who has termed the broadcasting industry "one

---

[4] U.S. Court of Appeals for the District of Columbia Circuit, case no. 19,409.

of the most discriminating industries in America today," has stated the intention of his office to "fight this case to the death." He submits that the station was allowed to submit only selected examples of its news and discussion programs rather than a fair cross section, and that his office was allowed to study station logs for only parts of six days, thus limiting its effectiveness in examining evidence. With a Ford Foundation grant, Parker is prepared to go as far as the Supreme Court in his pursuit of justice.

Broadening the Base

While the United Church of Christ concentrates on its now-famous case, it is broadening the base of its monitoring efforts. As a result of this extended monitoring more petitions may be filed with the FCC. Meanwhile the church is beginning to look at the employment practices of the stations in terms of discrimination, and the UCC has appealed to other denominations to press for the opening-up to Negroes of some 1,500 jobs in mass media in local areas across the country. While encouraging the churches to train Negroes, the United Church of Christ recognizes that such training will be to no avail unless the employment practices of local stations encourage Negroes' appointments. Thus the involvement of the churches must be directly with the power structure itself in order to effect change.

In all this activity there is no attempt to apply pressure either on the FCC or the industry simply for the sake of harassment. But the UCC example points up many important factors in new church activity. It illustrates the need for competent research. For too long the churches have been content to speak of redemptive action in the world without doing their homework. In both the UCC and Methodist examples there is clear evidence of careful research. This same element was present, and accounted for the success some twenty years ago of the Sheffield Industrial Mission in England. It was because the missionaries themselves could enter plants and lecture on industrial and technological change that the secular world took them seriously.

The Jackson case also illustrates the need for professional counsel. It carries as well the possibilities of conflict. Although it is seldom mentioned, it is understood that some of the UCC's sister denominations do not wish to become too closely associated with the case. The UCC has also had to face the possibility that its activities may bring it into conflict with its own members. Someday it may turn up dis-

Hugh Downs, the Rev. Robert Howell, American founder of the FISH Organization, and Joe Gargiola on the *Today Show*

crimination in a station owned by a leading church member. So the risk of such involvement with power structures may be brought to the surface sooner than expected. Perhaps almost a by-product of the Jackson investigation has been the church's contribution to the whole dilemma of broadcast control. At the end of their dissenting report Commissioners Cox and Johnson wrote these words:

It would appear that the only way in which members of the public can prevent renewal of an unworthy station's license is to steal the document from the wall of the station's studio in the dead of the night, or hope that the courts will do more than merely review and remand cases to the FCC with instructions that may be ignored.[5]

It is worth noting that the churches did not invent the demand

[5] Quoted by Robert Louis Shayon, "TV-Radio," *Saturday Review*, August 24, 1968, p. 54.

for better television programming in the public interest. Samm Sinclair Baker, a retired advertising executive, has said:

No TV station has ever lost its license. Regulations exist to keep a station from renewing its license every three years. The laws can be made meaningful only by eviction action. In this way, television can become public air, not advertisers' air. Harmful and unbalanced programming, overabundance of commercials, most of which are tasteless, insulting, and debasing, should not be permitted to foul up the public premises—any more than landlords should be allowed to let rats, lice, and pollution infest their buildings. . . .

If you want TV improvement, your outcry must grow louder across the land. It must swell from the current comparative whisper into a roar sure to be heard and honored, to amplify Minow's challenge: *"As a people we must insist on television's fulfillment and we must reject its debasement."* [6]

Whisper it may yet be. But it is being amplified by the actions of such groups as The United Methodist Church and the United Church of Christ. Such action is not without risk from within and beyond the churches themselves. But it represents a new style of living for the Christian, one which challenges him to personal sacrifice in the name of full human growth. It requires no theological apologia. It merely requires courage and tenacity.

Concrete Help for the Viewer

One of the most significant outcomes of the UCC-WLBT case and the extended monitoring encouraged by the church has been the publication recently by the UCC Office of Communication of a fourteen-page booklet entitled "How to Protect Citizen Rights in Television and Radio." It is intended as a guide to help citizens and organizations evaluate the extent to which stations in their communities render service in behalf of community interests and issues, and to act to improve program services. It reminds its readers of the impact and social importance of radio and television; outlines the intention of the communications Act of 1934 and the powers and responsibilities of the FCC, the broadcaster, and the viewer; and gives the viewer concrete help in improving television programming.

The criteria given for assessing the performance of a television station are worth summarizing in the hope that readers of these pages

---

[6] Samm Sinclair Baker, *The Permissible Lie* (Cleveland: World, 1968), pp. 103, 12.

Barbara Walters, the Rt. Rev. Stephen F. Bayne, first vice-president of the Executive Council of the Episcopal Church, and Hugh Downs discuss theological freedom on the *Today Show*.

will become sufficiently interested to obtain copies of the booklet itself:

Does the station make a serious effort to consult with representatives of community groups about the kind of programming it is providing and how it might improve its service? Is the program schedule balanced in terms of the FCC's description of local needs? Are local controversial issues aired with all significant views represented? Do announcers or guests on call-in programs attack individuals or groups? How much time is given over to public service and nonprofit groups in the community and at what hours? Are the interests of minority groups adequately served? Do Negroes receive treatment equal to that of whites?

If the answers to any of the questions posed indicate a failure of responsibility, the reader of the booklet is referred, by name and address, to groups which can help him correct the situation. It is hoped that wide circulation can be given to what is clearly a document for which the United Church of Christ deserves the gratitude of Christian and non-Christian alike.

IV. TELEVISION'S FUTURE AND THE CHURCH

Public Television

As the Christian churches began to discover their new involvement with commercial broadcasting in America, a dramatic move by Congress provided Americans with the first option to the system they had known for four decades. On November 7, 1967, Congress approved the Public Broadcasting Act of 1967, an act intended to

amend the Communications Act of 1934 by extending and improving the provisions thereof relating to grants for construction of educational television broadcasting facilities, by authorizing assistance in the construction of non-commercial educational radio broadcasting facilities, by establishing a non-profit corporation to assist in establishing innovative educational programs, to facilitate educational program availability, and to aid the operation of educational broadcasting facilities; and to authorize a comprehensive study of instructional television and radio; and for other purposes.

Public television, a concept long discussed in America, became a reality. And while its full impact lies in the future, its implications for churches, with their traditional concern for all forms of education, indicate at least a brief consideration of the Carnegie Report on Public Television, which formed the basis for the present act.

The report of the Carnegie Commission on Public Television, published early in 1967,[1] grew out of a conference three years earlier of the National Association of Educational Broadcasters, at which a proposal was presented to establish a commission to study the financial needs of educational television and how they might be met. The concept grew to include "a broadly conceived study of noncommercial television." A commission was formed and financed by the Carnegie Foundation and went to work in 1965. In endorsing the general objectives of the commission, President Lyndon B. Johnson wrote:

> From our beginnings as a nation we have recognized that our security depends upon the enlightenment of our people; that our freedom depends on the communication of many ideas through many channels. I believe that educational television has an important future in the United States and throughout the world. . . . I look forward with great interest to the judgments which this Commission will offer.[2]

After a year of meetings and conferences with educational broadcasters, commercial broadcasters, and allied fields, discussions on manpower, programming, and financing, the commission clarified the types of broadcasting which fell within its study. It saw commercial television as mass oriented, emphasizing entertainment programming. At the other end of the spectrum it placed instructional television, which is directed at the classroom-type learning experience. In the middle it described public television which, in the minds of the commissioners, "includes all that is of human interest and importance which is not at the moment appropriate or available for support by advertising, and which is not arranged for formal instruction." [3] Leaving commercial television to develop on its own and suggesting another study of instructional television, the commission produced and published its 254-page report in January, 1967. A very readable document, it should be studied by all churchmen who pretend to any concern with television in America today. The basic conclusion of the commission was that "a well-financed and well-directed educational television system, substantially larger and far more pervasive and effective than that which now exists in the United States, must be brought into being if the full needs of the American public are to be served." [4] The commission recommended the establishment of a

---

[1] *Public Television: A Program for Action* (New York: Bantam Books, 1967).
[2] *Ibid.*, p. vii.
[3] *Ibid.*, p. 1.
[4] *Ibid.*, p. 3.

network of noncommercial TV stations incorporating the present National Educational Television stations and financed by the federal government. It would transmit programs of high quality, which might not always attract a mass audience, in the fields of news, education, and special events. President Johnson endorsed the commission's report and recommended to Congress the establishment of a public television network at an initial governmental investment of $10 million.

Program Goals

The program section of the commission's report reflects a set of goals which do not exist elsewhere in American television. It suggests that public television can and should reflect the community to itself, televising home meetings and other forums, providing a voice for community groups that might otherwise not be heard. For all Americans it "should remind us of our heritage and enliven our traditions," looking "at our achievements and difficulties, at our conflicts and agreements, at our problems, and at the far reach of our possibilities." The report looks at the potential of new communications technology such as satellite television and stresses that public television "should take us into other traditions, should expose us to other histories, should let us see how we and the world look from other vantage points on the globe, and should let us reflect on the quiet achievements, raging crises, and the joys and pains of ordinary life elsewhere in the world." [5]

So the document continues, listing a new set of opportunities in a new kind of television system. Public television merits the churches' careful study, particularly in the light of the report's concluding words:

If we were to sum up our proposal with all the brevity at our command, we would say that what we recommend is freedom. We seek freedom from the constraints, however necessary in their context, of commercial television. We seek for educational television freedom from the pressures of inadequate funds. We seek for the artist, the technician, the journalist, the scholar, and the public servant freedom to create, freedom to innovate, freedom to be heard in this most far-reaching medium. We seek for the citizen freedom to view, to see programs that the present system, by its incompleteness denies him. [6]

[5] *Ibid.*, pp. 92, 93.
[6] *Ibid.*, pp. 98-99.

Paradoxically the concept of freedom is sometimes a threat to Christians and others who see difficulty in defining the point at which it becomes license. Add to the freedom demanded for artist, technician, journalist, and public servant the element of governmental involvement, and some Christians are threatened from two sides. It should be remembered, however, that the term "public television" is carefully chosen to indicate that the intention is simply that of the oft-forgotten Communications Act of 1934, that the airwaves belong to the public. It is true that government involvement in broadcasting amounts in some countries to censorship. Nevertheless it is equally true that the majority of television systems in the world today are financially sustained through federal funds yet remain publicly owned corporations operated without any political interference. The Canadian Broadcasting Corporation is such a publicly owned system which has consistently won awards for its programs in international competition. It is worth noting in passing that because the Canadian system is partly commercial it is unable to fulfill all the goals suggested by a group like the Carnegie Commission, and a separate educational TV network is being actively discussed in Canada.

Public Television and the Church

What should the stance of the churches be toward this development and on what levels? One Christian, the late Kyle Haselden, former editor of *The Christian Century*, was clear in his endorsement of the Carnegie Commission's goals just quoted. In his book *Morality and the Mass Media*, Haselden said:

> The churches should support this proposal. (Indeed it should also be supported by commercial broadcasters, since it would relieve them of pressure to put cultural and public affairs programs in prime time and might—to the commercial broadcasters' profit—recultivate the television habit among the affluent and the better educated people.) If the churches are genuinely interested in morality in the broad, deep sense of the word, they should adopt, without changing a word, the announced goal of the Carnegie Commission on Educational Television. The constant concept in this declaration is freedom, and freedom . . . is the habitat of authentic morality.[7]

It is possible even at this stage to predict benefits to the churches on the level of programming itself. William G. Harley, president of

[7] (Nashville: Broadman Press, 1968), pp. 137-38.

the National Association of Educational Broadcasters, in a speech to the National Council of Churches' Broadcasting and Film Commission in September, 1968, told of several series on educational stations which reflect the concern of the churches for the racial crisis in the United States. KSPS in Spokane developed a series which em-

Courtesy of the Broadcasting and Film Commission
An evening with the Free Southern Theater in New Orleans was part of the *Look Up and Live* television series

ployed role-playing to discuss communications barriers between blacks and whites and to reconstruct thinking in the community. Taking a different problem with each program, a black acts out the situation as he thinks the white would live it. Then the white acts out the situation as he thinks the black experiences it. Each participant has an opposite race counterpart who interrupts the dialogue if the roles are not being played accurately.

WETA-TV, Washington, has directed a series at finding jobs for inner-city residents. The format includes two hosts: a black with a prison record who knows the ghetto and a white who has worked with the Office of Economic Opportunity. Guests are invited who know the job scene and are prepared to talk honestly, and listeners are invited by a black girl to phone in their questions for answer by the guests.

WFSU, Tallahassee, contributed a dramatic approach by casting two children, one black and one white, in a series about young children called *Maybe Tomorrow*. Through the eyes of young children the only race seen is the human race in which all are brothers and sisters. It gives a glimpse of what the world can become, maybe tomorrow.

These are random examples of the programming being undertaken in just a few centers across the United States by educational broadcasters. The possibility for churches to cooperate in such programming, which while it commands a smaller audience than commercial boardcasting is still far in excess of many present church-produced programs, demands consideration. Churches can develop program ideas often arising out of church activities in social issues and can cooperate with local stations in their production. And churches can encourage long-range program strategies in collaboration with the stations themselves in the communication of community needs and aspirations.

It is clear to church broadcasters, and it must become clear to other divisions of church life, that old methods of communication to which the church has been fettered right up to the present must give way to competent mass communication. The work of just a few church employees within communications departments is beginning to bear fruit in open invitations from broadcasters to form a partnership in addressing the community with the concerns which all men share. In approaching this partnership the Christian need feel no apprehension about sacrificing the Christian dimension. The secular broadcaster understands the Christian bias when he extends the invitation. The only condition he places upon such cooperation is that the church must be as concerned with the world (and not with denominational credit) as he is.

Here is William Harley again, speaking to this point before the BFC:

Churches are functional and useful instruments within our society to the extent that people are engaged in them, and to the extent that they are involved with the people. Radio and television move the church to the people; not only what the church is but what the church does. The mission of the church can reach people where they are. We would hope that you would see in the NAEB [National Association of Educational Broadcasters] a means of arranging for further exchange of ideas, development of new program concepts, and professional development of current and potential religious broadcasters.

It would be difficult for the churches to find fault with that position and negligent of the churches to overlook it. But it would be equally negligent to see in public television a solution to all their frustrations in working with the commercial system. Commercial television will continue to attract the mass audience. Its personnel will continue to wrestle with the limitations of their own situation. Dialogue in this area will remain a prime responsibility of the Christian communicator. Samm Sinclair Baker expresses a warning the churches should heed:

Regardless of what strides are made in non-commercial television, efforts should be increased rather than lessened toward improvement of commercial TV programming and quality of commercials, including amount of time allotted to commercials. . . . The goal sought is that prime-time programming be set up on a fair percentage basis to please and elevate all major segments of the public.[8]

New Resources Needed

How can the churches avail themselves of the number of new opportunities held out to them by broadcasters? This question brings into focus a dilemma within the churches themselves. In many cases national churches have developed communications offices without fully understanding their purpose, beyond perhaps the extension of the church's image through the mass media. The missionary abroad continues to be for many churches the "living agent on the frontier." If church boards and committees have failed to grasp the proper role of the communications personnel in their midst, the communicators themselves have too often failed to communicate the potential of their work for the church. In very few cases have budget increases in communications work been commensurate with amounts spent in traditional work. It is easier for the man in the pew to relate to and be moved to support a real, live person in the mission field than a piece of video tape. Or so we thought.

Now new opportunities are upon us, and we do not have the manpower nor the financial resources to meet them. God really was standing waist-deep in the mass media after all, summoning us to full partnership with him in claiming the media for the fulfillment of man. At the risk of offending their brothers in other areas of the church's mission, Christian communicators must now press for an understanding of their own work as a primary area of mission which gathers up and

[8] Baker, *The Permissible Lie*, p. 106.

makes sense of all church endeavor. Goals for Christian communications work must be seen not merely in the context of the communications department but in the total context of all the church's efforts. Strategy in every area of church planning must include communications strategy.

A Canadian experience may serve to illustrate the need for manpower and resources. For five years Religious Television Associates, a production unit of the Anglican, Roman Catholic, and United Churches of Canada produced a half-hour telecast about the church in the world across the CTV network, which is an entirely commercial enterprise. Costs were shared by the three churches and the network. After two years at 11:00 A.M. Sunday morning, the churches successfully pressed the network to move the program to a better time slot. One o'clock on Sunday afternoon was the best the network would offer. After three more years at the time the churches threatened to remove the program unless better program time was forthcoming. The network declined, and the churches canceled the program and withdrew its staff to work on pilot programs and hold discussions with stations and networks about needs and possibilities.

The day after the cancellation was announced publicly the churches were approached (1) by the competing network asking that the staff be assigned to coproduction and cooperative promotion of a regular network series and a series of TV spots, (2) by the commercial network itself asking that the staff prepare and produce four specials during the season to be aired in prime time, and (3) by the National Film Board of Canada encouraging the churches to allow the communications staff to work jointly with Film Board staff in their *Challenge for Change* series in which communities are encouraged to make films of themselves and their own situations and reflect on where change is needed.

Obviously the churches have neither the resources nor the manpower to take up each of these opportunities, none of which would have been available five years ago. And the choice facing the churches is either to develop communications staffs and encourage co-operation with secular broadcasters or, in some cases at least, watch their present staffs drift off into secular communications work. If the churches respond positively within their own structures, they will attract rather than lose staff.

If churches are to respond to the opportunities for involvement with the structures of commercial and public television, they will need far greater resources than those now designated to the field of communications. And the need for an adequate communications strategy becomes even more acute as both systems come under the influence of space communications technology.

Although practical space technology is a very recent development, its rate of growth has been so rapid and its implications for Christian communication so penetrating that it is necessary to attempt a brief summary at this point.

Future Possibilities—The Communications Satellite

The history of space technology spans a single decade, yet its development has been so rapid that a brief review is essential if we are to find any perspective for its potential in global television. How long ago, for example, was Telstar? Yesterday? Or was it shortly after World War II? Actually it was in the summer of 1962 that Europe and America exchanged television pictures for the first time. By August of the same year Congress had passed the Communications Satellite Act of 1962 establishing a new and unique private corporation to enable the United States to develop a communications satellite system with other countries of the world as quickly as practicable. The services of the system were to be made available to all countries without discrimination. The Act expressed hope that the new system would contribute to world peace and understanding.

Satellite development has been dramatic. America was into the race in 1958, and by 1960 Pioneer V had set a record of continuous transmission over a distance of 20 million miles. Two years later Mariner II had boosted the distance to 54 million miles. During Telstar's lifespan that same summer more than 400 television programs were exchanged between Europe and America.

In 1964 Syncom III became the first of the stationary communications satellites achieving an orbit 22,300 miles above the earth. Such a long-range satellite, moving in rotation in conformance with the rotation of the earth and thus achieving a stationary altitude, eliminates the multitude of tracking stations required for short-range satellites. Sycom III relayed the Tokyo Olympics to more than 50 million viewers in Europe.

Discussions between the United States and a wide range of countries resulted in 1964 in the establishment of the International Telecommunications Satellite Consortium (INTELSAT), which by 1968 included more than sixty nations of the world. From 1965-69 INTELSAT has launched four satellites to make television service available to more than two thirds of the globe. Early Bird, the INTELSAT I satellite launched in April, 1965, has since been joined by another over the Atlantic and two more over the Pacific. At the time of writing, the more powerful INTELSAT III satellites are scheduled for launching over the Atlantic, Pacific, and Indian Oceans to complete the satellite coverage of the globe. The same rapid development has been reflected in the construction of earth stations. From a mere three at the launching of Early Bird in 1965 the number had grown to nineteen stations in fourteen countries by 1968. The number of stations is expected to stand at forty by 1970. Drawing on electronic research which has been undertaken only in our own generation, INTELSAT was able to report 100 percent reliability for its satellites throughout 1967; the reliability of associated earth stations and land lines was above 99 percent. Already the INTELSAT IV satellites are under development, with the promise that each satellite will cover one third of the globe and have the capability of changing its coverage pattern on a signal from earth.

The principal advantage of the communications satellite is its versatility. It is the only communications device capable of transmitting simultaneously radio, television, telephone, telegraph, data, or facsimile. Its cost is rapidly falling below that of cable, and it has the additional capacity of being able simultaneously to interconnect a large number of points scattered over one third of the world's surface —a feat which would require an exceptionally complicated cable network.

Despite claims by network news executives that flying TV film by air is as fast and economical as sending it by satellite, international television through space has already become routine. The average number of monthly hours of live satellite television has more than tripled since 1965, and the average number of programs telecast per month has increased more than sixfold. One such telecast of the Winter Olympics in 1968 was described by *Time* magazine.

The dour visage of *le grand Charles* picked up by the color cameras was fed to a control unit at the Olympic stadium, beamed to ABC headquarters in Grenoble, relayed by cable to Paris, and then to the French satellite ground station. . . . There the video signal was converted into a radio signal, bounced off the Early Bird satellite hovering 22,300 miles over the Atlantic, picked up and reconverted by a receiving station in Andover, Me., relayed by cable and

95

microwave through ABC in New York City to 187 stations and several million homes across the U.S., and to a ground station at Brewster Flat, Wash. There the signal was ricocheted off the Lani Bird 2 satellite 22,300 miles above the Pacific Ocean, picked up in Ibaraki, Japan, and relayed . . . to an additional 600 stations and millions of homes. From stadium to Scarsdale . . . to Tokyo, the entire 100,000-mile journey took only a little more than half a second.[9]

If this example doesn't suggest the challenge for a global church in global communication, consider the project being planned for India by INTELSAT members. It involves the building of an educational system for India by satellite. The proposal, developed by the Indian joint study group on satellite instructional TV, is aimed at linking India's 560,000 villages with an educational network. Four separate systems are under study in the project, three of which demand the employment of a space satellite. India is at present seeking U.S. aid to build and launch the spacecraft required for the system. It will be a synchronous satellite positioned over the Indian Ocean and will provide for utilization by other Afro-Asian nations on a time-sharing basis.

Courtesy of the Broadcasting and Film Commission
A scene from *Liberation Day Picnic,* written by Jan Hartman, the first of a series of three television plays dealing with the subject of peace and violence

[9] "Olympian Operation," *Time,* February 16, 1968, p. 51. Courtesy *Time;* copyright Time Inc. 1968.

In pursuing a policy of ground-system television by cable and microwave the Indian government could expect a television coverage of only 25 per cent of the country by 1981, whereas the whole country could be covered from the moment a satellite is launched and made operable. The UNESCO mission, drawn from the United States, France, and Russia in 1967, recommended satellite coverage for all of India by 1972 if the Indian government approved. The satellite plan for India involves a minimum of 50,000 television receivers, 35,-000 of which would be community and school sets distributed on a basis proportionate to the urban, semi-rural, and rural populations living near the transmitting stations. The remaining 15,000 receivers would be scattered in more remote areas for community reception. Some receivers would be geared to take the signal from earth stations, others direct from the satellite. With a population of 510 million living largely in 560,000 villages, it is anticipated that a realistic long-range target would be 10 million sets, the majority of which would be produced in India. The proposed $50 million budget includes $10 million each for the cost of the satelilte, its launching, and the provision of receivers, with a further $8 million required to equip community receivers for direct reception from the satellite.

In reporting to its members on this project, the World Association for Christian Communication sees its potential in making possible

an extended use of communication for the promotion of national goals in both in-school and out-of-school education, food production, community development, health and family planning. Moreover, the introduction of satellite-based television, with its immediate impact, could also break the isolation of individuals and communities, particularly in the rural areas, and instill a sense of participation in a wider national and world-wide environment. The use of satellite communication for the upbuilding of society is a concern of the World Association for Christian Communication, and although there is so far no mention in the UNESCO report of using the satellite for religious broadcasting, there is a great deal in this operation which is of concern to us.[10]

At present in India there are only 6,500,000 radio sets and no television system beyond a small educational system around New Delhi serving about 5,000 TV receivers. The churches at present operate seventeen recording studios in the country. If the present UNESCO plan goes through, the construction of facilities and training of staff will begin almost immediately, and India may literally leap from

[10] World Association for Christian Communication, *Newsletter*, September, 1968.

illiteracy, over the print era, into visual education by television within five years. In the past decade Indian centers like Dhurgapur have been transformed from small villages to automated industrial cities without passing through any form of industrial revolution such as Western countries experienced in the last century. The social implications of instant communication for India present an urgent challenge for the churches and demand an understanding of the potential for communication by satellite.

The use of satellites in eliminating illiteracy in many parts of the world is already under discussion. And the churches, which have established their commitment to education throughout the world, would be advised to study the educational potential of satellites. Churches have traditionally separated their departments of Christian education and communication. As secular education makes greater use of communications media, the need for close liaison of church departments on the national and local levels becomes imperative. All over North America children are learning through media—by producing films and filmstrips, watching television on closed-circuit systems, and developing audio and video tape. Content and communication techniques can no longer be distinguished from one another.

Nor should the church be unaware of satellite potential apart from carrying television signals. Recently nine computer centers in the United States were linked via satellite with a center in Paris. Instead of the normal 2,500 words per minute, which is common today, transmissions were possible at 50,000 words per minute. Financial or marketing information which would normally require eight hours of transmission was completed via satellite in thirty minutes.

By linking computers via satellite it will soon be possible to make available complete libraries from one side of the globe to another. Businesses with international operations will shortly be maintaining inventory control and billing customers simultaneously on a global scale. Regional, national, and international computer services will be available to even the smallest companies through regional computer centers.

Experiments have been conducted with illiterates recording a few words of vocabulary on tape, then transferring the same sounds into printed words by means of computers and print-out devices. In some cases practical literacy has been achieved in just a few weeks. If the required computers are not available in the country requiring them in such experiments, they can be instantly linked to the necessary computers in another country by satellite. The benefits for a church in maintaining and developing contact with remote mission fields are apparent.

Experiments are also underway in the use of a centrally located computer with 200 audiovisual typewriters located in various parts of the continent. Daily drill in arithmetic, spelling, and reading is possible across the world using satellite channels. Universities in the United States and Latin America are sharing and solving design problems through satellite. Complete newspapers have been transmitted in a fraction of a second, the entire Bible in little more than a second, by communications satellites. Passenger and air-cargo information crosses the Atlantic ahead of an airliner, thus reducing customs procedures at the landing point.

Aware of these and many other possibilities for satellites, Joseph Charyk, president of Communications Satellite Corporation, issued this caution to the United Nations Conference on the Exploration and Peaceful Uses of Outer Space in Vienna late in 1968:

We are faced with a golden opportunity to bring to mankind new hopes and new aspirations for a better life. The technology is here. But we must not permit the onrush of science to outstrip social and political advancement. Society must be responsive to this new technology, for social and political considerations are inseparably linked with its future. Space has presented us with a unique opportunity. We must exploit the potentials it holds in store promptly and fully. If we fail to do so, we may never have the same opportunity again.[11]

The political considerations are real and should not go unnoticed. The objective of INTELSAT is a single global satellite communications system. Membership in the organization is open to any country. Voting power, however, is consonant with financial investment and this has given an implied control to the United States. The launching of Early Bird was followed within a few months by the launching of the Molniya satellites by Russia. Though primarily intended for domestic use spanning the distance between Vladivostok and Moscow, the Molniya satellites can also be used for international television transmissions. In 1967 the Soviets announced that a number of socialist countries had agreed to cooperate for the advancement of space research and peaceful uses of outer space. The agreement included the

---

[11] Joseph V. Charyk, "Commercial Communications Satellites" (a paper presented to the United Nations Conference on the Exploration and Peaceful Uses of Outer Space; Vienna, 1968).

establishment of a satellite communications program open to all countries that are willing to join. In addition, individual countries such as Canada, Japan, India, Indonesia, and Brazil have announced domestic distribution programs. In the spring of 1968 Russia challenged American dominance of satellite communications by inviting forty-one nations to become members of the Soviet inter-Sputnik system. The Russian invasion of Czechoslovakia a few months later seriously diminished Soviet hopes for a rival system to INTELSAT. All of which makes the satellite situation generally unclear, since it operates on three levels: the political level, the level of international communications carriers, and the broadcast program level. Once again we face the dilemma of technological development far outstripping the political, legal, and distribution development. In fact, with the advancement of laser beam technology we are literally on the perimeter of a totally open society in which direct television transmission can be as common as present shortwave radio. In other words, it will soon be technically possible for an American to sit in his living room and dial Tokyo or Moskow on his set. It is because of the technical potential that broadcasters are anxious to see some resolution of the political problems that presently beset satellite communication.

Governments must now face the potential and the urgency of international agreements. Otherwise, broadcasts which start out in good faith from one point in the world may be totally unacceptable on arrival in another area. For example, no program originating in the United States under the sponsorship of a cigarette manufacturer would be acceptable in Britain where such advertising is forbidden on television, unless the commercials were removed. Libel laws, too, vary greatly from country to country as do laws regarding copyright and performers' rights. And language remains a difficulty.

It should be noted, however, that the international broadcasting community is more adept at solving such problems than the legislators and politicians. The *Our World* program, broadcast June 25, 1967, required almost two years of preparation, and the actual transmission involved thousands of technical and program staff. It included live contributions from Europe, North Africa, Canada, the United States, Mexico, Australia, and Japan and was seen by 500 million viewers in twelve languages in twenty-four countries on five continents. Similarly, the CBS *Town Meeting of the World* programs were built on the idea of a simultaneous multi-origin live satellite transmission on current events by prominent personalities. They were so arranged that when a question was asked in America the person to whom it was addressed was seen on American screens giving his answer. The same procedure applied for the European viewer. Audience questions and answers were also seen on both sides of the Atlantic simultaneously. These programs were worked out and transmitted despite the multitude of difficulties they entailed. It is worth noting, however, that the Soviet bloc countries withdrew from the *Our World* program at the last minute because of what they termed the Western political position in the Arab-Israeli conflict earlier that month.

In the *Our World* program the participating organizations managed to agree on a number of basic principles: there would be no political content, and no politicians or heads of state would be included; no item would be included in the program without the full knowledge of the participants; the entire program would be live; and the general balance of the program would be based on the content of the contributions and not upon geographical representation, with the project editor having the final say in program decisions.

The program overcame such obstacles as time zones, technical standardization among a variety of systems, and language. In the case of language, broadcasters claim that extra voice channels to accommodate different languages, simultaneous translation, and electronic subtitles are all possible solutions. *Our World* chose separate voice circuits.

It is well to remember that while the *Our World* type of spectacular is possible and desirable in terms of international understandings; it is also extremely costly. Perhaps the most important use of satellite television is in providing an instant worldwide hotline. It is in the transmission of the world's events as they occur that its greatest strength and urgency lie. And it is in this area that previous negotiations and agreements are essential, since the intricate planning of *Our World* is not possible in the provision of daily news events.

There are many problems yet to be resolved in the satellite-television picture. But authorities agree that they are capable of resolution and that satellite transmission does in fact hold the promise of a global village. Richard K. Doan feels that the broadcasters themselves could speed up the implementation of satellite communication: "The hang-up here at home, it seems, is a kind of parochial lack of interest in what's going on anywhere away from home shores except in that fought-over strip of land in Southeast Asia." [12]

[12] *TV Guide*, January 27, 1968, p. 9.

101

There can be little doubt that visual contact with the battlefields of Vietnam and the anguish of a Biafran village has shaped our understanding of the world. Television is making us different people. Speeding up the direct flow of information from event to receiver will change us further and faster. Through the ingenuity of Czechoslovakia's broadcast personnel and the European Broadcasting Union we watched the Russian tanks roll into Prague. It is significant and understandable that the Czech Broadcast Center was the first target of the invading forces.

The fact is that we can and we will see the world for what it is through television. We have been horrified to watch the murders of our leaders the very instant they occurred. With the tendency of all mass media toward the more sensational in the news, we face at the moment the possibility of a worldwide distortion of the real meaning of human existence. It must be stressed that such imbalance of the way things really are is seldom intentional. If a network newscast faces heavy competition from another network at the same hour, the temptation grows into necessity to include film footage from Vietnam or some other trouble spot in the world. The pressure is on the producer and the foreign correspondent to fill the time at all costs. With the start of global instant television the pressure will increase. If the churches still recognize their role as the conscience of society and the bearer of truth and hope, they cannot avoid involvement in this new dimension in television.

We have traced some of the possibilities and obstacles in satellite television. One fact is quite clear: it will come to pass. It is time for the social action units of American churches to consult with their communications personnel in shaping a strategy of involvement with television on a global scale. In recent years the churches' social action units have been in the vanguard not only of published briefs and government resolutions but in concrete strategy and action in such issues as war, race, and poverty. Now they must collaborate in an adequate strategy in the field of attitude formation through mass media.

A number of steps must be taken. Church communications personnel themselves must keep up to date on developments through published articles and United Nations papers on satellite development. They must have regular contact with specialists in the field in government, international communications organizations, and network broadcasting. They must have the kind of international liaison and information-sharing that is possible among Christians when it is difficult for governments. They must be prepared to interpret for other sections of the churches on all levels the meaning of communications language. They must help to cut through the mystique that is growing around what appears to the layman as an area beyond his competence and understanding.

This kind of involvement is the real role for the Christian in the future of broadcasting. It is sheer fantasy for the churches to imagine themselves owning their own satellites for the broadcast of a Christian program schedule in television as is the case for shortwave radio in some parts of the world. The churches must accept the secular development of the media and find their contribution within that development. If a *Town Meeting of the World* can include statesmen, politicians, and representatives of the arts, it can include Christians in all these fields as well as church leaders. By developing competent personnel in communications some American churches have begun to bridge the former gap between secular communications and the church. The number of church communications people who are now welcomed as consultants and in some countries even as producers of network programs is an indication of the growing confidence and acceptance of the Christian contribution within the media.

If there is any truth in the claim that there is a "kind of parochial lack of interest in what's going on away from home shores," this constitutes a serious threat to America's responsible behavior as a world power. Many of America's northern neighbors whose daily television diet is dominated by American television feel totally isolated on trips to the United States where scarcely a mention is made of major news events in Canada. And part of the doubt that persists concerning America's ability to assist in the development of other nations arises from the absence within American mass media of non-American cultures and values. Global television must take into account, on a much more profound level than was apparent even in a program like *Our World,* the essential value of cultures which have remained foreign to most Americans. NBC markets its programs in seventy countries, a fact which contributes enormously to the American image overseas. How often, in recent years, have the television programs of any of those same countries been seen in America? Only in the ghetto-time broadcasts of the churches themselves and in the low-rating programs of educational broadcasters is the sharing of cultures and values apparent.

Time and again we are confronted with the need for goals in television which meet the human condition. In private and public television and now in satellite communication the churches must provide catalytic action in formulating such goals.

EPILOGUE

In the Convent of Saint John the Divine in Toronto, where these thoughts about television and the church have been committed to paper, the life of the Christian community moves at the signal of bells which summon to worship as well as declare times for movement into worldly duties. When the bell rings, it sounds three times as a reminder of that communication which motivates creation—the communication between the Father who gave us life, the Son who gave meaning to life, and the Holy Spirit who sustains life. The purpose of all life is communication. The author of Genesis knew this when he recognized that even the perfection of the Garden was incomplete without humans in dialogue and relationship with one another and with their Creator. All progress in human pilgrimage is toward the reestablishment of the communication which is ruptured by the human will. And the characters of the biblical record of this quest use every communications technique at their disposal to convey the meaning of God's message. Jeremiah acts out the destruction of Jerusalem by dressing in rags and making a hole in a wall. Paul sends letters to be read aloud wherever Christians gather. At "various times . . . and in various different ways" the people of God declare their message. And that message proclaims the discovery by man that greater love is possible through proper human communication.

But the biblical record is realistic in its understanding that communication does not occur automatically. It involves respect for the needs of the receiver and a careful study of how to encode our message in such a way that it is intelligible. Our task is not to win acceptance of a particular point of view; that is not the goal of communication. In a story from Vietnam an American marine expressed his difficulty in understanding the South Vietnamese. Even when they spoke English, he could not cope with their thought patterns. In a particularly poignant passage he told of an incident in which American troops were evacuating by helicopter from a clearing. A Vietnamese woman ran to the aircraft as it took off, and two marines dragged her aboard. The woman wore only a blanket which fell off as she tumbled into the helicopter. The troops had to leave her and turn to the guns to protect their retreat. The young marine joined them, pondering the leaflets that had been dropped on Vietnam to win over these people and his anguish over a war which communicated words but overlooked human dignity. The problem of communication in Vietnam or anywhere else is not an American one; it is a problem

The Lambeth Conference 1968; BBC cameramen cover the opening service at Canterbury Cathedral

of our human condition. We cannot imagine human unity without conformity to our way of thinking and speaking. We overlook the real need of the receiver and how to serve it.

In the world today there are 162 million television sets and 490 million radios, and still communication in Christian terms eludes us. Communication for the Christian means communion, a unity within diversity. And now, as we climb up the eighth day of creation to the village of the universe, using God's communication gifts to tie us together as we press outward from the earth, we hear again the command of God to bring his people once more into harmony and love. It comes no longer from a boiling pot or an almond branch but from the persistent voice of a satellite, holding God's promise within our grasp at last.

In the midst of our confusion the church has no pat answers. And that is good. The church has only the sense of need and the command of its God to meet that need in a world that is now open. And new instruments, more powerful than any God had heretofore bestowed upon his people, belong to his people.

Television is such an instrument, but it is only one. And a sound strategy for Christian communication will recognize the multitude of media which can be employed together to re-create human dialogue and concern. A study of human poverty, to take but one issue, will begin with research. It will explore the issue in local and national as well as international terms. It will then apply its findings to the available media. Print will be used to give background information to church congregations for study groups where dialogue and concern will be generated. The same material will be heard from pulpits. Graphic artists will take the material and turn it into posters for subway stations and buses as well as for church porches. Folk songs will be written about it and recorded for sale. Groups of Christians will unite with non-Christians to study the problem and shape strategy which will change legislation, where necessary, on all levels of government. Films will be made in color for group showings and for television. Slides and filmstrips will tell the story in Sunday schools and in secular groups. Long-distance telephone circuits will bring the voices of world leaders into the midst of conferences on poverty. Leading advertisers will be approached to donate billboard space, and agencies will donate their time to produce the billboards. While all these media are being coordinated to convey the message as broadly as possible, radio and television will incorporate into their daily

107

The closing press conference of Lambeth 1968, televised on *Lamp unto My Feet*. Left to right: Michael Delanio, the Archbishop of Canterbury, and Bishop Dean

schedules sports, interviews, and programs which will keep the issue constantly before the public. Some of the programs will be open-line shows and will take the issue down to the personal level. The voices of the poor themselves will be heard instead of experts talking about poverty. Automobiles will carry bumper stickers, and people will wear buttons.

A secular issue, it will call Christians into dialogue with their non-Christian brothers in all the media. And the word "gimmickry" will not be a problem since the media themselves will involve more people more deeply than ever before. Gimmicks are really shorthand means of communicating and should hold no fear for the Christian who takes seriously the immediacy of modern communications.

It is impossible to predict the impact of the media used in this way since multimedia exploration lies in the future. It remains for the churches themselves to move quickly from the exclusive use of older forms of communication, and even from the exclusive use of one new form in isolation, to test the multimedia approach for their mission of servanthood. In doing so the churches will find themselves in new company with a new involvement in the world. And the gos-

pel of reconciliation will find expression in the ocmmunicating instruments God has prepared for his people in this age. The columnist
whose remarks opened this section of the book expects the churches
to be involved in television, and the world awaits the Christian
presence in the media.

Such a thrust will require courage on the part of the churches because risk is involved, the kind of risk that demands that Christians
give up special privileges and attitudes and dissolve into the world.
It will mean that the church will find its recognition by its very
anonymity. But perhaps there is real wisdom and strength in the
words of Duke Ellington, who declared following his concert in
Grace Cathedral, San Francisco: "Communication itself is what baffles
the multitude. It is both so difficult and so simple. Of all man's fears,
I think men are most afraid of being what they are—in direct communication with the world at large. They fear reprisals, the most personal of which is that they 'won't be understood.' Yet every time
God's children have thrown away fear in pursuit of honesty—trying
to communicate, understood or not—miracles have happened." For
such a miracle the world awaits. Like the animals in the Garden, God
is turning over to his people the control of his new creation. In faith
the church must respond.

PART II

RADIO
AND
THE CHURCH

EVERETT C. PARKER

I am grateful to my colleagues of the staff of the Office of Communication of the United Church of Christ for help in the preparation of this manuᵢ script. Dr. S. Franklin Mack gave invaluable aid in the preparation and criticism of the writing. Dr. Ralph Jennings conducted research and generously permitted the use in Chapter III of material gathered for the writing of his doctoral thesis.

I.   RADIO: WHAT KIND OF COMMUNICATION PHENOMENON?

Before the advent of radio a man was his own weather caster. On-the-spot experience of distant events was undreamed of. Chief contributors to the development of American culture were the home, the school, and the church. Newspapers, magazines, books, lectures, the burgeoning movies (which were just learning to talk in the 1920s) were adjuncts of the cultural milieu. They provided information, a spur to the imagination, a link to the world outside self and community. But they did not dominate either intellectual development or the use of leisure time. Nor did they demand or get instant response.

Radio changed all this overnight. News reporters and commentators, actors, comedians, musicians and vocalists, stylists, writers, philosophers, preachers, and other communicative personalities suddenly became familiar to thousands and shortly thereafter to millions. Night after night their voices came into American homes. They were accepted as welcome guests. They demanded—and got—attention, to the exclusion of all else. They purveyed opinions, tastes, courses of action. They opened vistas of culture and knowledge. Above all, they entertained.

113

The radio personalities became innovators, almost without thinking about it. They changed long-entrenched ideas almost overnight. They homogenized culture, moving it in the direction of urban complexity and sophistication and away from the Protestant and rural ethic that had dominated the life of the nation throughout its history.

At first the relationship between broadcasters and audience was one of innocent and delightful discovery. Each doted on the other. Each

Associated Press Wirephoto
President Franklin D. Roosevelt in the early days of radio

strove mightily to please the other. The performers did their best to entertain, inform, enchant, enthrall their listeners. The audience showered its favorites with messages, gifts, and confidence. It was a relationship of openness and mutuality.

By the mid-1930s a subtle change had begun to take place. Radio began seriously to exploit the personal and emotional relationships between performers and audience for commercial gain. Gradually the performers began to change their roles, to sound a new note. The warm, friendly announcer for whom a place had been made at the fireside was discovered to be a salesman who had worked his way into

Fibber McGee and Molly

the living room. Radio began to condition Americans to look upon themselves primarily as consumers. Everything was made to appear to be a commodity that could be bartered and consumed—not only real products like soup and soap, but sex, politics, art, vocation, social position, and even the souls of men.

The people listened to the heady new advice: to strive after "gracious living" (a far cry from living under the grace of God!), to amass material comforts ("You owe it to yourself"), to buy, *buy, BUY.* They tried the new products of mass production that radio touted— the soaps, the cigarettes, the deodorants, the automobiles, the packaged

115

foods, the stomach remedies. They liked them. They liked the shows and the people even more: Amos and Andy, Fibber McGee and Molly, the Shadow, the Green Hornet, the Helen Trents and Doctor Malones of the soap operas, the Lone Ranger. The listeners never stopped to ask what *The Lone Ranger* was doing to children's conceptions of democratic government, what the daytime serials might be doing to family relations, what distortions of Negro life and culture *Amos 'n' Andy* was purveying, what effect cigarettes might have on the national health, what radio was doing to a dozen other cultural imperatives. Radio was just there. You took it like it was.

Religion was not appreciably different from the rest of society; it too largely took radio like it was. Both Christians and Jews were quick to seize upon radio when it came along, seeing in the new medium the opportunity to reach a wider—even a universal—audience. Religion had an important and unquestioned place on radio in its formative period. Virtually every station had its religious programs. *National Radio Pulpit* was one of the very first network programs and is today the oldest continuing program on the air. The Federal Radio Commission and its successor, the Federal Communications Commission, unquestioningly designated religious programming as a service stations needed to provide to serve the public interest.

The involvement of church groups in both programming and the ethical aspects of broadcasting has extended throughout the entire period during which radio and television have been establishing and exercising their influence upon the people of the United States. Regrettably, this involvement has ranged over a broad spectrum from the principled to the venal, as will be shown in Chapter III. Suffice it to say here that religion, as much as any other institution in American culture, has suffered neglect, degradation, and denial of access to the vast audience for radio and television as the broadcasting industry has more and more neglected its public service responsibilities in its cynical drive for higher and higher profits.

The Status and Function of Radio Today

Once television was introduced and began to catch on, people, including radio broadcasters, believed that radio was on its way out. For a time radio languished. Then it staged a remarkable comeback, so remarkable that in America 98 percent of all homes have radios, most of them with two or more sets in use. Fifty million cars have radios, many of them now with both AM and FM tuners. With transistors taking the place of tubes, radios are smaller, lighter, more portable, and less expensive than ever before. More radios than television sets are sold each year.

In programming, radio has been flexible; in fact it appears to be in constant flux. FM was slow to develop but now, as will be seen, can ignore the competition of television and can challenge the supremacy of AM. Stereo has given radio a new dimension of quality. Sophisticated receiving, amplifying, and sound-reproducing techniques offer "wall to wall sound" of a quality acceptable to the most discriminating enthusiast.

Radio has also made a highly profitable alliance with the phonograph industry. Radio and records support each other. Radio stations depend heavily upon records, both popular and classical, for programming material. On the other hand, radio is the number one sales promoter of records. Both youth and hi-fi enthusiasts have both radios and record players as their constant companions. A recording that makes the top ten or even the top forty is assured of astronomical sales, and radio takes its share of the credit and the profit.

Radio is far ahead of television in the broadcasting of music, both in range of sound quality and the amount of what it has to offer. Television, because of its preoccupation with the picture, provides sound that is far below the quality of radio.

Radio also enjoys a mobility and a flexibility that often give it an advantage over television in news reporting and other on-the-spot coverage. Miniaturized tape recording and transmitting equipment permit radio reporters to get in and out and on the air ahead of television and newspaper correspondents.[1] But it is the transistor and the battery that give radio a mobility advantage over all other mass communication media. Again and again emergencies, such as the massive power blackout in the eastern states, reveal how dependent people are upon radio for news and information. In New York City during the power failure, transistorized, battery-powered radios can be credited with averting widespread panic and disorder. Thanks to their portable radios, thousands of people stranded on the upper floors of office buildings, in railroad terminals, and other places far from their homes were able to take the experience in stride, and even to find some humor in it. Radio kept them in touch with the world and, more im-

[1] Solid-state television equipment is beginning to close this gap. Religious broadcasters should study the new technical developments and take advantage of them.

portantly, with what was being done to unravel the mystery of the failure and repair the damage.

This episode points up another distinctive quality of radio. It is an intimate medium. There is an unique impersonal-personal relationship between the radio performer and the listener. To the inexperienced radio broadcaster the audience may seem to be an amorphous mass entirely impervious to the program fare that is being fed into the transmitter. All broadcasters must face the harrowing reality of being unable to know what the listeners are thinking and doing and how they are reacting to what is being broadcast. But the experienced broadcaster knows to whom he is talking. He is not speaking to an indefinable mass of people, or a measurable crowd, or an audience in the accepted sense of the theater or lecture hall or church. He is talking to one person—or at most two or three—sitting in an automobile, a kitchen or a living room, riding a tractor, lounging on a beach, even walking on a city street. It is to this one person, not to a mass audience, that the radio message—talk or music—must be beamed.

The listener, on his side, has no doubt about his relationship to the broadcaster. It must be very personal; otherwise a twist of the dial wipes the program out of existence. The listener uses his imagination to create a mind image of the personality and physical appearance of the broadcaster, all based upon the quality of the voice he is hearing. Almost always, if his interest is held, he has the sense that the performer is speaking to *him,* and to him alone. If one doubts this sense of personal rapport between the listener and the radio performer, one should listen to the call-in programs. Thousands of lonely people are solaced or excited by the familiar voice of the program's host who chats with them briefly. Many a call-in program owes its success to the fact that people often find it easier to talk to a radio personality they will never meet than to a close friend or a counselor. Television performers do not invoke this sense of intimacy between themselves and the audience members because it is apparent from the picture that they are surrounded by other persons on the set and that they play to the camera, not to the audience members.

The understanding of radio's one-to-one relationship was slow to evolve. Each new communication medium is first perceived as simply adding a new dimension to what is already being done. It takes time and experience for a medium to develop a self-awareness and a character of its own. Radio was no exception. It began by amplifying and adapting the spoken and written word and standard musical performances—very much as the silent movies metamorphosed into "talkies" simply by adding sound to mime and as television was to do later by adding pictures to radio. Of the first religious broadcast on record, the airing of a Sunday morning church service in Pittsburgh, the pastor said, "We simply put a microphone on the pulpit; we didn't make any change in the service."

Only very slowly did broadcasters come to the realization that radio was different from any communication medium previously known and must be programmed with respect to its unique qualities. In its prime, aside from its immediacy and speed and the personalized nature of the communication, radio functioned best as a storytelling medium. It did this because the listener was blind to physical details of the story. In order to participate at all, he had to employ his imagination to the utmost. Actually, he was the co-author of the script, a heady and exciting role. The scene was usually set in a few words. The listener obliged by using his imagination to decorate and people the set to his own satisfaction. Cued by sound effects, he moved the action forward in accordance with his own fancies. The 1938 dramatization by Orson Welles of H. G. Wells's fictitious invasion from Mars is the classic example of the perceived reality of radio drama. The hearers convinced themselves.

When television came along, starved for material, it adapted the more popular radio shows, transforming them almost literally to the screen. When these shows went from radio to television, they became less real. There was little or no room left for the imagination. Most popular radio shows were based upon quickly recognizable situations that were constantly repeated. When a show like *Fibber McGee and Molly* got on television and the closet crammed with junk had to be pictorially opened each week, it could no longer be the listeners' closets. The repetitive aspects of the program quickly became shopworn, and the series failed. Unfortunately, the take-over of popular radio shows by television not only set television back materially; it killed radio drama too. The sound medium never has recovered its eminence as a medium for drama, although a modest attempt to revive radio drama is now under way.

Audiences

In its heyday radio was top dog among the mass media of communication, attracting millions of listeners to the more popular network

119

shows. Immediately after World War II television began its assault on the radio audience at the same time that a large number of new radio stations came on the air to compete for listeners. Successive changes in living patterns related to rapid social change, especially the expansion of transportation, affected the tempo, the length, and the content of radio programs. Long programs that required the close attention of audience members throughout became largely a thing of the past. So did elaborate, costly productions.

Associated Press Wirephoto
Left, Bob Hope during one of his first network broadcasts; right, TV star Bob Hope today—an example of the multimedia personality

Mass audiences for radio disappeared when network radio succumbed to the power of network television. Economics and competition made it necessary for individual stations to program for small, specialized audiences. More will be said about the distinctive character of individual stations and their methods of specialization. But the reason any station programs as it does is financial. There can be several times as many radio stations in a given market as there are television outlets. Each radio station must compete not only with television but with all other radio stations for its share of the available audience. Even the clear-channel stations cannot hope to attract audiences comparable to those of pretelevision days. Small, specialized audiences that may appear insignificant to a television station can be the lifeblood even of a large radio station.

Changing Factors in Religious Programming

Since singing and preaching were the two things the church did best, they dominated religious radio programs for more than two decades. Network pressure brought the church service into the studio and modified its form to a mini–church service. It was easier and cheaper for the network to handle religion this way. From 1935 onward a rising chorus of dissenting voices challenged the powers that controlled national religious broadcasting, insisting that there were other and better uses to be made of the limited opportunity the churches had to be on the air.

There was a growing suspicion that religious broadcasting was oriented to churchgoers—and the older people among them. (It was not until 1954 that the Communications Research Project at Yale Divinity School revealed the truth of this surmise.[2] Radio was frosting on the cake for them, the argument ran. While they had a right to expect a certain amount of spiritual enrichment from radio, and those who were house-bound had obvious needs, the primary use of radio by the church should be to extend its ministry to persons who could not be reached through the standard program of the institutional church and to exploit the uniqueness of radio as contrasted with pulpit and print.

Some progress was made toward this latter end, especially from 1940 until the time television killed network radio. All over the country local religious broadcasters experimented with formats and nondevotional content. The Joint Religious Radio Committee was formed by the Congregational, Methodist, Presbyterian U.S.A., Evangelical, and Reformed Churches, and the United Church of Canada. Out of it, for national distribution on records, came the first children's program, *All Aboard for Adventure,* and the first documentaries about missionary work and worldwide relief needs, along with the first dramatic series on the Bible, *The Radio Edition of the Bible.* Religious news programs and news commentaries appeared, most of them handi-

---

[2] Everett C. Parker, David Barry, and Dallas Smythe, *The Television-Radio Audience and Religion* (New York: Harper, 1954) .

121

capped by lack of news sources, a vacuum that still exists. Interviews, debates, panel and round-table discussions, drama, musical shows—all the formats used by secular radio became grist for the mill of religious broadcasting. All except one, and that one the most important in broadcasting, the spot announcement. Spots have been the lifeblood of commercial radio and television. But they have also been used for promotion by all sorts of civic organizations. Religious broadcasters have been the exception. Only within the last five years have any major religious bodies seriously tried to convey a theological message through the medium of spots.

Since the coming of television, religious programs in both media have more and more been shunted to odd hours when most of the available audience is asleep, at table, or in church. Partly, as will be seen later, this distaste for religion on the part of broadcasting stations and networks is due to the failure of religion to keep up with the times. Radio has changed radically in both format and sound. Yet the majority of religious programs are just what they have always been, devotional in nature, featuring a sermon and prayer by a minister.

The rapid technological and social changes that have radically altered the character of radio exert equally strong pressures on the broadcaster of religion. If he would make effective use of radio, he must keep abreast of change.

Whether radio and television are the instruments of social and cultural change or are themselves the symptoms and the product of change has been much debated. The consensus seems to be that the media of mass communication interact with culture, being sometimes the precursors of change, sometimes the active force that causes change, and sometimes the reflection of the society of which they are a part. If they have done nothing else, the electronic media certainly have accelerated change by communicating an instant awareness of tension and trouble and of variations from accepted patterns of thought and action. A classic example is the radio and television coverage of Martin Luther King, Jr.'s confrontation with police authority in Selma, Alabama. Within hours, without being formally summoned, thousands of persons from all over the country were pouring into Selma to become a part of the event being reported.

There is nothing new about rumors or happenings that are reported as news triggering a chain of events. The electronic media have speeded up the process phenomenally. Witness the fact that public demonstrations are now staged in the expectation that—and sometimes only if—

their effect will be amplified by exposure on radio and television far beyond the effect being achieved on the spot.

What is the influence of the church on culture and cultural change? This too is much debated. But there is a growing conviction that permeation, restructure, redemption, and renewal of the culture are proper functions of Christianity. Psychology and anthropology have joined forces to demolish the concept of man as an intellectual and spiritual being from the neck up and a physical animal from the neck down, and of the function of civilization and especially of religion as being to give the spirit dominance over man's "lower" nature. The realization is slowly dawning that man's hungers, impulses, drives, and satisfactions are not essentially evil but rather are necessary to permit men and women to achieve their full potential as mature human beings.

Individual and societal departures from inherited norms of thought and action and change itself have all come to be viewed in a new light. Now the burden of proof of "rightness," of superiority, is more on that which is old and accepted than it is on that which is new. Nevertheless, the relationships between man and his fellows and between man and God exist as before, and they have within them the seeds for potential growth both of great good and of equally great evil.

The theological dilemma of man is not erased by revolutionary technological developments and rapid social change; rather it is compounded. Therefore, the Christian interpretation of the meaning of the relation of man to his culture is both relevant and necessary. It should be the dominant concern of anyone who proposes to deal in the name of Christianity with the revolutionary new means of communication now in use and the even more revolutionary developments that are just over the horizon. A firm theological anchorage is essential for any Christian who works in mass communication, either as citizen-critic or as spokesman for the church.

II. RADIO AND THE PUBLIC INTEREST

The American system of broadcasting includes an interval paradox. According to the Communications Act of 1934, the airwaves over which radio programs are broadcast belong to the public. The Federal Communications Commission, which was established by the Communications Act, issues three-year temporary licenses to broadcasters who promise to operate their stations in the "public interest, convenience or necessity." When we say that a broadcaster has a "responsibility" to treat races equally or to seek out differing viewpoints on controversial issues, we are referring to this promise the broadcaster makes when he applies for a license.

The other side of American broadcasting is that the broadcaster obtains his license in order to serve the public, but he stays in business only so long as he is able to serve private interests. There is no inherent reason why he cannot do both, but at times his duty to serve the public—for example, by providing time for the discussion of all sides of a live local issue or for the airing of unpopular political or religious views—may interfere with his own and his advertisers' desire not to alienate any listeners. In such a case the temptation to put private interest ahead of public interest is very strong for the commercial broadcaster. Radio, as we noted earlier, is an intensely competitive business.

In 1966 the nation's commercial radio stations divided advertising revenues of $872 million and profits of $97.3 million, according to statistics compiled by the Federal Communications Commission. These sums were not divided equally, however. Forty-three radio stations earned profits of more than $500,000 and 2,810 stations reported lesser profits. But an additional 1,102 stations lost money, a total of $31,098,316.

The competition for the advertising dollar affects the religious communicator in several ways. There is growing reluctance to do unsponsored public service programming of any sort in salable, let alone prime, time. Nor is a station likely to accept programming that will lose audience because of its narrow appeal and thus lessen the station's ability to attract advertisers. The commercial broadcaster has a tendency to avoid controversial programming.

This indifference to public interest means that the religious broadcaster has several hurdles in his path. If he wants to do significant programming at a time when a substantial number of people would normally be listening, it will not suffice for him to remind station management of its public service obligation to the community. A more practical approach is to enlist station cooperation in devising programming that will attract audience and reflect credit on the station.

As a commercial medium with no accepted guidelines as to what constitutes a reasonable profit, radio has proved very attractive to investment capital. It is not surprising that in many instances station ownership and management, left to their own devices, have shown little regard for the public interest. "Good programming" is programming that attracts audience and provides a continuum on which may be strung a maximum number of commercial announcements. Broadcasters may be as public spirited as other leading merchants in their communities, but nearly all stations are overcommercialized, and only a minority subscribe to the self-regulatory codes of the industry's own National Association of Broadcasters.

Unlike the owner of a newspaper or a hardware store, the broadcaster does not own the airwaves: he is a custodian of something that belongs to the people. A merchant who sells shoddy merchandise may have to reckon with the Better Business Bureau. The broadcaster has to apply for license renewal only every three years. He knows from experience and observation that he is not likely to be disciplined for disregard of his public service obligation, or even for default on promises made to the Federal Communications Commission in a previous application. Unless the community takes steps to let him know that his stewardship is unacceptable, he is not likely to be called to account. There are communities in which good station relations on the part of the churches are a virtual impossibility unless and until community action has obliged station management to accept the obligation to program in the public interest. Churchmen may be obliged to initiate community action to bring pressure to bear on a particular station to protect this public interest.

Freedom of Speech—for Whom?

Much has been said and written to the effect that broadcasting stations should be entitled to the same freedom as the press. The rejoinder has been that the press is an independently owned and operated medium, whereas a broadcasting station has been given by the government, acting on behalf of the public, a franchise to use one of a relatively few frequencies. It could be said that the only time broadcasting really enjoyed "freedom" was in a brief chaotic period when stations preempted frequencies at will. It was this unprincipled behavior that necessitated the adoption of the Radio Act of 1927 and the appointment of a Federal Radio Commission. Later, in 1934, the Act was slightly revised, and the Federal Communications Commission was created by Congress. The FCC has the power of license revocation. It has conditioned the granting of a franchise upon a signed agreement by station management to broadcast, in the words of the Communications Act, "in the public interest, convenience or necessity."

As the market value of broadcasting stations has increased and as licensees have had their franchises renewed time after time, this concept of public ownership of the airwaves has become more and more odious to the broadcasting industry. Defiance of the FCC is spurred on by *Broadcasting,* the trade magazine, which has consistently opposed meaningful governmental oversight of broadcasting and stigmatizes public ownership of the airwaves as a meaningless fiction. Broadcasters who would like to exercise monopoly control over their assigned frequency and shut the public out are becoming more and more bold in their attempt to curb the regulative powers of the FCC. Their ambitions can be countered effectively only by an aroused public and a Congress that has been made aware that its constituents will not permit such a preemption by private enterprise of one of the most vital of all public assets.

The industry attacks the FCC at the point of most vital importance both to itself and to the public—the judgment of the quality of a station's performance. In theory at least the FCC makes original grants of licenses on the fitness of the proposed licensee, plus what programs he promises to broadcast, and the commission predicates the renewal of a license on what a particular station management promised to do in the public interest judged against performance. The industry loudly asserts that this kind of oversight constitutes an abridgment of a station's autonomy over the content of its own programming. It is true that under the Communications Act: (1) the commission is forbidden to censor and (2) stations are responsible for their own programming. The FCC may not interfere with what goes on the air. This genuine freedom of speech that stations enjoy gives them virtually absolute control over what they broadcast. It does not, however, exempt them from having thes FCC investigate and pass judgment on their total programming over the three-year period between license renewals.

When the FCC must choose between two or more applicants for one frequency, each with the requisite financial resources and management capability, it has only one other criterion by which to decide who gets the franchise. That is the relative impressiveness of what each applicant proposes to do in the public interest. When the time for license renewal approaches, the FCC, all other things equal, must make a judgment as to whether to renew or revoke the license on the basis of whether or not the station has lived up to its promises.

In actual practice, unless there is a competitive application or a strongly supported public protest, the FCC follows the path of least resistance and renews licenses automatically. But it is the commission's right and obligation to take into account promise and fulfillment. The commission has maintained that in requiring and evaluating such promises it is not in any sense dictating how a station shall program but only that it shall do so in the public interest.

This minimal oversight by the FCC is the only protection the public has against being arbitrarily barred from the air by the broadcast licensee. It is the public, not the broadcaster, that is always in danger of being denied its First Amendment right to freedom of speech. Unless the right of the public to have constant and widespread access to the air, over all stations, is zealously guarded, the broadcasting of

127

news, ideas, or opinion will be possible only at the whim of and in accordance with the views of the licensees.

The Fairness Doctrine

The presentation of news and public affairs programs is perhaps the single most important public service rendered to its community by a radio or television station. Through such programs, broadcasting fosters the dialogue that makes democracy work. The broadcaster's responsibility to the public interest accords him special obligations in this sensitive area. The FCC requires of the station another kind of program balance: fairness in the handling of controversial issues of public importance.

A broadcaster is not permitted to use his facilities solely for the presentation of his own point of view or of the views of those who purchase the time he offers for sale. He is obliged to provide coverage of controversial issues. Further, he has the responsibility to see that listeners hear all significant viewpoints concerning the issues presented. This policy has been enunciated by the FCC. It is known as the fairness doctrine.

In addition to these general requirements of fairness, if in the course of a discussion of controversial issues a personal attack is made upon the honesty, character, or integrity of a person or group, the broadcaster must notify those attacked and provide them adequate free time to reply. Personal attacks made upon public officials and foreign persons or groups, attacks by political candidates and their spokesmen on each other, or attacks made during bona fide newscasts or coverage of bona fide news events are excluded under this ruling. The commission issued the fairness doctrine and other clarifications of necessary response to the public interest clause in its *en banc* ruling of July, 1960. This opinion introduced the concept of fulfilling community "tastes, needs and desires," suggested fourteen program categories which the FCC sees as encompassing "public interest" (see p. 133), and required management to take steps to ascertain and implement the wishes of the community.

Enforcement

A number of reasons have been advanced as to why the FCC has often failed to enforce its own rules. The commission says in its own defense that it is underbudgeted, understaffed, and overloaded. This may be true. But the attitude of the commissioners is determinative of what happens or does not happen. Members of the FCC, seven in number, serve by presidential appointment for seven-year terms. The President appoints the chairman.

Among recent chairmen, Newton Minow and E. William Henry, his successor, were vigorous critics of the laxities and excesses of broadcasting. They tried valiantly to improve both regulatory procedures and the functioning of the commission. But changes in membership and the appointment of Rosel Hyde as chairman in 1966 ushered in a period characterized by a hands-off attitude toward the industry, with only a minority voice (Commissioners Kenneth A. Cox and Nicholas Johnson) left to be heard in protest against the shockingly callous neglect of the public interest that characterizes the vast bulk of broadcast policies and programming.

With billions of dollars at stake, the broadcasting industry has a powerful lobby dedicated to discouraging congressional action deemed inimical to its interests. The fact that senators and representatives depend on radio and television for exposure in order to stay in office and the further fact that not a few senators and congressmen, and even a former President, have heavy investments in broadcasting, also weigh against a strengthening of the FCC. The industry rightly assesses the disposition of the FCC to "get tough" in terms of the kind of men appointed to the commission and funds granted or withheld.

While it is true that senators and representatives are beholden to radio and television for access to the public, and the public now places more dependence upon radio and television for news than upon the print media, it is not the broadcasters who elect but the people. Hence it follows that the best way to clarify the role of the FCC is for the public to shed its apathy, become informed, and make its demands upon its elected representatives for tighter supervision of broadcasting. If there is relentless public pressure for effective regulation of broadcasting, Congress will quickly respond with adequate money to run the FCC and Presidents will appoint men of probity as commissioners.

Fortunately, the local community is not without recourse. Foundation grants have made it possible for the Office of Communication of the United Church of Christ to offer the help of field representatives to communities sufficiently up in arms over station excesses to request it. Experience has shown that a local committee widely representative of community interests, when given sufficient information as to what citizens' rights are and what has been done in other communities, can bring remedial influence to bear upon station management to force improvement in service.

Who Speaks in the Public Interest?

One of the most tantalizing problems in broadcasting is how to define what actually constitutes "programming in the public interest." The 1960 *en banc* ruling of the FCC, since made mandatory, requires station management to ascertain the "tastes, needs and desires" of listeners and to give proof that it has taken this information into consideration in its programming. It is sobering to reflect that no other community agency—neither newspapers, public utilities, the chamber of commerce, the service organizations, nor the council of churches—has a constituency potentially as representative of the total community as does a broadcasting station, nor are other institutions *required by law* to think in as all-inclusive terms about service to the community.

Radio and television go into the homes of the poor and the rich, the disfranchised and the elite, into homes harboring all varieties of political opinion, religious belief, and social orientation. A broadcaster, to meet the expectations of the total audience in his listening area, must reckon with the widest conceivable range of taste as well as of program preference. To enter fully into his problem and to be of significant help to him in meeting the "tastes, needs and desires" of the community, churchmen will have to forget for the moment about denominationalism or even religion as such. They will have first to find out what kind of people with what kinds of needs and desires live on this radio highway that runs through virtually every living room in the community.

If station managements get the impression that spokesmen for the community's religious institutions are interested primarily in more religious programs at better times and are both uninformed and unconcerned about the total range of community interests, the church will have little influence with broadcasters. The voice of special privilege will carry little weight over against the voice of popular demand.

A Matter of Taste

This reflection brings us face to face with the fact that most of the people most of the time look to radio and television for information, entertainment, and diversion. There is much significance in this for the Christian communicator. This almost universal turning to radio and television in leisure time is not simply a characteristic of the "lower classes." A similar tendency is exhibited by many among the intelligentsia, including preachers and university professors. To the extent that they turn to radio, escape is usually what they look for. This is certainly what the younger members of their families prefer most of the time to serious, thought-provoking programming, whether "religious" or otherwise.

The educated elite have a wider range of interests and more sources from which to derive sustenance than do the less well educated, whose number is legion and whose dependence upon the broadcast media is undoubtedly much greater. There is little question as to who constitute the vast majority of potential listeners in almost any signal area.

A better understanding of "tastes, needs and desires" of the community on the part of churchmen who are concerned to see broadcasting services improved is essential. It is common practice for the cultural elite to dismiss as either "highbrow" or "trashy" and "worthless" programming that is not to their own personal taste.

Taste is undoubtedly one of the least understood characteristics of human personality. Dog and cat fanciers go to great lengths to cater to the whims of their pets and to feed them whatever suits their tastes. But most of us are unwilling to grant to our fellowman the right to like what he likes whether anyone else likes it or not. Much time and energy is spent criticizing the tastes of others and trying to persuade them to conform to one's own taste in food, dress, hair style, reading matter, and broadcast programming. Nothing could be more futile. A husband cannot hope to change his wife's preference for more salt than suits his taste or to dictate his son's hair style or his teen-age daughter's choice of apparel any more than family or friends can hope to dictate his food preferences or his taste in reading matter. Taste comes close to being an inalienable right, a basic ingredient to "life, liberty, and the pursuit of happiness." To grasp this as a fact and to govern one's attitudes accordingly is to be truly mature. This grasp is essential to the application of Christian principles in dealing with what broadcasting stations have to offer.

This is not to say that taste cannot be cultivated, broadened, and even changed markedly. There is an implicit challenge to "taste and see" in the fact that others enjoy what I do not. A legitimate criticism of both radio and television is that they offer too narrow a range of satisfactions for potential listeners and viewers. It can easily be proved

131

that listeners prefer one type of programming to another if the choice offered is sufficiently limited. No one can really say whether or not he likes something he has not experienced. Broadcasting has a nasty habit of offering only programming that suits the commercial interests of the broadcasters, then claiming they are giving the people what they want because viewers make pollster choices between two or more equally bad programs. They have no opportunity to choose something better. Nevertheless, radio has opened new windows on the world for millions, and in the process many have become avid listeners to programs for which their liking is newly acquired. Taste intolerance is as unchristian as racial intolerance. A liberal-minded person should want to know what it is that others see in programs he does not care for.

The religious broadcaster is facing a moment of truth when he asks himself: If I have my way and my program is accepted, what will be the reactions of other, quite possibly majority, elements in the station's audience? Such questioning may not keep him from urging that his program be aired. It is manifestly impossible to please all of the people all of the time. But attention to audience taste will help him to put forward his program proposals in a proper perspective. It will remind him that the obligation of the station program manager is to the entire community.

Taste and Station Service

What we have been saying assumes that the Federal Communications Commission requirement that station management must ascertain and strive to satisfy the tastes, needs, and desires of the community applies equally in all situations, a point that has never been resolved by the commission. In a one-station community, a broadly inclusive service to the primary listening area may be demanded by the public with some likelihood of FCC backing. But even in the one-station community AM signals from surrounding communities may supplement what is offered locally. In multiple-station markets the FCC makes no pretense of demanding the same type of service from each station. Rather, the working principle seems to be to recognize a station's primary audience (listeners who prefer it to others for whatever reason) as the constituency whose "tastes, needs and desires" are to be met. However, every station is under an equal obligation to serve the public interest. In the original license application and subsequent renewal forms management is given the opportunity to say to what extent and in what manner it proposes to program. The FCC has evolved the following fourteen public interest categories:

The major elements usually necessary to meet the public interest, needs and desires of the community in which the station is located as developed by the industry, and recognized by the Commission, have included: (1) Opportunity for Local Self-Expression, (2) The Development and Use of Local Talent, (3) Programs for Children, (4) Religious Programs, (5) Educational Programs, (6) Public Affairs Programs, (7) Editorialization by Licensees, (8) Political Broadcasts, (9) Agricultural Programs, (10) News Programs, (11) Weather and Market Reports, (12) Sports Programs, (13) Service to Minority Groups, (14) Entertainment Programming.

It is *not* required that programming be done in each or even in any stated number of these areas, nor is there any prescribed length of time that must be devoted to "public service" programming. It is implied rather than specifically required that "public service" programming be done without charge. No station is *required* to broadcast religious programs.

It is difficult to predict how the Federal Communications Commission will act in the future, but its work load and the disposition of its majority membership to pander to the industry and ignore the public interest have been such as to make it unlikely that very close scrutiny will be given to the public service content, or lack of it, in license applications and subsequent programming. On the other hand, there has been an insistent demand by a vocal minority of the commission's seven-man membership that it crack down on stations that fail to fulfill the needs of their communities for diversified broadcast services. Therefore, it is important to bring to the attention of the FCC any stations that are seriously neglecting their public service responsibilities.

Responsibilities of the Public

What the public has a right to expect from its radio and television stations has been discussed. With rights come attendant responsibilities. Just as we are concerned with the kind of education that is offered in our schools, the police and fire protection provided in our community, and the health care available in our hospitals, we should concern ourselves with the radio and television fare which is served up in our homes. Citizens have an obligation to examine and evaluate the broadcasting being done in each community. Most electorates get the public officials they deserve on the basis of the way they fulfill citizenship re-

133

sponsibilities. By the same token, most communities get the broadcasting service they deserve.

The following questions should be considered in evaluating the broadcasting by stations in your community:

1. Does each station make a serious effort to consult with representatives of community groups about the kind of programming it is providing and how it might improve its service?

2. Does each station present a balanced program schedule, offering programs in as many of the fourteen areas enumerated by the FCC as are needed to meet local needs?

3. Is there adequate discussion on the air of controversial issues that are important to the community? Does this programming give opposing points of view? Are members of minority groups featured in discussions of community issues? Are news and documentary programs wide ranging, or are they biased toward one viewpoint or a limited number of viewpoints?

4. Do announcers or others who appear on the air attack individuals or groups? Are there call-in programs on which anonymous callers are allowed to make attacks on individuals or organizations? If such attacks are made, does the station offer those attacked an immediate opportunity to reply?

5. How much time does each station devote to public service broadcasting for nonprofit organizations within the community? Are these programs aired during hours when people are likely to be listening, or are they on the air at times when people are in bed, at meals, in church, or watching television? Are the public service programs aimed at a variety of audiences, or are they dominated by a particular segment of the community?

6. Are the interests, tastes, needs, and desires of minority groups, such as blacks and Spanish-speaking persons, adequately served? Do blacks, for example, receive treatment equal to that accorded to whites? Do they appear regularly on the stations on all types of programs at all times of day? Are racial issues and the affairs of the black community dealt with fairly and objectively? Do black leaders have regular access to each station to present their views? Are the lives and problems of blacks portrayed to the whole community with depth and meaning?

If the answers to any of these questions indicate that one or more stations may not be living up to their responsibilities to the public, you may want to pursue the matter further. Throughout this chapter stress is laid on what the church can do. But in challenging a station's misuse of its franchise the church may be able to serve best as a catalyst. There is strength in numbers. Although any person is entitled to complain to the FCC, the more representative the suggestion or complaint is of the public as a whole, the more likely it is to be given serious consideration.

The concerned citizen will seek out other individuals and organizations in the community who share his concern. He will join with them in deciding what practices in broadcasting are objectionable and how radio and television service can be improved. He must remember, however, that he is exercising an important responsibility. If he seeks to use his organization's power merely to censor unpopular broadcasters or to keep points of view other than his own from being heard, he will make a mockery of the right of the public to freedom of speech on the air.

The best way to make sure a station will act responsibly is to let its management know you are interested in its performance. Keep station management informed about your suggestions and complaints, but also about the things you like about its programming. Sometimes you will be able to talk things over and improve your broadcast service. However, it is possible that the broadcaster will reject your overtures. He may even deny that you have any right to interest yourself in broadcasting affairs.

If you or an organization to which you belong feels that one or more of the radio or television stations in your community are not meeting their responsibilities to the public and that station managements are unresponsive to the suggestions or complaints of substantial segments of the public, there are organizations that can help you have views considered by the stations. If you write for help, be sure to describe your problem in detail. The following is a list of organizations that are helping community groups to achieve balanced programming:

American Civil Liberties Union
156 Fifth Avenue, New York, New York 10010

American Jewish Committee
165 East 56th Street, New York, New York 10022

Anti-Defamation League of B'nai B'rith
315 Lexington Avenue, New York, New York 10016

Broadcasting and Film Commission
National Council of the Churches of Christ in the U.S.A.
475 Riverside Drive, New York, New York 10027

Catholic Interracial Council
Southern Field Service
8017 Palm Street, New Orleans, Louisiana 70125

Institute for American Democracy
Suite 101
1330 Massachusetts Avenue, N.W., Washington, D.C. 20005

Office of Communication
United Church of Christ
289 Park Avenue South, New York, New York 10010

The address of the FCC is:

Federal Communications Commission
1919 M Street, N.W., Washington, D.C. 20554

III. THE ETHICAL DILEMMA OF THE CHURCH WITH RESPECT TO RADIO

Church bodies and individual Christians have been uneasy about the ethical aspects of broadcasting from the very beginning. Regrettably, this involvement with ethical questions has ranged over a broad spectrum from the principled to the self-serving and venal.

In the early days of radio, church spokesmen hailed the new medium and viewed it with alarm in about equal numbers. The viewers-with-alarm questioned the amount of time people were spending listening to radio, the quality of the program fare and its effects on traditional morality, and how healthy it was for large numbers of people to have their tastes and morals influenced by faceless radio performers. One self-serving moral charge was raised against radio by churchmen early in the life of the medium and is still heard today. This was that radio was immoral because it enticed people to stay home and listen during the hours of Sunday morning church services and on weekday evenings when church meetings were being held.

The first radio shows for children generally won the approval of churchmen for their moral purity. They tended to feature storytelling and simple music, with a great deal of emphasis placed on honesty

137

and good standards of behavior. Shows like *Topsy Turvy Time* had emblems to wear, a secret club with a slogan based on the initials TTT (what else but "Tell the Truth"?) , and a rigid code of behavior to live up to on pain of losing the right to wear the emblem. But these shows were too good to last, even in that innocent time of the late 1920s. Soon the westerns, the mysteries, and the horror shows were attracting the small fry. Church spokesmen were ahead of the child psychologists in pointing out the possible danger to children of exposure to violence during much of their leisure time, day in and day out.

Strangely, in the one area where radio sinned most deeply the church was silent until it was too late. Religious social actionists who were keenly aware of the moral shortcomings of the economic system of the 1930s and highly vocal about them failed either to observe or understand the moral problem posed by the wedding of mass communication to the huckstering of the products of industry. The hedonistic cult of the consumer was firmly entrenched in American culture before the ethical spokesmen in the church knew it existed.

The practitioners of religious broadcasting from the beginning to the present day have been less concerned with the ethical influence of radio, and later of television, than they have been with reaching the largest possible audience with a religious message. Religious broadcasters early established a liaison with the owners and managers of stations and networks, to the mutual satisfaction and often the profit of both sides. No one acquainted with certain religious programs conducted by independent ministers and evangelists, largely for personal profit, can fail to recoil in distaste from the sordid attacks launched by these brethren on respected church leaders and denominational and interdenominational bodies and from their deliberate manipulation of the faithful and the unwary for purposes of raising money. It is to the shame of both the church and the broadcasting industry that these so-called religious programs have been permitted to proliferate and flourish on the air over a period of decades.

There have been others in religious broadcasting—certainly not venal in any real sense of the term—who have been willing to accept all the shortcomings of broadcasters in return for time on the air for themselves or their organizations. Over the years they have seen their programs pushed deeper and deeper into ghetto time periods. Their productions have been neglected, their messages emasculated. Yet in exchange for the dregs of the programming schedules, they have been silent when their voices should have been heard in protest, or worse still, they have been ready and uncritical apologists for the broadcasting industry whenever a public voice has been needed to defend industry practices and interests.

Probably the classic example of subservience of religious broadcasters to the industry was the testimony in opposition to the chain broadcasting rules—reportedly written for him by NBC—given in 1941 by Frank Goodman, who controlled the radio work of the Federal Council of Churches. At one point Goodman was interrupted by an exchange with Senator Homer T. Bone, of Washington:

SENATOR BONE: Dr., is your statement an attempt to analyze the proposed regulations and their possible effect, or is it blanket opposition?
DR. GOODMAN: Absolutely a blanket opposition. We do not possess any knowledge in any way to discuss the issues involved except that we are going to lose something if there is confusion. We feel that way about it. Does that answer your question, Senator? [1]

Goodman's testimony had been preceded by a petition to President Roosevelt signed by virtually every Protestant preacher who used NBC facilities, including Harry Emerson Fosdick. The petition, which was endorsed by the Federal Council of Churches, condemned any Federal Communications Commission regulation of the networks. Even today, when religious programming is at a nadir due to the cynical disregard by networks and stations of the interest of people in religion, with consequent starvation budgets for religious shows and programs aired to minimal audiences, persons entrusted by religious organizations with oversight of broadcasting are so fearful of losing what little time on the air they have that they are reluctant to criticize the broadcasting industry, even for the most flagrant violations of public taste and trust.

The Church as Critic of Broadcasting

Fortunately, there has always been another side to the relationship between religion and broadcasting. While religious broadcasters have sought "friendship" with the industry, those men and groups in the

[1] U.S. Congress, Senate Committee on Interstate Commerce, *Hearings: To Authorize a Study of the Radio Rules and Regulations of the Federal Communications Commission* (June 2 to 20, 1941), 77th Congress, 1st Session, 1941, p. 599.

For a further discussion of the relationship between the Protestant churches and broadcasting, see Ralph M. Jennings, "Policies and Practices of Selected National Religious Bodies as Related to Broadcasting and the Public Interest, 1920–1950" (unpublished Ph.D. dissertation, New York University, 1968).

church that are genuinely concerned with ethical considerations and the involvement of religion with man in his everyday pursuits have consistently spoken out for the public interest. They have advocated a stewardship of the great natural resource—the airwaves—which would preserve it for the purposes of the people.

As early as 1931 *The Christian Century* began to view with alarm the close relations between leaders of religion and the broadcasters. (It still does!) In a lengthy discussion of "Freedom of the Air," Paul Hutchinson, the *Century's* editor, solemnly warned that freedom was being lost as far as the public was concerned. He demanded that churches and other public institutions remain aloof from the broadcasters who gave them time, be vigilant in watching the Federal Radio Commission, and be vocal in their criticism of broadcasting.[2]

The Federal Council of Churches (predecessor to the National Council of the Churches of Christ in the U.S.A.) published a book, *Broadcasting and the Public*, in 1938. It was a careful, conservative assessment of the place of radio in American life and of the public policy needed to direct its course. The first chapter stated: "The churches have a valid concern with radio quite apart from its specifically religious use. Nothing that affects the social well-being can fail to be of concern to organized religion." [3]

The book opposed censorship of individual programs from any source, but it also spoke out forthrightly for FCC evaluation of the overall program service when station licenses came up for renewal:

We believe that the Commission should consider the quality of the programs offered in the past by an applicant for renewal of a license, as a prime factor in evaluating his claim to the use of a radio frequency. . . . When a broadcasting license is up for renewal, it would become the responsibility of the Commission to evaluate the claim of an applicant for a license in terms of the trade practice codes and on the basis of his demonstrated capacity and willingness to serve the public interest.[4]

It also advanced the novel idea that the community should participate in licensing procedures:

The community itself should have ways of seeing that the broadcasting privilege is exercised by agencies that have the greatest proved capacity and

---

[2] *The Christian Century*, XLVIII (March 11–April 22, 1931) , 340-48, 376-79, 407-9, 441-44, 512-14, 545-50.
[3] Department of Research and Education of the Federal Council of Churches, *Broadcasting and the Public* (Nashville: Cokesbury Press, 1938) , p. 7.
[4] *Ibid.*, p. 186.

willingness to serve the public "interest, convenience, and necessity." . . . We believe the most effective way to achieve equity and to maintain liberty is to provide for co-operative action on the part of disinterested groups of educators, social workers, religious leaders, and other cultural associations looking toward the enrichment of radio programs through the assignment of frequencies to those applicants who are most responsive to public opinion and most sensitive to social needs. . . . Unprejudiced testimony, well documented, publicly given as a matter of . . . public record, furnishes, we believe, the best basis for responsible democratic administration of the law in the assignment of broadcasting rights.[5]

Similarly, the Federal Council enunciated the principles of the fairness doctrine and the personal attack rules long before they occurred to the FCC:

We believe it would be in the public interest if provision were made regularly, on all stations, for the presentation of at least two points of view on all controversial questions that are discussed over the air. The effective operation of such a plan would be facilitated if records, open to the public, were kept of all applications for the use of time under this arrangement. The policy of the major networks and some individual stations not to sell time for the discussion of controversial issues is admirable. It must be recognized, however, that if news commentators take sides vigorously in their talks, or if such discussion is included in the advertising, a new situation arises. The rule that any person attacked shall be given an opportunity to state his side of the case is a valuable safeguard. But it is not adequate to meet a changing situation in which controversial discussion is injected into news commentaries or advertising. Lesser networks and many individual stations are frequently quite willing to sell time for controversial broadcasts. This is likely to mean that the group with the most money to spend has the greatest opportunity to broadcast its side of a given controversy.[6]

But support of the public interest required action as well as words, and no church agency made support of the public interest in broadcasting a part of its regular program until 1944. In that year, the Congregational, Christian, Methodist, Presbyterian, Evangelical, and Reformed Churches formed the Joint Religious Radio Committee. The committee had two major activities: (1) production of recorded dramatic and documentary programs and educational programs for children and (2) support of the public interest in broadcasting.

The committee spoke out on important issues confronting radio. It gave vigorous support to the reservation of FM channels for education-

[5] *Ibid.*, pp. 187, 188.

[6] *Ibid.*, pp. 194-95.

al use. It commented publicly on the FCC's "Blue Book": "On the basis of this statement of principles, the FCC stands as the vanguard of protection for the listener." And it mourned in public when the FCC abandoned the enforcement of the Blue Book provisions.

Freedom of access to broadcast facilities was a primary concern of the committee. Taking a position unpopular with some churchmen, it supported the FCC's controversial 1948 Scott Decision [7] against congressional critics:

> Certainly every minority group—including atheists—should be permitted to answer direct attacks upon them. . . . The decision of the Commission in the Scott case clearly defines this right. It is a strong decision, also, because it protects the majority groups and the stations from efforts of publicity-minded minorities in whom the public has little or no interest to force their way on the air under the guise of being denied freedom of speech.[8]

Also in 1948 the committee argued before the FCC in support of the original Mayflower Decision,[9] the first time a church agency testified against an industry position. The committee told the FCC that:

> The licensee [is] wholly unjustified in using a medium of publication for the furtherance of his private views:
> "The committee believes that the licensee already has wide power to control the views expressed through his broadcast facilities both through pre-broadcast review of scripts and, more important, through determination of the program schedule."
> [The spokesman] qualified the stand of the committee against editorializing with an allowance for station advocacy "through the medium of the forum or other discussion program where views other than those of the licensee are also expressed."
> In regard to the matter of fairness, the Committee insisted that the licensee's right to exploit the broadcast facility for his private gain could be justified only by "maintaining through his broadcasting facilities a medium for the unrestricted interchange of information and viewpoints about his community." [10]

By the following year churchmen were divided over the issue of private advantage versus public interest in broadcasting. The Protes-

[7] 11 FCC 372 (1946) .

[8] Everett C. Parker, "Parker Comments on Scott Decision," *The Church and Radio* (September 30, 1948) .

[9] FCC 399 (1941) . The ruling denied broadcasters the right of advocacy.

[10] Summary of testimony by the Joint Religious Radio Committee appearing in Leon Seymour Stein, "Editorializing by Broadcast Licensees" (unpublished Ph.D. dissertation, New York University, 1965) , pp. 681-82.

tant Radio Commission, successor to the Joint Religious Radio Committee,[11] petitioned the FCC not to establish a special class of FM radio stations for religious use. The proposal, put forward by the Southern Baptist Convention, would have intruded upon unused frequencies reserved for education. The Protestant Radio Commission said in opposition:

(1) The setting aside of a band of radio frequencies for the exclusive use of religious organizations would constitute a violation of the "establishment of religion" clause of the First Amendment to the United States Constitution.
(2) The denial of religious organizations of the right to compete for broadcast licenses upon equal terms with other applicants on the basis of the statutory considerations of public interest, convenience and necessity would constitute a violation of the "freedom of religion" clause of the First Amendment.
(3) Any encroachment, at this time, upon the channels now set aside for non-profit educational broadcasting would not serve the public interest, convenience and necessity but, on the contrary, would be adverse to the public interest, convenience and necessity. In general, there is no objection to the allocation of FM frequencies, other than those now assigned to non-profit educational broadcasting, to a special category of non-profit broadcasting stations for which religious organizations may compete upon terms of equality with non-profit organizations not of a religious nature.[12]

Diversity in broadcasting received further support from the churches when in 1951 the Broadcasting and Film Commission of the National Council of Churches, successor to the Protestant Radio Commission, expressed its support for reservation of television frequencies for educational purposes.[13]

The hearings which preceded the FCC's 1960 programming statement [14] drew active participation from the church. The Broadcasting and Film Commission spoke out strongly for the FCC's obligation to concern itself with programming. Even though the FCC was precluded

[11] The Protestant Radio Commission superceded the Joint Religious Radio Committee in 1948, uniting twelve interdenominational agencies and ten Protestant denominations.

[12] U.S. Federal Communications Commission, Docket 9470, "In the Matter of the Joint Petition of the Radio Commission of the Southern Baptist Convention and the Executive Board of the Baptist General Convention of Texas," *Brief of the Protestant Radio Commission,* December 1, 1949.

[13] See, for example, "The Week in Religion," Religious News Service, March 31, 1951, which summarizes the brief of the Broadcasting and Film Commission and the rationale behind it that the churches were not making a plea for themselves but "for all people, whatever their creed or need, in every American community."

[14] "Report and Statement of Policy re: Commission *En Banc* Programming Inquiry," 20 Pike and Fischer, R.R. 1901 (1960).

by law from censorship, it was, nevertheless, required by law to protect the public interest.

Its role in guaranteeing fairness in broadcasting of controversial issues was supported.[15] The Broadcasting and Film Commission later participated in the FCC's revision of license renewal and application forms to provide more detailed program information and offered specific suggestions for further improvement.[16]

The 1960 report of the Study Commission on the Role of Radio, Television, and Films in Religion appointed by the General Board of the National Council of Churches stated in part:

The churches, along with other elements of the responsible public, have an obligation to speak representatively to the Federal Communications Commission and Congress and to urge the FCC to fulfill its legal mandate to supervise and regulate the radio and television stations in the public interest. . . . Particularly we urge that the FCC improve its disposition to enforce and its means of enforcing the power it already has to grant or withhold licenses on the basis of the demonstrated readiness of stations to operate in the public interest. We would encourage the FCC to set up local boards of review and to hold public hearings at the local level to evaluate the performance of radio and television stations in those cases where questions have been raised as to their operation in the public interest. Wide public participation in local hearings should be encouraged.[17]

In 1963 the National Council of Churches issued a policy statement[18] pointing out that "since television, radio and motion pictures exert powerful influences on the opinions, tastes, and values held among the people of the world, the functioning and effect of the mass media are of inescapable concern to all Christians," and advocating that "the churches should look upon participation in mass communication in much broader terms than they now do." Addressing itself to broadcast regulation, the pronouncement said:

[15] "NCC Spokesman Testifies at Federal Communication Hearing," Religious News Service, December 7, 1959.

[16] U.S. Federal Communications Commission, Docket 13961, "In the Matter of Amendment of Section IV (Statement of Program Service) of Broadcast Application Forms 301, 303, 314, and 315," Comments of the Broadcasting and Film Commission of the National Council of the Churches of Christ in the United States of America, 1961.

[17] National Council of the Churches of Christ in the U.S.A., The Church and the Mass Media: Report of the Study Commission on the Role of Radio, Television, and Films in Religion (New York: National Council of Churches, 1960), p. 9.

[18] National Council of Churches, "The Church and Television and Radio Broadcasting," a policy statement adopted by the General Board, June 8, 1963.

The churches, as responsible institutions in Society, should speak out against any lack of accountability in the communications power structure. Among actions required to further the public welfare are:

1. Continuance by the Federal Communications Commission or regional hearings for periodic review and reappraisal of performance by broadcast licensees.
2. Enforcement by the Federal Communications Commission of the provisions of the Communications Act of 1934 requiring that station licensees shall operate "in the public interest, convenience, and necessity."
3. Enforcement of the Federal Communications Act of 1934 to place networks under the oversight of the Federal Communications Commission. The practicalities of operation, especially in television, give the networks substantial control over much that is broadcast by individual stations; therefore they should also be held accountable for broadcasting in the public interest.
4. Action by the Federal Communications Commission and other appropriate governmental agencies to ensure integrity of advertising on television and radio. . . .
5. Action by Congress to eliminate conflicts of interest among its own members in the enactment of laws relating to control of mass communication.
6. Action by the Congress to prevent members who participate in ownership of stations, networks, or common carriers from sitting on Congressional committees charged with oversight of communication policies.

The 1963 pronouncement was not universally accepted. The broadcasting trade press deplored it. Paul M. Stevens, director of the Southern Baptist Television and Radio Commission, said:

The National Council of Churches is a powerful organization. It stands in a vital vantage point between government on the one hand and the public on the other. In my opinion, it would do much better to take the harder task of raising public tastes to a righteous and God-pleasing level, rather than the easier and weaker way of appealing to government for legislation.[19]

For the churches, choice was still as it had been: between public relations and denominational aggrandizement and the public interest, for or against an active concern with the ethical issues posed by broadcasting.[20]

After the issuance of the pronouncement the National Council and some of its member denominations joined to demand that broadcasters prove service to the public interest. In the BFC, a Government and Industry Committee was formed in 1964. That same year the

[19] "The Sword of State Versus the Public's Pen," *The Beam*, August, 1963.
[20] These issues are discussed in Desmond Smith, "The Church and the Airwaves," *The Christian Century*, March 24, 1965, pp. 364-67.

BFC was joined by Methodist, Presbyterian, and United Church of Christ spokesmen in testifying before the Federal Communications Commission to urge the creation of new license-reporting forms for broadcasters which would require them to spell out in detail what they considered to be the needs of the communities they served and how they proposed to serve those needs. The commission adopted this proposal, which at last has given each community an opportunity to compare the licensee's *performance* against his promises.

Three years later the BFC testified before Congress in support of the Corporation for Public Broadcasting and marshalled considerable support prior to passage of the Public Broadcasting Act of 1967. This Act, likened in importance to the College Land Grant Act of a hundred years earlier, makes possible an entirely new broadcasting service, both radio and television, which need not be hampered by the economic considerations which restrict commercial broadcasting. Thus, although some Protestant broadcasters still are primarily interested in maintaining good public relations, the more progressive large denominations have opted in favor of concern with the ethical issues of broadcasting as a whole.

The Activist Role of Churches in Defending the Public Interest

The first national denomination to make defense of the public interest in broadcasting a basic church policy was the United Church of Christ. On the eve of its formation in 1957 its Office of Communication circulated a policy statement to delineate what action might be expected from the new church in the field of mass communication. The statement said in part:

> What is the pertinence of the Christian Gospel for both the producer and the consumer of television and radio? Certainly the principles of Christian ethics apply in this field as elsewhere. . . .
> Perhaps our most important task is not that of being broadcasters ourselves, but of awakening the consciences of the men who control the broadcasting facilities and of the public to the appalling results that can come from the misuse of television and radio.

Coupled with the determination of the United Church to make the drive for racial justice and civil rights a primary concern, this communication policy led naturally to an effort to establish the right of black citizens to receive service from the media of mass communication.

Nowhere was the public interest more neglected than in the treatment of blacks by both television and radio stations, especially in the

146

South. A survey of Southern stations revealed there was little concern for the presentation of black viewpoints or an explanation of black needs, desires, and hopes. Especially contemptuous of the needs and wishes of the blacks who constitute 47 percent of their viewers were the television stations in Jackson, Mississippi. Observation of these stations over a period of several weeks was followed by a monitoring study in which the stations were watched by monitors and all programmatic material was recorded for a period of one week, March 1–7, 1964. Analysis of the monitored period led to a petition to the FCC to deny renewal of licenses on the ground that "the Negro population of the area is deprived of proper enjoyment of the available broadcast frequencies and the entire population, Negro and white, receives a distorted picture of vital issues." [21]

Other specific charges included exclusion of blacks from the programming of the stations, failure to use courtesy titles for blacks, bias against blacks in the treatment of civil rights issues, and outright advocacy of segregation and of resistance to laws and judicial decisions favoring integration. Station WLBT-TV was especially active in opposing integration and in airing segregationist views.

The charges and evidence were too serious for the FCC to ignore. For more than a year the commission debated on what to do about the unprecedented appeal from the public group for disciplining of stations that were flouting the Communications Act. Finally the commission majority granted a three-year renewal to one station and, in spite of a detailed dissent by Chairman E. William Henry and Commissioner Kenneth A. Cox, a probational one-year renewal to WLBT. In both cases the commission majority denied standing to the United Church of Christ and its fellow petitioners from the Jackson area on the theory that the public had no right to intervene in license renewal proceedings.

On appeal to the United States Circuit Court resulted in a landmark decision overturning the FCC on all counts. A hearing was ordered on the renewal of the WLBT license. More importantly, the court ruled that the public has the right to standing in license renewal procedures.

---

[21] U.S. Federal Communications Commission, BRCT 326, "In the Matter of the Application of Lamar Life Broadcasting Company for Renewal of Its License to Operate Television Station WLBT in Jackson, Mississippi," *Petition of the Office of Communication of the United Church of Christ, et al., to Intervene and to Deny Application for Renewal,* April 8, 1964.

The court made one of the clearest declarations on record of the status of the public in relation to the activities of broadcasters:

Unless the listeners—the broadcasting consumers—can be heard, there may be no one to bring programming deficiencies or offensive over-commercialization to the attention of the Commission in an effective manner. . . . We cannot believe that the Congressional mandate of public participation . . . was meant to be limited to writing letters to the Commission, to inspection of records, to the Commission's grace in considering listener claims, or to mere non-participating appearance at hearings. . . . Consumers are generally among the best vindicators of the public interest. In order to safeguard the public interest in broadcasting, therefore, we hold that some "audience participation" must be allowed in license renewal proceedings.[22]

As this is written, the WLBT case is on its way to the Supreme Court for final adjudication. It has shown that espousal of the public interest is a costly, frustrating, almost endlessly long process. The government, in the person of the majority of the members of the Federal Communications Commission, will put every possible obstacle in the way of any public group that seeks to champion citizens' rights. Yet, as Robert Lewis Shayon has pointed out, religious, educational, professional, labor, and civic organizations have been alerted to the rights and responsibilities of the public under the Communications Act. They have discovered that action pays off, that "evaluation of [station] performance versus promise, as the court stated, can provide 'a means for reflection of listener appraisal' of a licensee's statutory obligation to operate in the public interest." [23] Future regulatory procedures depend upon the vision and will of the public and the vigilance of groups that feel a responsibility to represent the public's interest. It is inconceivable to think that any governmental agency can long limit the rights of citizens and frustrate the will of citizens in the face of relentless public pressure for enforcement of the law.

Such pressure is building up on the FCC. In the short time since the court first ruled in the WLBT case (March, 1966) the Anti-Defamation League of B'nai B'rith has sued to prevent the renewal of the license of station KHYM, Inglewood, California, for carrying anti-Semitic propaganda, more than a dozen prominent church and civic organizations in the Philadelphia area have forced the Carl McIntire–controlled WXUR into a hearing before a FCC examiner, and nearly

[22] *Office of Communication vs. FCC*, 359 F. 2d 994 (D.C., 1966).
[23] "Historic Reversal for the FCC," *Saturday Review*, May 7, 1966, p. 102.

a hundred residents of Paradise, California, have petitioned the FCC to deny renewal of the license of a station in that community which has specialized in airing extremist attacks on community leaders, especially ministers and teachers.

Church organizations are stepping up activities to protect the public interest in broadcasting. Agencies of the United Church of Christ, United Methodist Church, United Presbyterian Church in the U.S.A., Roman Catholic Church, and the American Jewish Committee have filed briefs in federal courts opposing attempts of the Columbia Broadcasting System, National Broadcasting Company, and other broadcasters to have provisions of the fairness doctrine declared unconstitutional. In April, 1967, agencies of the United Church of Christ petitioned the FCC to issue a rule forbidding stations to engage in discriminatory employment practices on the basis of race, religion, or national origin. The Broadcasting and Film Commission of the NCC, Baptist, Methodist, Presbyterian, Episcopal, Roman Catholic, and Jewish support of this petition was immediately registered with the FCC, followed by that of councils of churches from all parts of the country, the NAACP and the NAACP Legal Defense Fund, the American Civil Liberties Union, more than a score of other national civic organizations, organizations of attorneys, the U.S. Department of Justice, U.S. Civil Rights Commission, U.S. Equal Employment Opportunity Commission, state and city Human Rights Commissions, more than twenty senators and representatives, and a number of private citizens. In July, 1968, the FCC voted unanimously its intention to issue such a rule. The churches had generated the kind of relentless public pressure that even the industry-oriented majority of the FCC commissioners cannot afford to ignore.

The Rights and Responsibilities of Broadcast Licensees

The American system of broadcasting and the Communications Act of 1934 which governs it are based on a philosophy that was painstakingly worked out and exhaustively debated in Congress prior to its enactment. Anyone who takes the time to read those debates will know that the drafters of the Dill-Rayburn Bill knew exactly what they were doing. There were any number of ways they could have created a broadcasting system. The easiest would have been to establish an American version of the government-controlled British Broadcasting Corporation. But Congress worked out a uniquely American plan. It specifically withheld property rights in the broadcast spectrum, implicitly making it public property. At the same time, it placed the use of the spectrum in private hands. Broadcasters were given temporary but exclusive use of frequencies as the reward for operating "in the public interest, convenience and necessity." No additional price, monetary or otherwise, was exacted of them.

For more than a quarter of a century the broadcasters have sought to rid themselves of the minimal jurisdiction placed over their operations by the Congress through the FCC. Their latest attempt is the full-dress attack in the courts against the fairness doctrine, already mentioned. The Protestant, Roman Catholic, and Jewish organizations who oppose that attack said in their brief to the U.S. Circuit Court:

The First Amendment not only permits but requires that broadcast licensees be regulated so as to insure that all viewpoints are heard. The Government interferes with the right to speak when it grants exclusive licenses to use the airwaves to some while excluding others. This primary interference cannot be sustained under the First Amendment unless it is accompanied by conditions that effectively protect the free speech rights of those excluded.[24]

The broadcasters have maneuvered the public into the position of a permissive parent listening to the arguments of a spoiled child. The broadcasters, like the child, wheedle and coax, test now this tactic, now that one—all for the purpose of convincing someone of something that really is not true. The perplexed parent, once hoodwinked into acquiescence, loses control of the child. The public, once it accepts the broadcasters' premise on constitutional freedom, will lose control over broadcasting and thus risk losing its own freedom.

The question is not: Should broadcasting be removed from public control? It is rather: How can the public reassert its authority over broadcasting so as to protect the freedom of speech of the citizen and his right to access to the broadcast media?

The broadcasters claim that any oversight of their activities is a violation of their right to freedom of speech under the First Amendment. The fact is that if we are to enjoy the fruits of the system of broadcasting so painstakingly worked out by Congress, someone must judge whether or not the station licensee is delivering his share of

[24] U.S. Court of Appeals for the Seventh Circuit, "Columbia Broadcasting System et al. vs. U.S. of America and Federal Communications Commission," *Brief of the Office of Communication of the United Church of Christ et al., Amici Curiae,* 1968.

the bargain. Inevitably, this means some governmental agency—judicial, legislative, or executive—is going to pass judgment on his past acts. Unquestionably, such judgment opens up the possibility of oppressive governmental requirements, even of persecution and censorship; but it is nonsense to suggest that one can have regulation without judgment or effective service without some regulatory agency to measure promise against performance.

Even *Editor and Publisher* recently editorialized for at least minimal controls over freedom of the broadcast licensee:

> The effort of the broadcast industry to have itself declared a coequal with the printed page under the First Amendment's guarantee of a free press seems to be rather schizophrenic. . . . Certainly, broadcasting must operate in the future as it has in the past, with the broadest degree of freedom, but a license is a license which by its definition means control no matter how slight.[25]

Property rights held sacred a generation ago have yielded to the demands of human poverty, human labor, governmental necessities, and the complexities of modern business. Few would suggest that a man has lost control of his factory because he must bargain with his workers. Is it too much to suggest that the broadcaster has not lost his freedom because he must make a place for the multiple views of the public he serves?

[25] "What Is an FCC License?" *Editor and Publisher*, September 21, 1968, p. 7.

IV. THE EVOLUTION OF RELIGIOUS RADIO PROGRAMMING

In the early history of broadcasting the religious program was easy to identify. It began with a choir singing a popular hymn. Then came scripture-reading and prayer followed by the *pièce de résistance,* an inspirational message from a well-known minister, then more prayer and the fade-out on the choir. Most stations then, as now, opened and closed the broadcast day with a prayer and the "Star Spangled Banner." A few programs were devoted entirely to "religious music," and there were a scattering of bulletin-type programs which told the "good news" of meetings held and resolutions adopted by organized church bodies.

The assumption behind this type of religious broadcasting was that there were many people who wanted to attend church services but for one reason or another could not do so. Radio brought the church to the home, and in the name of the church, some of the nation's most popular preachers and singers. Much religious broadcasting today still adheres to this pseudo worship-service format. The Billy Graham broadcasts, *The Protestant Hour,* and *National Radio Pulpit* are examples. These programs have their devotees who feel that their lives are enriched by their listening.

Other and newer religious programs are less easy to identify. Spot announcements, created by commercial advertising producer Stan Freburg and sponsored by the United Presbyterian Church, carry a religious message but do so in the form of amusing skits that last a mere thirty seconds. Humor is not something traditionally associated with religious programming.

The United Church of Christ sponsors daily five-minute programs featuring congressmen and senators who discuss issues related to world peace. The only thing that associates *Congressional Comment* with religion is the tagline at the end of the broadcast identifying the United Church of Christ as producer.

The United Methodist TRAFCO *Night Call* program allows persons throughout the country to call in and discuss with authorities their views on social problems. The show usually does not deal with religion as such but with issues of war and peace, racial and social justice, human equality, and with what it means to be a black man in white society.

Objectives and Audience Reaction

The difference between the new kind of religious broadcasting and the old kind is that Christian communicators are increasingly seeing the boundaries of God's kingdom as being the boundaries of society; that God is concerned with what is happening in the *world,* to the "least of these"; that the church is the people of God working in his name wherever they may be; that the congregation is not an end in itself but is the incubus from which Christians move into the world to do God's work.

A second reason for change has been a growing realization that the home radio cannot take the place of a church sanctuary, no matter how many prayers and sermons are broadcast. A sanctuary is designed for one kind of communication, communication with a specific group of persons gathered in one place and consciously sharing a community of interests. Radio communication is directed to an audience of isolated individuals diffused throughout the various strata of society. The symbolism, lighting, acoustics, a sense of togetherness, and the minister's presence in a church sanctuary all help to convey the gospel message. These elements cannot be transferred to the air. Therefore, they get in the way of a radio broadcast; they do not enhance it.

Many religious broadcasters realized this fact early in the development of radio. The origins of *The Lutheran Hour,* for example, can be traced to a realization on the part of the Lutheran Laymen's League that its programs had to be produced specifically for radio. Morton Wishengrad's unforgettable *Eternal Light* programs, broadcast under the sponsorship of the Jewish Theological Seminary of America, pioneered in the use of radio drama with religious themes.

All Aboard for Adventure, a fifteen-minute program dramatizing incidents in the life of the apostle Paul, reached children in a way that traditional church services transferred to the air never could. It was significant too in its recognition that young radio listeners preferred short, punchy programs but could absorb highly sophisticated intellectual content.

Thy Kingdom Come, a half-hour Saturday night NBC series featuring a brass choir and a double quartet in startling arrangements of traditional hymns, and with actor Ray Middleton reading selected scripture passages, had a phenomenal audience impact. The mere fact that churches would sponsor such an offbeat program seemed to impress people.

It has now become obvious that the less obviously religious a program is, in the sense of being keyed to a church service, the less likely it is to be tuned out in favor of a secular broadcast. Many people instantly reject everything that sounds churchy as being irrelevant. Yet these are the people the church is trying hardest to reach through radio, not the committed Christians who are already in the church pews.

Make no mistake, slick, shallow entertainment-type programs under religious auspices will not communicate either. Listeners reject them with the same impatience and disgust as they do the pious daily devotions. There is a vast difference between what people look upon as a "religious" program and what they look for from religion on the air. Listeners want hard-hitting religious programs that deal with the real issues—as Jesus dealt with them. If the program be dramatic, let the drama treat of the realities of the grim humor and stark tragedy of human life. Youths want guidance for their lives; married couples want help for family problems; old people want assurance. All want reliable information, standards, guides to action. Above all they want some honest source to tell it like it is. This is the mission of religious broadcasting.

Although most religious programs continue to be devotional, sermonic, or a combination of the two, there have been serious attempts to

154

broaden religious radio formats to meet a broad spectrum of listening audiences. In addition to the United Methodist *Night Call* and the United Church of Christ *Congressional Comment,* the American Lutheran Church has developed a program especially for teen-agers called *Silhouette,* which intersperses current popular rock-and-roll music with comments which relate to the teen-agers' world. A number of seasonal spots have been developed, such as *A Moment for Thanksgiving* and fifteen-second to one-minute spots for the Christmas season, Easter, and other special days. *Guideposts,* a series of twenty-six fifteen-minute dramas, deals with factual human interest situations; *American Profile* and *Man with the Mike* provide stations with short interviews of people who have helped others.

In addition to these programs, most of which are syndicated through the National Council of Churches, the BFC continues three network programs of "old-style" radio. The oldest is *National Radio Pulpit,* continuously aired over the NBC network since 1923. It is the oldest network radio program on the air. For more than forty years it featured Ralph W. Sockman, pastor of Christ Church Methodist in New York City. Audience research as early as 1950 showed that the audience for the program had grown small and that it would remain small.

Courtesy of the Broadcasting and Film Commission
Dr. Ralph Sockman and singers for the *National Radio Pulpit*

Nevertheless, the National Council's BFC has clung to the program, based on the conviction that it should provide a ministry to the widest possible spectrum of audiences, including the relatively small but loyal audience to whom *National Radio Pulpit* ministers. Each year more than 350,000 sermons from this program and *The Art of Living*

Courtesy of the Broadcasting and Film Commission
Art of Living speaker Dr. Norman Vincent Peale

are mailed without charge, on request, thus giving direct evidence of an interested audience. Further evidence was received in 1968 when for a few months WNBC, the NBC network flagship station in New York, moved both programs to before 7:00 on Sunday mornings; the station management received more than a thousand letters protesting the move, and before the end of the year the programs were returned to a more convenient time.

A third cooperatively sponsored program is *The Protestant Hour,* a syndicated half-hour show on tape which goes under BFC sponsorship to several hundred stations each week. Five member communions of the BFC divide the fifty-two Sundays among their leading preachers. Their selected spokesmen go to the Protestant Radio and Television Center in Atlanta to record the programs; the music is added and the tape duplicates sent from Atlanta to the cooperating stations. This program, like *National Radio Pulpit,* appeals to a minimal audience.

The BFC also has a radio news program which it offers free to stations. *Church World News* is a fifteen-minute weekly program contributed to the BFC by the Lutheran Church in America. The analyst and producer of this useful news roundup is Richard Sutcliffe, director of television and radio for the denomination. It is distributed on discs.

Courtesy of the Broadcasting and Film Commission
Richard Sutcliffe of *Church World News*

Another weekly radio news service, *News-Script,* is sent to subscribers in script form, with each item timed for broadcasting. It is a project of the Department of Communication of the Massachusetts Council of Churches.

157

The avowed purpose of the BFC in continuing to offer these and a number of other programs for radio is twofold: (1) to provide opportunity for the best of radio preaching and church music, of counseling and high-caliber news reporting to be heard nationwide and (2) to set a standard for such programming. Also, it provides an outlet for denominational talent that might otherwise be put on the air competitively.

When the question arises as to whether or not to continue a program such as *National Radio Pulpit,* the argument is made that speakers who have been heard over a period of years have attracted a following of faithful listeners who feel a sense of rapport and who insist on their right to hear their favorites. (In a divided Protestantism it may not be without significance that there is a means provided whereby the public can hear men of many communions preaching the same gospel.) But there is no proof, based upon research, that these arguments are valid.

The same nostalgic plea is made when one man has been on the air locally over a period of years. There is no disputing the fact that people newly in town or visiting from communities in the signal area may be attracted to the church of a minister they hear on the air. It is also true that to make an impact, one must broadcast regularly over a long period of time. This situation poses a difficult problem for a council of churches desirous of seeing this type of program continued only if there can be a sharing of the radio time by all qualified preachers. Unless the time is allotted in substantial blocks, the continuity of the programming is lost, and the audience attracting-and-holding power may be correspondingly diminished.

Syndicated Programs

There is always the danger in discussing the national and local use of radio for religious programming that what independent broadcasters are doing with radio will be left out of account. In actual fact, what independent religious broadcasters are doing through nationally distributed syndicated programming far outweighs in sheer volume all the programming being done nationally and locally by councils of churches and ministerial associations. Almost all this independent programming is aired on purchased time, so the producers know on what stations and at what times their programs can be heard. (This information is often difficult to get on programs aired in sustaining time, as practically all council programs are.)

Most of the independent programs range from theologically conservative to right-wing extremist. Their number is legion. Anyone who travels south of the Mason-Dixon line and listens to his car radio will be hard put to find other than revivalist programs in seemingly inexhaustible profusion. In Los Angeles at one time it was estimated that there were 365 paid religious programs being aired on radio every week.

H. M. S. Richards, director and speaker of *The Voice of Prophecy*

Some of these programs are entirely reputable, even though they might not be considered to be good radio today. Among others are the Billy Graham program, *The Lutheran Hour, The Bible Study Hour, Back to God, Back to the Bible,* and the Seventh-Day Adventist program, *The Voice of Prophecy.* The Adventist program is a sound educational venture. It draws listeners into a variety of correspondence courses dealing with Adventist beliefs and biblical and allied subjects. It maintains a staff large enough to deal personally by correspondence with all who respond. The speaker, H. M. S. Richards, also maintains direct contact with thousands of listeners through an intensive speaking and Bible-teaching schedule. The Adventist program is not designed to attach persons to a church-of-the-air but is one that seeks to relate the responsive listener to a fellowship of like-minded Christians locally. While this technique may not be readily adaptable to a single community, the Adventist preparation, performance, and follow-through attest to the seriousness with which the churches' use of radio should be approached. At least the method, which combines education with evangelism, is one that should be given serious consideration by cooperative religious broadcasters such as councils of churches.

A study of syndicated religious broadcasts will reveal that there are no nationally sponsored Jewish programs and that such Roman Catholic programs as may be heard are sponsored by orders or other semi-independent agencies and not by the National Catholic Organization for Radio and Television. Both Jews (*The Eternal Light*) and Catholics (*The Catholic Hour*) still depend for coverage upon the rapidly diminishing facilities of the NBC radio network.

By far the largest number of syndicated religious radio programs are traditional in format and therefore can be presumed to have audiences limited very largely to "believers"—persons who respond to the particular preacher. Joseph T. Klapper and other researchers maintain that "a program selects its audience." [1] The person who listens to the broadcast of a church service is a person who would attend if he could. The often heard claim that so-called "gospel broadcasts win people to Christ" is not borne out by findings that can be validated. Klapper says what broadcasting *can* do is to strengthen beliefs and opinions already held. Others not as closely oriented to the value system of commercial broadcasting contend that broadcasting

---

[1] *The Effects of Mass Communication* (New York: The Free Press, 1960).

content, if cast in terms and format that listeners will accept, can *introduce new ideas and concepts* and can inspire even more listeners to act in areas that are important to their aspirations and values.

More and more the religious broadcasting of the future must be designed not to duplicate what is already being done in the churches but to permit radio to do what radio can do best. This trend is being accelerated as a result of interdenominational cooperation. Those who continue to go it alone are slower to recognize the need for change.

Cooperative Religious Broadcasting

From the inception of broadcasting in the 1920s there have been churches and individuals that have operated their own stations or aired their own church services. Some who tried to get their programs accepted by a network and failed have created their own networks by syndicating programs to stations willing to accept them. At the same time there has been a steady increase in cooperative interchurch planning and programming, both nationally and locally. The Protestant agency for this cooperative ministry is the Broadcasting and Film Commission of the National Council of Churches. (Paralleling and cooperating with the BFC is the Catholic National Commission on Radio and Television and, at various times and in relationship to one or another network, representatives of the Jewish Theological Seminary of America, the American Jewish Committee, or the New York Board of Rabbis.) The BFC deals with networks nationally, with the national communications offices of denominations, and with state and local councils of churches. It does not operate in relation to local stations.

By mid-1968 there were forty-two state and city councils of churches with staff employed to maintain liaison between the churches and local radio and television stations. Most of them have radio production facilities and production budgets, and several have more than one staff member assigned to radio.

The Broadcasting and Film Commission came into being as a merger of the Protestant Radio and Film Commissions in the fall of 1950 as the National Council of Churches was formed. It had a staff of four persons and a modest budget devoted to network radio broadcasting. Few communions then had broadcasting departments. In most instances this responsibility was assigned to persons who also had other staff responsibilities. The potential of broadcasting began

161

to be appreciated as top church leaders became more and more involved in planning through the BFC and in on-the-air appearances. In a remarkably short period of time in the late 50s and early 60s denomination after denomination established departments of radio and television and employed full-time staffs. Each new denominational broadcasting head felt the need to do some creative programming on his own. Each had also to be absorbed into the cooperative fellowship of the BFC, dependent as it was upon denominational underwriting for its support. Out of this ferment came many new program ideas, but a diminution of cooperative production. The denominations began to go it alone, and still do.

Today nearly all denominational offices have burgeoning educational and program-production projects for their own constituencies, which have a prior claim on budget and staff over the needs of the BFC. Most of them recognize the need to plan together and to share one another's plans, and while there is no intention to pool production money, there is a tendency to pool the productions themselves by coordinating their distribution through the BFC. Nevertheless, this pooling of resources falls for short of what would be necessary to make the BFC the powerful bargaining agent with networks and stations and the representative spokesman to government that it was originally designed to be. At best, some experience is being gained in clarifying goals and objectives, based upon a growing understanding of the role of mass communication in society and of the use the churches should be making of the mass media.

Radio-TV staffs of state and city councils of churches share their problems and aspirations in the National Association of Council Broadcasters and through committees of the BFC. These independent local cooperative agencies contribute to the national agencies a keen awareness that all radio is local. Recognizing that geographical boundaries mean nothing in broadcasting, they are now working in terms of what broadcasters and advertisers refer to as market areas. The Pittsburgh council broadcasting department, for example, has become the Inter-Church Broadcasting Commission of Western Pennsylvania. More inclusive of denominational loyalty and resources than the national agency (BFC), these state and city council broadcasting departments have brought into cooperation communions not members of the National Council of Churches, numerous cooperatively disposed, religiously oriented community agencies (the YMCA, for ex-

162

ample), and in some instances Roman Catholic and Jewish bodies as well.

One of the first casualties of this growth of cooperation in the larger cities has been network religious radio. Major emphasis is being put on "live-local" program origination. This type of programming is encouraged by the FCC. Council broadcasting staffs feel they can do almost anything locally that can be done nationally and do it just as well, given the financial resources. With locally originated programs they can choose optimum available time for their presentation. They can capitalize on the interest in local personalities to make their programming seem more relevant to local "tastes, needs and desires" than programming from outside would be. This policy poses a difficult problem of adjustment for the Broadcasting and Film Commission. It further complicates the BFC's transition from being *the* broadcasting agency of the churches to whatever may be its future role and function nationally.

In the early days of network radio there was every reason for the churches to take advantage of network prestige, the infrequent network assumption of production costs, and network dissemination of programs to affiliated stations, often at some expense to the network. On the other hand, it was to the network's advantage to have prestigious programs to offer in religion as in other fields. In the earliest days of radio the network had reason to be profoundly grateful to the churches, for they provided good programming for time that had to be filled on Sundays and even during the week. This mutual advantage diminished progressively as commercial sponsorship developed and the money-making potential of broadcasting began to be appreciated. It was not long before religious programs began to be relegated to less salable time, the Sunday ghetto. Now the radio networks themselves have gone the way of all flesh. Their chief purpose—certainly one of major importance—is to disseminate news. There is also some demand for special events, such as sports broadcasts. But the network is no longer the chief or even a major source of local radio programming. Religion, like the local station, must depend largely upon its local resources to provide adequate representation on the air.

V. THE NEW SOUND IN RADIO

Radio today is a different medium from what it was in the years 1930 to 1947, its golden era. The nationwide networks of thirty years ago with their audiences numbered in millions no longer exist, or continue in name only. The composition of the audience for radio has changed. Today radio deals with audiences—not audience—and those audiences have different needs, different preferences, and different expectations of what radio is and should be than did the audience of twenty years ago.

Above all else, radio has become a *local* medium. Only a quarter of the nation's 6,250 radio stations retain affiliation with the principal national networks (ABC, CBS, MBS, and NBC). Those stations still affiliated rely on network programming sources at most for news, a few feature programs (*Dimension* on CBS, *Monitor* on NBC), and special events coverage. All stations are largely dependent for program fare upon shows produced in their own studios and syndicated recorded programs.

Radio once dominated family use of leisure time. Its big shows strove for universal appeal across generation and class lines. The family often listened as a unit, especially to the popular evening network shows.

164

Now television has the universality in program appeal and the mass evening audiences. There are no longer millions of prospective listeners for any given radio broadcast.

Bob Hope and Bing Crosby, stars of network radio when audiences numbered in the millions

Nonetheless, the aggregate audience for radio is great, perhaps even larger totally than it was in the years of network radio. Millions of persons do listen to radio. The RADAR study, a 1967 survey made by broadcasters, claimed that 94.7 percent of the nation's adult population listens to radio sometime within any given week. But this audience total is divided and subdivided into thousands of audiences attuned to thousands of individual stations. Any given broadcast is more likely to attract only a few hundred listeners than it is to garner an audience numbered in the thousands. Walter E. Nixon, a broadcasting specialist with the United Community Funds and Councils of America, has analyzed audience statistics to show that on the *average* a single radio station attracts only 2,500 listeners during a quarter-hour of broadcasting. Obviously, some stations attract many more listeners than do others who compete with them. The audience claims very enormously between stations in a single community and from one hour

165

to another on individual stations. The important fact is that any station, even a 50,000-watt clear channel outlet, is limited in the audience it can attract.

How do people listen, and to what do they listen? A 1968 Gallup Poll of adults taken for the National Association of Broadcasters found that nearly two thirds of the respondents generally have a favorite station and prefer to listen to it. Three fourths are even more selective; they tune in for a specific program. Two thirds of the people interviewed reported that they listen to radio without doing anything else at the same time, a remarkable concentration record, if true. As to programs, 87 percent of those questioned listen to radio for news reports. Other program preferences, in order of audience interest, were found to be music, sports, news discussions, interviews with well-known or interesting people, religious programs, and advice and informational shows. Many people reported they simply want to have the radio turned on.

Station Personality

Since radio is so keenly competitive, each station tries to develop some unique means of attracting enough of an audience to make its operation profitable. Most stations strive to create a station "personality" that will commend itself to an audience of a particular class with a particular set of interests.[1] We are all familiar with the stations that specialize in programming classical and semi-classical music, with those that play rock and roll all day long to cater to teens and subteens, with all the all-news format, and with the stations that feature hour after hour of random telephone conversation on the call-in shows.

One interesting example of a successful personality station is WBAI-FM in New York City. This station is supported by listener contributions; therefore it must satisfy its listeners or go quickly out of business. WBAI thrives on controversy. It broadcasts the vews of John Birch Society members and of Communists, of religious fanatics and fanatical atheists, of black militants and white racists, and all shades

---

[1] This practice is not new, although it is a necessity for radio stations. The mass media have always fostered cultural and psychological subgroups whose interests and loyalties can be exploited for advertising revenue. The adolescent girls who feed on the celebrity magazines and middle-aged women who fancy confession magazines are two such groups. *Playboy* magazine has successfully developed for young men (not adolescents) its peculiar social image of a "valued mode of existence." Television has recently succeeded in abstracting men as an audience subgroup through its extensive use of sports broadcasts.

of opinion between these extremes. Almost anyone with something interesting or shocking to say becomes grist for the WBAI mill. The first show of the day comes on the air anytime from 7:00 A.M. (official sign-on time) to 8:30 A.M., depending upon when engineer and announcer make it to the station. Audience members sometimes listen to silence for as long as an hour waiting for their favorite station to get on the air.

The audience of other stations may not be so loyal, but one mark of today's listener is that he tunes to a station not to hear a specific program (the results of the Gallup Poll previously cited, notwithstanding), but because he knows that the station generally broadcasts programs he wishes to hear.

The religious broadcaster, to get his program on the air *and have it listened to,* must tailor it to fit the format of the station he approaches for time. A rock-and-roll music station will not be inclined to broadcast a thirty-minute theological discussion, but an FM station which concentrates on playing classical music and presenting lectures by learned men might be interested. Similarly, an all-news station would not air a program of favorite hymns. Its listeners would not be interested; they tune to the station for news.

It is a waste of time today to produce a program which does not conform to the specialization of the station over which it is to be broadcast. Even if the station can be pressured into giving or selling time for the program, it is unlikely that many persons will listen.

AM and FM Program Services

The religious broadcaster should be familiar with the two basic kinds of radio service in use today, amplitude modulation (AM) and frequency modulation (FM). There are complicated technical differences between the two, but for the layman the important thing to remember is that AM transmissions can be heard over great distances from the transmitter but are subject to electrical and other forms of interference (static), while FM transmissions can be heard only within the horizon range of the station antenna but provide high-fidelity static-free sound reproduction. FM is, therefore, a superior service for the broadcasting of music or of any other sound that requires fidelity and full-frequency range in reproduction.

Until recently, FM receivers cost more than did AM sets, and they were sometimes hard to tune. They worked well as part of a fixed high-fidelity sound system but were impractical for use in automobiles or even as kitchen or bedroom sets. Lately FM receivers have been transistorized and simplified. One sees them swinging from shoulders at the beach and sitting on the bedroom dresser. The writer has an excellent FM receiver housed in a portable unit that also has AM and shortwave receiving bands.

The earlier problems of FM made it inevitable that the vast majority of radios sold should be AM receivers; therefore the majority of broadcasting outlets were AM stations, and even when FM transmitters began to be common, advertisers preferred the larger audiences to be found on the AM band.

In the hope of attracting the affluent, who would be the ones most likely to experiment with FM, most FM broadcasters programmed more cultural material than did the AM stations. Symphonies, operas, lectures, book and theater reviews, and formal instruction were all part of standard FM fare. The station AM programming became popular music, short newscasts, and the call-ins often interspered with a good many paid religious programs. In many cases an AM station also holds a FM license. It has been common practice in such cases for the same programming to be carried over both stations.

A recent ruling by the Federal Communications Commission has banned this latter practice. A station management which holds separate AM and FM licenses must now broadcast substantially different programs on the two stations or risk the loss of one of the licenses. This FCC ruling should mean that FM stations will become more independent of AM dominance and will carry a greater variety of programs than they have in the past. Add to this situation the growing number of FM receivers and the tendency of FM stations to specialize in stereo reproduction, and one can conservatively predict that FM will soon equal and in time will succeed AM as the primary radio service.

Today, however, the religious broadcaster who wishes to get his message to the largest possible audience still must concentrate on AM stations. In doing so, he will pay a certain price. His program will be judged first on its merit as entertainment, then on its religious content and the service it can render to the audience. The religious broadcaster may wish to produce a discussion of the moral values in contemporary society. The station will reject it in favor of a two-minute sermonette. He may wish to begin his program with a Bach chorale. A popular and lively hymn tune will win the day.

Most AM stations today—and an increasing number of FM—are

168

programmed so that he who listens may be on the run. One of the most important sources of audience is people in cars, going to and from work, shopping, or taking a long trip. Another audience is people who tune in for news bulletins, weather reports, and time signals while they are dressing in the morning and undressing at night. Still another is the large number of persons who we have seen are interested only in news bulletins. Except for broadcasts of sporting events, people do not turn to AM radio to be entertained over a period of time, as they do to television, or to be informed "in depth" or culturally enriched (also a form of entertainment) as they do to FM or the hi-fi set. The attention span for AM may be expected to be short. Therefore, AM stations tend to program in short segments: the single musical number preceded and followed by disc jockey chatter; the 4½-minute news and weather wrap-up; 4½-minute commentaries, such as *Dimension;* and spots, spots, spots. Some stations limit the length of a program segment to 4½ minutes. An exception to the rule of shortness is the call-in show, which may last for hours, but even so, a single conversation wih a caller seldom exceeds a minute or two in length.

If the religious broadcaster wishes to plan his programs to satisfy the average FM station, he may have the opposite problem. FM stations characteristically try to appeal to the more cultural tastes in a given community. Their program formats allow for half-hour and even hour-long presentations. Their listeners are accustomed to pay attention to what they hear. FM listeners also expect to hear good music. Somet FM stations will turn thumbs down on programs that deal with the Bible and with matters of Christian faith. With them, the Christian communicator needs to be careful not to be entrapped into treating issues of faith in generalized, objective terms, thus watering down his presentation to a thing of little more than academic interest.

The biggest drawback in FM broadcasting is that the audience is likely to be small. The question facing the religious communicator is often whether he wishes to reach a small audience with a detailed, reasoned program of considerable length or a larger audience with a simple, short presentation.

One does not have to prostitute the quality of religious broadcasting to cope with either of these limitations. There are ways, as will be seen in Chapter VI, to make spot announcements convey the deepest Christian insights. Some Christian broadcasters successfully employ

169

formal educational techniques to present such issues as ethical responsibility and peace to highly secularized FM audiences.

The point to be remembered is that radio is not an electronic plum waiting to be picked by any wandering Christian who wishes to use it for his own purposes. It is a specialized medium with unique potentialities and limitations. The Christian broadcaster must be aware of these restrictions and be prepared to produce programs that can achieve his purposes over radio stations that are determined to hold rather than to drive away their audiences.

Audience Choice

As indicated earlier, the religious broadcaster must decide first what audience he is determined to reach with what he hopes to communicate. Next, he must study the personality of the stations which are accessible to him and the audience tastes to which they cater. Finally, he must decide whether or not what he has to offer on the air fits into the format of one or another of the stations.

The general audience for religious programs is large and is spread over a cross section of society. This writer and associates who have done research on audiences for religion have found that the more than 60 percent of households that regularly listen to religious programs are no different in social and intellectual characteristics than are the families that do not follow religious broadcasts. While the whole audience for religion is generalized, the specific audiences for individual religious programs are far from being cross sections of society. Each religious program selects its own audience, which is specialized in both size and social composition. Research has shown that in cities of 250,000 and over, network and nationally syndicated religious programs have audiences about equal to a large church congregation. Listeners are more likely than not to be church affiliated. They are almost without exception church oriented; that is, they have a background of religious training and church attendance, even though they may at the moment be using radio as a substitute for active church membership.[2]

Religious broadcasters often err in failing to take into account this predilection of their programs to be self-selective of audiences. Queried about their target audiences, spokesmen for religion almost invariably specify all-inclusive groups: all the unchurched, all families, all adults,

[2] Parker *et al., The Television-Radio Audience and Religion,* pp. 201-6.

the unsaved. They think that when they go on the air their audiences are as universal as the gospel itself, that they are speaking to everybody. They make the mistake of believing that because radio reaches audiences numbered in the millions, it automatically delivers an audience that is representative of universality.

Duplication of pulpit material or of in-church communications—which is what most religious broadcasts do—will attract only the same class of audience the communicator will get in his church, and in decreasing numbers, since they do not need to duplicate their church experience. Furthermore, the attraction of radio will not automatically rub off on an amateur performer; nor will it make a man who cannot inspire in the pulpit inspire on the air. Any religious spokesman who aspires to use radio successfully must undergo the discipline of becoming as much a professional in broadcasting as he is in religion. He must also understand the needs and tastes of the various available audiences and their readiness to absorb a religious message.

The obligation of stations to serve the public interest has been stressed in detail. There is a reciprocal obligation that rests on the religious broadcaster and all others who speak in the name of public organizations to make an intelligent, understanding, and cooperative approach to stations with programs that will conform to the tastes, needs, and desires of the audiences of the particular licensees.

Some religious leaders shy away from trying to put religious programs on stations that concentrate on popular music and news or stations that offer narrowly one-sided programming of whatever sort. However, the primary reason for using radio for the promulgation of the Christian faith is that broadcasting affords an opportunity to communicate with persons who are inaccessible to the church by any other means. If the purpose of Christian proclamation and evangelism is to sensitize the insensitive, to stab awake the indifferent, to challenge misconceptions, and to communicate to troubled and despairing persons that God cares, then the place for such a message is in the place where these people are open to receive it, namely through mass communication.

The experience of Christian broadcasters on mission fields abroad is instructive at this point. At the end of World War II the government of China was prepared to provide an almost unlimited amount of time on its radio stations for any form of commercial broadcasting, including religion. Rather than use the powerful stations controlled by the Chiang Kai-shek regime, Christians in Shanghai and Peking

171

demanded and obtained, from American missionary agencies, the establishment of Christian stations, all of which have since fallen into the hands of the Communist regime. The Chinese Christian leaders complained that when they spoke on Kuomintang-controlled commercial stations, they were preceded and followed by "sing-song girls," the Chinese equivalent of today's rock-and-roll interpreters. These Christian spokesmen never considered the fact that sing-song girls were the chief radio attraction in China at that time and that their greatest opportunity for reaching a maximum audience of non-Christians was to be side by side with those popular programs.

Since 1947 numerous Christian stations have been established throughout the world, especially on the shortwave bands. Except for stations sponsored by conservative and fundamentalist bodies, which do not demand proof of performance, such stations have found that if they are to attract any significant audience, they must devote 60 percent or more of their time to programs of news, indigenous music, agricultural information, child care, and other public welfare interests not originally conceived of as having religious broadcasting significance. Religious broadcasters in such places as the Philippines, India, Southeast Asia, Japan, the Middle East, and Ethiopia have come to the realization that whatever enriches life or sheds light in dark places must concern them as much as formal religious subjects. Their broadcasting is keyed by audience demand to the thesis that right living is essential to a right relationship to God and one's fellowman and to the understanding that listeners demand service, not just indoctrination.

In the United States and Canada the emphasis on local programming plays into the hands of the creative Christian communicator who wants to make maximum use of radio but who may have little money to spend. The amount of time that is available to religion through network programming is small and is diminishing. But local radio stations throughout the country are looking for entertaining and informative programs to fill their broadcasting schedules and to meet their public service requirements. Radio today is like a new medium of communication. It is dominated by the necessity of obtaining and holding a dependable segment of the audience in a fiercely competitive market. The religious broadcaster who can produce programs that are excellent enough and interesting enough to help the station build up its audience in measurable quantity stands the best chance of getting time to air his message.

VI. PROGRAM PLANNING AND PROGRAM TYPES

Communication is a complex affair, but it is never abstract. It takes place only on the basis of an encounter in which there is a clash of mind with mind. Even in cases of conflict, if anything is to result from the encounter, the exchange must take place within an atmosphere of mutuality and attentiveness in which there is the expectation that response will be both given and elicited; for exchange alone is not necessarily communication. Comprehension and acceptance occur when the parties involved share a common universe of discourse, a mutual desire for contact, and sympathetic understanding of their common involvement in the predicament of man. Only in a real I-Thou encounter is anything really communicated.

Roger Mehl calls communication "the fundamental human fact." It is more than that. Communication is profoundly the fundamental religious act.

No people can function constructively without a faith that gives both individuals and the whole society a secure basis for action. Each generation thinks and acts within an overarching faith that is developed out of a complex of beliefs, ideas, and institutions whose linkages are derived from the system of communication. The input to the communications media of thought, suggestion, analysis, and interpretation has great influence in determining the faith of a particular culture, especially one that is dominated by mass communication as is ours. Therefore, the process of community-wide opinion-forming can be one of the most important of our religious activities, and the church has a ministry to public opinion and to the instrumentalities through which public opinion is influenced. Religious broadcasting provides means for the church to address itself to the issues that influence the community mind-set. Since these issues and both the specific decisions of the individual and the flow of common life are operative within a prevailing climate of opinion and complex of compelling motives, this ministry calls for a religious interpretation of the underlying emotions, ideas, and incentives that determine the events of our lives as a people. Consequently, the purpose of religious broadcasting is not just to voice an opinion about this or that but to inseminate the expectancies and guiding images through which people will handle life. This teaching and preaching should be carried on boldly and vigorously, in such a manner that it demands response from the auditor which indicates he understands that it makes a difference in his life if he accepts the Christian interpretation of meaning and being.

Mass communication can be employed to make religious motivation and faith the pulse of a civilization and the seedbed out of which cultural renewal and redemption will grow. This concept of the role of religion in mass communication should dominate program planning.

How to Get Time on the Air

There are two ways for a church or a combination of religious bodies to get on the air. They can buy time, or they can convince the station management it should give the time as a public service.

Radio stations stay in business by selling air time to organizations that wish to broadcast some sort of message. The message may be commercial advertising from an appliance store or a religious program from a church. The time-buyer has certain advantages over the public service organization that gets free time to air its program. For example, it is almost certain that no question will be raised over the purpose, format, or content of the program. The commercial sponsor has control of his program, whereas the public service client may be subjected to all sorts of strictures under the guise of station policy. Time is another vital factor. The best available time is held for sale. Conversely, the buyer of time can choose when he wants his program to appear, while the public service program is assigned time when the smallest audiences are available.

Radio is relatively inexpensive as an advertising medium, especially in comparison with television. Yet its impact can be every bit as great as that of any other medium. Many stations publish rates of less than $100 for an entire hour of broadcasting. Spot announcements often can be bought cheaply also. Usually stations sell time to local organizations at substantially lower prices than the ones they list on their national rate cards. There are always discounts for quantity purchases. One mistake to avoid is buying time in the Sunday morning religious-ghetto hours because it is cheaper in price than anything else. The audience does not justify the expenditure.

It goes without saying that a church or denomination that wants to advertise its own program will be expected to buy time from most radio stations. Free time usually goes to councils of churches or ministerial associations, which represent the whole religious community or at least the majority of Protestant church membership. But the possibility of obtaining free time is not the sole—or even the most important—reason for having the churches do their radio broadcasting cooperatively. The nature of mass communication mitigates against the narrow sectarian content of most denominational broadcasting and in favor of an ecumenical programming that emphasizes the oneness of Christianity, the overall Christian concept of man and society, and the relation of man to God. Furthermore, the churches, with their always limited financial resources, cannot afford to be competitive with one another on the air. Together they can pool their money to hire producers, writers, and other technicians needed for the presentation of effective programs. Alone, even national denominations find it well-nigh impossible to pay the costs of top-notch programming.

Above all else stands the fact that listeners are impatient with sectarian radio programs and tend to reject them, just as non-Christians in missionary lands turn away from the sectarian divisions among missionary agencies. While sectarian programs do attract listeners, studies of religious broadcasting show that the majority of them are persons who are already convinced of the rightness of the message.

Even the council of churches, with its limited funds, is faced with the question of when its programs are to be aired if it limits itself to sustaining time, as against the possibility of reaching substantial audiences by buying time in prime periods. Audience surveys indicate

175

that it is hardly worthwhile for churches to expend man hours and money for production costs on programs that are aired on Sunday mornings, when most religious programming is heard. If stations will not fulfill their public service responsibilities by providing time in the better hours of the day for important community institutions such as the council of churches, the religious interests in the community might better serve their cause by buying time for their programs, in the short run, while putting pressure on the stations by persuasion and legal action, if necessary, to fulfill their public service responsibilities under the Communications Act.

How to Decide What Should Be Programmed

It has been well stated that every radio broadcast is a show and must have essential qualities of showmanship if it is to garner an audience. If the elements of showmanship are present in a program, if something catches the ear that appeals to some basic facet of personality or to something that is close to the self-interest of the listener, he will stay with that program. People will listen to something that sounds alive. They are willing to be informed—even to be educated—if at the same time their imaginations are piqued and they are lifted outside themselves into a fascinating world of wonder and interest. This is entertainment in its most constructive sense.

Religious programs are no different in kind from any other radio shows. They cannot be planned in a vacuum. The producer of a religious radio program cannot ignore (1) what the listener wants from radio, what his emotional and intellectual concerns are, what is going on in his life with which the program can make connection, and how willing he is to listen to a religious program, or (2) the generalized kind of radio communication that the listener will not merely put up with but eagerly take in. This latter factor is directly related to the "personality" of individual radio stations.

It is fruitless for churches or councils of churches to go on radio for the purpose of garnering prestige for the institution or for selected clergymen. Nor should they fall in with program proposals advanced by stations for the purpose of establishing a good record for their reports to the Federal Communications Commission at license renewal time. Religious programs will exert impact only if they have something worthwhile to say to the people of a given community and if they say it in terms that the people will listen to and understand. These standards do not require religious programs to aspire to the lowest intellectual level among listeners. They do make it apparent that religious communicators may have to modify their ideas of what is good for the audience to relate to what the audience thinks is good. This kind of compromise is always necessary in the communication of ideas through the mass media, since we can enter the consciousness of the listener only through reference to his experience and comprehension of his readiness level.

The Planning Committee. Effective radio programming requires careful planning. A council of churches should have a broadcasting committee made up of persons who are broadly representative of the interests of the community, theologically sophisticated, educationally oriented, and knowledgeable about broadcasting policies and techniques. It should have laymen, laywomen, and clergymen as members. This committee should address itself to at least these seven tasks:

1. Study of the needs and interests of the people of the community to determine the issues that religion should and can speak to via radio

2. Setting of goals for religious broadcasting

3. Conduct of station relations (programs should be handled by producers)

4. Deciding what programs should be broadcast under the auspices of the council

5. Auditioning of proposed programs, considering them in the light of the goals adopted

6. Making general plans for each series of programs—their preparation, production, and promotion—leaving the actual work of production to qualified writers, directors, and performers

7. Arranging for financing of programs, approval of budgets and supervision of their expenditure

Analyzing the Community. The planning committee should look at community needs and the needs of the churches at least once a year, basing the study on grass-roots testimony. The issues and ideas that are agitating other units of the council should be examined. Community leaders in all walks of life should be asked to help the committee determine what are the pressures and problems and religious needs as of a particular year, month, and week. The ideas and events that are in motion in the community are the raw material from which to fashion religious radio programs.

The broadcasting season will probably run from September to June. The yearly analysis should be begun in the early spring and completed

177

by the end of May. It should be followed by a planning institute in which the next season's programs, except for special events, are blocked out to allow for adequate preparation. This planning should not prevent the committee from being flexible enough to change its programming to meet emergency needs.

Setting Goals. Goals should be concrete; for example: to eliminate discrimination in employment in the community; to have white children understand black children and their problems and aspirations; to increase church school enrollment by a stated amount; to create a climate of opinion that will lead to the elimination of air pollution; that all churches shall have racially open membership; to develop emotional identification between listeners and Christian missionaries and thus foster support of missions.

Goals should be broad enough to allow for a variety of interpretations of beliefs, ideas, and issues, but planners must guard against allowing programming objectives to stray from the fundamental truths on which all Christians agree. The ultimate goal of our broadcasting is communication of the gospel. The good news that "God was in Christ reconciling the world to himself" is the core message. God is dealing directly with "the world"; the gospel is directed to the stuff of human existence: travail, suffering, joy, love. Religious programming can do no less than to treat of the world and its meaning if listeners are to be led to relate themselves to God's reconciling will.

Delineation of the underlying theology and method of Christianity is necessary to guide a sustained ministry carried on through broadcasting. Grasp of the faith on the part of the planning committee must be related closely on the one hand to the analysis of the community and on the other to the programs that finally appear on the air. Certain questions—some intellectual, others concretely related to broadcasting procedures—need to be asked and answered before goals are decided upon and program preparation begins: What are the values and practices held precious by Christians? What are the core experiences of the Christian life? How are these values and experiences communicated? What are the strategies of Christianity that need to be communicated? What is the Christian interpretation of the events that are buffeting people now? Of coming events? What is the Christian judgment on the decisions people are making? What are the needs of people in this community that pose a peculiar challenge to the church because they can best be met by the church or will not be met unless by the church?

Coupled to these questions is the concrete query: What issues for which the church has a peculiar responsibility can be dealt with effectively by radio better than by other available means, or by radio in conjunction with other available means? This question is not easily answered. Decision requires insight into the listening habits and tastes of the persons with whom one wants to communicate, together with an assessment of their readiness to attend to programs designed to speak to their needs. The importance of facing up to this problem cannot be overemphasized. Too much of what passes for religious broadcasting is entered into without any such preliminary assessment.

Planning Programs to Achieve Goals. Once the planning committee has decided upon its objectives, it can choose programs that may be expected to achieve them. The program plan should include all shows that the committee originates locally plus those that may enter the community via a network, as does *The Art of Living,* or by means of syndicated recordings, as is the case with Richard Sutcliffe's weekly news report. It is important to know just what religious programming is being heard in the community, aside from the programs sponsored by the council of churches. In part, this information is needed so the committee will know what competition it has; in part, the knowledge will make possible the utilization of some programs that fit into the committee's policies and plans. Since there is hardly any community into which radio signals do not come from other places near and far, the needed information cannot be had simply through picking up the local newspaper and scanning the week's listing of radio programs. Getting it requires a listening project, which in turn requires the enlistment of concerned laymen and laywomen to be reporters.

The listening project should be extended to include general observation of all radio stations in the community. The results should reveal what each station's personality is: what community "needs, tastes and desires" it is trying to serve; what audience it is reaching; the format, length, and content of its programs; what religious programs are being aired, and at what hours.

Whatever the outcome of these studies may be, they will provide the information without which one cannot hope to get very far in planning new programming. The writer's own experience in studying radio stations shows that in the average community one may expect to find a large number of syndicated religious radio programs which buy air time. They range from conservative devotional-evangelistic programs to the talks and commentaries of the right-wing religious extremists,

179

such as McIntire, Hargis, and Bundy. These commercial programs tend to monopolize the choice broadcast time devoted to religion. Network programs sponsored by the National Council of Churches, such as *National Radio Pulpit,* and syndicated programs distributed by the *major* Protestant denominations, such as programming of the local council of churches, are most often consigned to the Sunday morning ghetto hours.

Besides finding out what is on the air, the planning committee should study the programs that are available to them from the National Council of Churches, denominations, state and local councils of churches, the American Bible Society, and similar sources. Such programs can lighten an otherwise burdensome production load. Usually they will be of a type or quality that is beyond the ability of local resources. But such outside programs should not be used automatically just because they are easily obtainable and usually are given without charge. They should be aired under local auspices only if they fit in with the objectives of the planning committee. Do not let outsiders do your programming for you. However wise and skillful they may be, they do not know your community and its needs.

How can you be reasonably certain a particular series of programs will achieve a stated objective? First, by writing out (in one sentence, if possible) the general objective being sought by each series of programs and the specific purpose (always in one sentence) of each individual program. Second, by planning the programs in accordance with the purposes. If you are using recorded programs, examine each one before it is broadcast to make sure it is suitable for your needs. Find out from the Broadcasting and Film Commission what is going to be on the network shows you are endorsing. For your home-produced series, write out the ideational content of each program for the guidance of the producer. Keep your statements of objectives in the form of concrete *ideas* that can be used as guidelines by writers and performers in preparing shows. Remember, they are not the specifics that appear in scripts.

The programs that are finally prepared for broadcast should develop from an appraisal of the interrelationships between your goals, the audience to be reached, and what needs to be said to attract and hold listeners. The committee should consider such questions as these: What do the listeners know about the subject of the program? What more do they need to know? How much of what we want to say can we expect them to assimilate? What must we do to prepare them to listen to us? What beliefs do we want to change? What action do we want the listeners to take? How can this action be most clearly defined? What is the most vivid means of presenting the subject matter?

Asking such questions is not a *pro forma* exercise. They are asked by every advertising agency as it creates material to be used through mass communication in behalf of a client's product. If religious broadcasting is to be something more than a recital on the air of pious platitudes, if it is to vivify the unique revelation of God in Christ in our time, if it is to stab awake and scandalize, upset and redirect lives, and teach men how to praise God in the secular world, then the religious broadcaster must subject himself to an even more rigorous discipline in both preparation and performance than that which the commercial broadcaster goes through as a matter of routine. Detailed preparation is essential to success in broadcasting, and even then success is not assured. Only after such preparation is the planning committee in a position to consult with its producer on the format and content of the programs that will actually be aired.

Program Types

The possibilities for a creative radio ministry are almost endless. The church can do anything secular broadcasters can—and do it as well—from sending a roving reporter around town with a tape recorder to talking turkey to teen-agers through jingles written by Stan Freberg. As a rule of thumb, the more simple a show is in format, the more effective it is likely to be on radio. Programs that are not overloaded with production frills give the performers and the content a chance to shine. It is what is said, how it is said, and by whom that count on radio, rather than the package in which the message is delivered.

The Relation of Format to Content

"Format" is a term borrowed from printing. It means "the shape, size, and general makeup of a publication." Applied to a radio program, "format" describes the program design into which the content is inserted and through which the content moves. Format is how you play what you have to say.

The format is secondary in importance to the purpose and content of the program. Some shows, such as *Meet the Press*, develop formats that become their identifying signatures. Even so, the format is only a vehicle for the transmission of the content; it does not make the show what it is.

It is true, of course, that programs are conducted primarily on the basis of format, with content subordinated to form. A good many religious programs are of this type. *The Eternal Light* is a dramatic series; content must be fitted into the form of drama. Similarly, with *National Radio Pulpit* format is paramount, with content conformed to the mini worship-service design.

The subject matter should determine what format a program will assume on the air. Since religious programs aim mostly at communicating ideas and values, it is well to decide on objectives and content before choosing the format for the performances. Once you know what you want to do, format will follow in due course, with the decision hinging on the question of what type of program will best communicate the chosen message to the desired audience. Subordination of format to message may lead to the use of two or several formats within a given series of programs.

All too often religious programs are planned the other way around. A station offers a council of churches a spot for a "devotional" program, meaning a rotation of ministers as speakers with church music for filler. Automatically the offer is accepted. The speakers begin to appear and to speak their unconnected pieces without serious consideration having been given to (1) what such a program will accomplish in the religious life of the community, (2) what *ought to be said* on the particular station at the time being offered and by what means it should be said, (3) what audience the program will reach, if any. Or a planning committee may hit on a program format that seems to be popular—interviewing, for example—and put a show on the air only to find that it is worthless in terms of religious values because nobody thought to ask the fundamental question: Interviews of whom, for what purpose?

Program Forms and Practices

Imagination and a willingness to experiment, coupled with a sound grounding in radio techniques, are necessary for the development of programs that will catch and hold a substantial number of listeners. A church body might develop a program of community analysis that few people could ignore by sending someone everyday to interview and observe at city hall, in hospitals, among the poor, in business offices, on the street, and then to report on the air about the ethical problems encountered. Or the council of churches might turn over a time period to its youth department for a series in which the young people might say anything they wished. Think what that might do to start dialogue across the generation gap! Or one series of programs could ignore formal religion entirely and each week present an interview with a community leader who would talk about community affairs and what listeners can do about them. Or church women could run a consumers advice program for mothers of young children who do not have the time or facilities to shop around. Or a series of organ concerts could be recorded, using only the best organs and organists in the community, and then aired on FM. Or the best teen-age rock-and-roll combinations could record weekly and be aired with the minister who best knows how to talk to teen-agers as master of ceremonies. He would know what to say between numbers.

All the foregoing are programs that are feasible for a council of churches to produce at small cost and with talent that is apt to be available. They would fit into a variety of formats.

A balanced schedule of religious broadcasting will include programs in a number of categories, some of which are concerned solely with content, others of which are closely identified with format. No program practices are suggested here that are beyond the scope of the talent and money available to a council of churches.

News. There are two sides to the broadcasting of news about religion. The first and most important thing to do is to see that religious news is carried regularly on newscasts of the various stations. Church bodies have a tendency to take their news releases to the local newspapers and let it go at that, ignoring the news desks of the radio and television stations. The audience for broadcast news is greater than the readership of most newspapers. Most people depend upon radio and television for the bulk of their news and information.

News releases need to be written in broadcast style for use on the radio. Otherwise they can contain the same information that is transmitted to the newspaper. If the local radio stations do not use news of religion, interviews should be arranged with the news directors. Often men in that post are unaware of the fact that churches are important community institutions. More frequently, like the city editor of the newspaper, they must be educated to understand that church bodies generate hard news through their acts and their expressions of opinion and that a large number of people want to hear news about church activities.

183

Programs devoted entirely to news of religion can have an important place in any religious programming schedule. They should be prepared from reliable news sources, such as the reports of Religious News Service. They should be written in radio news style and voiced by someone who has experience in news broadcasting. If a news commentary is attempted, it must be done by a person who is expert in analyzing the news. His judgments must be based upon reliable information that is more detailed than material on a specific subject that can be picked up casually through mass communication.

The best weekly analysis and report of the news of religion that is distributed nationally is that of Richard Sutcliffe, director of broadcasting for the Lutheran Church in America. Mr. Sutcliffe is a professional radio commentator, and his reporting is well and accurately done. The programs are provided free to councils of churches as a service of his denomination. They may be obtained from the Broadcasting and Film Commission.

Spot Announcements. Ten-second, twenty-second, and one-minute spot announcements are radio's stock in trade. They sell goods running into uncounted billions of dollars every year. Spots are designed to catch the listener up and to hold his attention wholly, but for a short span of time. That is why the commercials come on louder than the rest of the program material. The advertiser wants to tear your attention away from everything else, even his own entertainment program. The important thing is that this technique works. People pause—at least mentally—and listen. They absorb the material in the spot, not just the name of a commodity, but even ideas and information.

Taking a cue from this fact, the Television, Radio, and Film Department of the United Presbyterian Church in the U.S.A. developed a series of radio spots aimed at young adults which tests have shown have a remarkable power to catch attention and drive home a message. These spots, one-minute long, were written and produced by Stan Freberg, one of the most successful Hollywood producers of commercial radio and television spots.

The Presbyterian broadcasting staff gave Freberg a formidable task. They demanded spot announcements that would stab people out of apathy and challenge assumptions that the church is irrelevant. They also insisted upon communicating a single theological tenet: that God *is* and God *cares.* Freberg used humor, a theme jingle—"Out on a limb without Him"—and crisp, satiric dialogue to achieve his effects. A situation was set up in each instance in which an interviewer (Fre-

184

berg) engaged a subject in conversation about the church. The subject rejected religion and the church as irrelevant, then was stung with a crisp question or comment designed to make him do a double take and realize his own isolated predicament. The spot closed with the jingle.

The production of spots as complicated and elaborate as these is beyond the resources of a local council of churches. (The Freberg spots can still be obtained from the Broadcasting and Film Commission.) But simple spots can be prepared locally, and they can be effective if enough thought is given to them. They can even be made humorous.

An example of a simple spot is the one-liner which lasts ten or twenty seconds. In some communities churches of the United Church of Christ are experimenting with one-liners that run something like this: "The United Church of Christ thinks a well-rounded education includes religious education. Is your child in Sunday school?" A clever writer can turn out any number of such short announcements. They need not all be voiced by the same person. In fact, the reader should be chosen to give maximum meaning to the content.

The Five-Minute Format. We have already pointed out that many stations do most of their nonmusical programming in five-minute segments—five minutes of news and weather report, five minutes of sports news, five-minute shoppers' guides, etc. Five minutes really means four and a half minutes; the last thirty seconds are always taken for a commercial spot announcement.

These short program segments may prove to be advantageous to religious broadcasting. There really is little audience for sermonizing. As we have seen, a skillful writer can pack a point and a punch into a one-minute spot, perhaps to better advantage. Important issues can be introduced and explained and solutions suggested in four and a half minutes. If the thinking is clear and the language is concise, the message will be driven home and remembered.

The Office of Communication of the United Church of Christ has recently been distributing several series of five-minute programs that have had widespread station acceptance and that may be a source of ideas to the planning committee of a council of churches. *Encounter* presents conversations about ethical issues between Morris Abram, president of Brandeis University, and Truman Douglass, vice-president of the National Council of Churches. *Congressional Comment* gives senators and representatives the opportunity to say anything they

185

please about American foreign policy and issues of war and peace. *Let's Be Friends* uses two formats, both featuring Edwin Randall as master of ceremonies. Sometimes Randall talks quietly about ethical and social issues from the standpoint of Christian beliefs. Sometimes he interviews interesting and important people.[1]

The five-minute format offers councils of churches the opportunity to develop "personality shows" in which someone who can speak about religious issues in terms acceptable to listeners can be featured. Personalities are just as important in local programming as they are on networks. The highly paid disc jockey is the prime example. A personality shines brightest and probably has the greatest impact and develops the greatest audience loyalty through a one-man show. Furthermore, a one-man program is the easiest, least expensive, and most foolproof production you can put on—if you have the man or woman! It takes great skill to do a one-man show, plus the dedication to give the hours necessary for preparation of content and the rehearsal required for each appearance.

Call-in Programs. There is no reason why this popular program format should be monopolized by uninformed listeners who discuss trivia with equally uninformed station announcers and by right-wing extremists who use call-in programs to attack community leaders and institutions. The call-in should be a natural for thoughtful local ministers to get into down-to-earth dialogue with listeners on subjects that really count.

The Television, Radio, and Film Commission of The United Methodist Church is demonstrating every night on a nationwide hookup of stations how this can be done. *Night Call*, with the noted Negro radio artist Del Shields as master of ceremonies, nightly presents people who come prepared to discuss serious issues (but not to chat) with callers who telephone in from all parts of the country. Thousands of calls that cannot be answered pile up every night, testimony to the fact that people want an opportunity to be heard on the burning questions of these troubled times.

Special equipment is needed for the call-in programs. The station must have enough incoming lines to receive hundreds of calls over a short span of time. Volunteers must be available to man the phones

---

[1] Samples of all the foregoing programs may be obtained free from the Office of Communication, United Church of Christ, 289 Park Avenue South, New York, New York 10010.

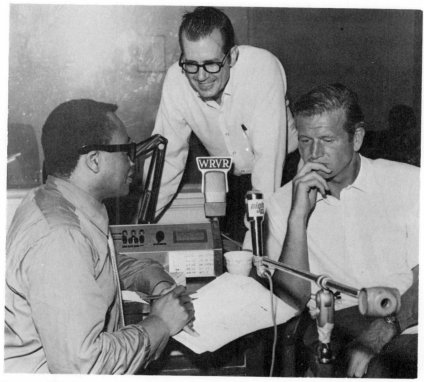

Courtesy of Wagner International Photos
Night Call's host Del Shields with producer Ben Logan and guest Mayor John Lindsay

and carry out preliminary interviews with callers. Their most important assets are tact and judgment, for they will decide which calls will be taken on the air. The station should have a tape recording system that allows a seven-second delay before remarks made on the telephone reach the air. This delay period allows obscene statements and other unsuitable talk to be withheld from the air.

The most important element in the show is the minister—or the team of ministers and lay experts—that responds to the callers. Like every other host on a call-in program, the religious representative on the phone must convey the impression that he likes people, is interested in their views as well as their problems, and will handle any

187

question with candor and without being noticeably embarrassed. He must be willing to engage in frank, no-holds-barred conversation. He must also be capable of quickly shutting off the trivial.

Anyone hosting a call-in program will find it advantageous to have a rolldex card file of information and quotations about issues that are frequently brought up on the air. Then when someone calls up and says something like: "What do you think of the superintendent of schools making that speech last Thursday saying we should send money to Communists to support them?" (an actual call-in question), the host can flip his file, find that the school official was endorsing gifts to UNICEF on trick-or-treat night, and say so, firmly.

Any minister who hosts a call-in program must also be prepared to be faced with a new and perhaps time-consuming ministry to people who hear him on the air and want to bring their problems to his study where they can talk to him in person.

Interviews. The interview is cheap and easy to produce, but it is not simple to prepare. It can be vividly exciting or deadly dull, depending upon the people who participate.

Courtesy of TRAFCO

Eric Robinson interviews for *Man with the Mike,* a United Methodist program produced in cooperation with the National Council of Churches

188

A good interviewer is a rare jewel. He must understand people, like them, like to talk to them. He must be able to draw out comparative strangers. His sensitivity to listeners needs to be equal to his sensitivity to the person he is interviewing.

A good interviewer always subordinates himself to the person he is interviewing. It is not the interviewer's ideas that people have tuned in to hear. His questions must be framed to give his guest the widest possible scope for reply. This means that the interviewer should know not only what his guest thinks and believes but also what his opponents stand for. Only then will he be prepared to ask "hostile" questions— queries framed from the viewpoint of the opponents. This is the only fair way to interview. Bringing out the opposition views gives a man the opportunity to develop and defend his own position.

Interviews need to be carefully prepared for but not rehearsed; otherwise they may lose their spontaneity. The interviewer should have in mind the questions he wants to ask. It is better not to reveal them to the subject, again in the interest of maintaining spontaneity and informality. Never let the subject read prepared answers or even work from extensive notes. It will destroy the sense of encounter and make the program sound stale and flat. If the person being interviewed knows his subject, he will have enough facts and ideas at hand to be exact enough in his answers. If he has the questions in advance, he will probably show it by being too pat and detailed in his answers and will spoil the naturalness of the conversation. Within the limitation that he should be asked about things he is expected to be familiar with, the more surprised he is by a question, the better his performance is likely to be.

Having learned all he can about his subject, the interviewer should put himself in the place of the listeners and bring up the questions they will want answers to. A good attitude for the interviewer to take is that of a man who has encountered an interesting person in a hotel lobby and wants to sound him out as to who he is, what he does, and what he thinks.

Interviews fall into two general classifications. Some are reportorial, designed to elicit facts from an expert or from a person who has had a particular experience. They revolve around facts: "I was there." "I saw what happened." "I studied it, and these are my findings." Others are all personality. Their purpose is to introduce the listeners to someone who is inspired spiritually and can inspire others. The

189

person interviewed need not be famous. A school teacher who has the respect and love of her pupils, a man who looks upon his daily work as a Christian vocation, a mother who understands and can interpret the trials and rewards of family living—persons such as these, teamed with a skilled interviewer, can provide fascinating Christian witness.

In any interview success will depend largely upon the vitality, the integrity, and the aura of interest that flow from the person being interviewed to the individual listener.

Interviews can be conducted in a radio studio, but it is just as easy to take a tape recorder to a person's home or place of business and interview him in surroundings where he feels most at ease. Another favorite method is the "beeper phone" interview in which the station calls the subject and interviews him through the telephone. The FCC no longer requires the "beep," but some stations continue to use it because they think it lends documentary authenticity to the interview.

Discussions. Discussion programs are most likely to find places on FM stations. But their success, as always, hinges on choice of an issue that is important to the listeners, willingness of the participants to listen to each other and to help each other get their views expressed, and a clash of views that will bring all facets of opinion to bear on the problem.

The discussion leader is also a key factor. It is sometimes advantageous to have a radio professional in command. A member of the station staff who has built up a following brings with him a ready-made audience from among his fans. From his side, participation in a religious program with high intellectual standards enables him to be heard in a new setting that is complimentary to his public image. One hazard is that he may not be well enough versed in the subject or sufficiently interested to give the program the "bite" it should have. On the other hand, he may be able to probe with questions and comments at points where a clergyman leader might be fearful of giving offense. It is the task of the person in charge to bore in as may be necessary to get answers to questions the listeners want answered. He cannot afford to be either hesitant or overly nice to the participants. Nothing can be more deadly than to hear people on a discussion program being overly solicitous of each other and politely formal when the situation calls for candor and some degree of heat.

One mistake sometimes made in discussion programs is to pick a "best" solution for the problem and point all the argument and interpretation toward it. Seldom can a vital issue be solved in thirty to sixty minutes of conversation, especially if the participants are careful to air all points of view. The best that can be expected is to have the problems pointed up, the terms for meeting them defined, some *possible* solutions suggested, and the means for attaining them described. Such open-end procedure is good for the listener too. It gives him the opportunity to exercise his judgment, to find his own truth. However, if as infrequently happens, there is an open-and-shut solution that the participants agree on, it should be conveyed to the audience.

The formats suggested here as vehicles for religious broadcasting, especially the short, personality-centered, one-man shows and the interviews and discussions, are desirable because these are people-to-people programs. The feeling of isolation and loneliness that seems to pervade our society puts people in danger of losing their sense of community. They question whether or not it is worthwhile to live disciplined, responsible lives. They discount ethical, moral, and religious ideals which only a few years ago were assumed to be beyond challenge. Even in small towns, people do not know their neighbors as they did a generation ago.

The programming heretofore discussed channels documentary evidence and sympathetic ideology to listeners—material that may help offset defeatist assumptions. While the programs cannot all be positive in outlook and optimistic in tone, they will always put negative factors in proper perspective. More importantly, they can radiate that human warmth that radio can communicate so well. Without having met the performers face to face, listeners can be made to feel a rapport with them. There can be a basis for understanding and vicarious friendship. Such a relationship can be extremely important to the listener who feels isolated.

A feeling of rapport on the part of the listener is most likely to result from repeated appearances on the air by performers, although sometimes a single exposure may have the magical effect of communicating this feeling. This need not seem strange if we remind ourselves that one hearing of a gifted violinist, singer, poet, or actor can have an unforgettable impact and that one contact with a person can evoke a feeling of wanting to know him better.

There is a mystique about radio communication. Some of it is the verbal content of the message, but much of it has to do with the voice quality and the idiosyncrasies of manner of the performer. Difficult as

191

it is to define, this mystique is nevertheless easily recognizable. It is what the theologians have in mind when they say a person has charisma. Religious broadcasting should place a high value on the charismatic personality.

Will Rogers, a charismatic personality, on his Sunday evening broadcast for NBC

Worship Programs. If worship programs are a part of the schedule, they should be the most carefully produced of all. Music should never be amateurish. Its tonal quality should meet the most exacting hi-fi standards.

Sermonic material should be written especially for the program, not warmed over from the previous Sunday's pulpit appearance. And minister and choir should rehearse together long enough and earnestly enough to give a flawless, polished performance.

Putting each minister in the community on a devotional program in rotation is to be avoided at all costs. Participants must be chosen on the basis of ability to perform on the air. However, one good training ground for ministers can be a five-minute daily devotional program aired just after sign-on or before sign-off. Audience is admittedly minimal at those times, but the opportunity is given to the minister to hear and criticize himself.

Training

Even appearances on five-minute devotionals should be avoided by ministers who have no training in broadcasting. Standards of performance are so exacting and so widely recognized today that the neophyte has little chance of success.

Fortunately, there are training facilities available through most of the major denominations, some seminaries, schools of communication, and some councils of churches.

Courtesy of TRAFCO
A training workshop for *The Place*, TRAFCO's teen-age program

Station Relations

No community organization—including the church—has a *right* to time on the air simply because it wants it and asks for it. No station manager is justified in giving or selling time for programs that have trivial aims or are planned in haphazard fashion. He owes it to his

193

audience to demand programs that are interesting, that cater to audience tastes and needs, and that will be skillfully produced.

Therefore, the most important thing in station relations is to offer a program that is worth putting on the air. The best way to convince a station manager you can fulfill this requirement is to present him, in writing, with detailed plans of the series you propose to sponsor. Include your purpose, the audience you expect to reach, number and description of the individual programs, production plans, budgets, promotional plans, and at least one sample script.

Don't just mail him your plans. Take your document in and sit with him while he reads it. He will have questions; you can answer them. If he has objections, you can counter them on the spot.

A Summary to Guide Program Policies

All available research findings indicate there is a substantial audience ready to listen to religious radio programs and that these potential listeners constitute a cross section of the population in personality, education, social status, interests, beliefs, even in age. To reach such a multidimensional audience requires imagination and initiative, coupled with a detailed knowledge of listener interests and needs and a clear definition of the aims of any programs attempted. Most program formats generally in use in radio can be expected to attract audience as long as the subject matter is interesting and important to the listeners and the programs have skillful, believable performers. Unless religion uses whatever variety of programming it has available, it will limit its opportunity to speak to a maximum number of people. But never will there be one audience, for listeners are divided into diverse audiences that must be attracted and held by diverse programs aimed at particular interests and needs.

Whatever programs are produced, there should be an overall strategy into which each one fits. Each series, each show, should have a specific task to perform that can be set down in a declarative sentence that tells exactly what the program is about. Only through detailed planning and continuous evaluation can the sponsoring agency of religious programs have a yardstick against which to measure the success of its radio broadcasting.

APPENDIX—RESOURCES

Resources fall into at least three categories: (1) *consultative,* (2) *printed,* and (3) *available for broadcast.*

The first category consists of the denominational departments of radio and television, the Broadcasting and Film Commission of the National Council of Churches, and the state or city councils with radio-TV staffs.

Paid directors of broadcasting employed by councils of churches now have an important role in operating religious broadcasting. Their number is increasing steadily. They have formed the National Association of Broadcast Executives. They are recognized by the Broadcasting and Film Commission as an entity entitled to elect representatives to the Council Cooperation Committee and to the Board of Managers of the BFC. The interests of this professional group extend beyond the communities they serve to encompass the needs, problems, opportunities, and resources of the cities in relationship to the broadcasting of religion. They are interested in all that is encompassed by the term "Christian communication." Radio and television are seen as tools to be used in conjunction with other media, and planning a broadcast program as something to be done in the context of overall program planning.

These men and women represent an extension of the services and presence of the Broadcasting and Film Commission, though their own organizations are separate and autonomous. Their counsel and advice can be a valuable resource. It is entirely in order to invite a nearby council broadcaster to consult with leaders in a community which does not have a specialized staff of its own. The BFC can provide an up-dated list of names and addresses.

A. Organizations
Denominational offices of communication or of radio and television

Broadcasting and Film Commission of the NCC
475 Riverside Drive, New York, New York 10027

Council broadcast executives (Write to the BFC for a list of names and addresses or the names of those nearest you.)

Institute for American Democracy
Suite 101, 1330 Massachusetts Avenue, N. W., Washington, D. C. 20005
(For information on combating extremism in broadcasting)

National Association for Better Broadcasting
373 North Western Avenue, Los Angeles, California 90004
(For information on program evaluations)

National Association of Broadcasters
1812 K Street, N. W., Washington, D. C. 20006
(For the industry's self-regulating Radio Code)

Television Information Office
745 Fifth Avenue, New York, New York 10022
(For broadcasting data)

Anti-Defamation League of B'nai B'rith
315 Lexington Avenue, New York, New York 10016
(For action information)

Federal Communications Commission
1919 M Street, N. W., Washington, D. C. 20036
(For information on rulings)

Government Printing Office
Washington, D. C. 20002
(For printed copies of FCC decisions)

B. Publications

Broadcasting and Government: Responsibilities and Regulations. 1961
By Walter B. Emery. Michigan State University Press, East Lansing, Michigan.
Code of Standards for Protestant Religious Broadcasters.
The Consultation of Protestant Religious Broadcasting, Room 403, 2112 Broadway, New York, New York 10023.
Effects of Mass Communication. 1960
By Joseph T. Klapper. The Free Press, New York, New York.
Emerging Profiles of Television and Other Mass Media: Public Attitudes. 1950-1967
A report by Roper Research Associates. Television Information Office, 745 Fifth Avenue, New York, New York 10022.

How to Protect Citizen Rights in Radio and Television.
    Office of Communication of the United Church of Christ, 289 Park
    Avenue South, New York, New York 10010.
Radio Programming: A Basic Training Manual. 1968
    By Ralph Milton. Geoffrey Bles, London. Available through
    RAVEMCCO, 475 Riverside Drive, New York, New York 10027.

C. Available for Broadcast

The Broadcasting and Film Commission has excellent music resources in
three volumes of recordings entitled *So Will We Sing.* The BFC can also advise with regard to availability of network or syndicated programs to meet
special needs, including spots and other programming not channeled through
the BFC.

Denominational offices often have spots and other programs of various
lengths and may be able to supplement or amplify information supplied by
the BFC.

The television-radio departments of councils of churches are preserving
some of their best programs on tape for possible use elsewhere. Ask the BFC.

PART III

FILM
AND
THE CHURCH

JOHN M. CULKIN, S.J.

I.   INTRODUCTION TO THE MEDIUM OF FILM

It's the age of the moving image. Photography got it started. Film got it moving. Television got it into the living room. What began as a luxury is now almost a universal necessity. Celluloid fables have fed the dreams of the world for more than half a century. The moving image has been harnessed to the goals of commerce, propaganda, education, exploitation, entertainment, journalism. It is the dominant medium in the communications experience of most people in the developed world. Film and television are the forms of communication most wanted by most people everywhere. It's the age of the moving image.

Even sleeping giants like the schools and the churches are overcoming sixty years of lethargy or active hostility to search out the positive aspects of the media. The timetable is right on schedule. A couple of generations is just about the stimulus-response pattern of traditional and established groups to innovation. There is little fun, however, to be had in warming-over the tedious facts of the communications gap between the churches and the media. The weak man broods over the past; the strong man takes vengeance on it. It's a time for doing things, and there are some nice things to be done.

Films are what we will be talking about. Some of the learned cinematologists claim that we must distinguish among "films," "movies," "cinema," "motion pictures." These nuances may be necessary for students who have to pass exams, but they don't do much for the person who has to get a film program started in the local school or church. This treatment is intended not for theoreticians but for practicing fanatics. Theory will be provided as a context, but it will always be translated into a series of specific "for instances." Film is such an extensive field that there is always the hazard of going over all the ground without touching any of it. Through a number of case studies related to general themes or individual titles it may be possible to communicate not all about film, but what film is all about.

Students frequently make a distinction between educational films and "real" films. We know what they mean. The films that are out to get their point across and to instruct often lack the style, pace, and humanity of "real" movies. More importantly they often fail even to do what they set out to do. This book is about real films—the kind that get screened in commercial theaters and on *Saturday Night at the Movies*. It will also deal with the so-called short films, whose length and craft place them in a category all their own. There will be little or no discussion of the traditional instructional films about which more guidance is already available than most of us need or want. Besides, *Alfie* is more fun to be with than any of the teaching films. And realistically it is the *Alfies* which have to a degree become the teaching films in the age of the image.

The total information environment has become a giant teaching machine. The schools and churches operate within this ambience. They no longer control the information inputs into the lives of their clients. Nor can they pretend that their constituents have not already been conditioned by the facts, attitudes, and values disseminated through the new media. The traditional mediators of information and values have found that they are often responding to situations rather than creating situations. This new reality of the total information environment merits some attention at the outset. It has all happened so fast that most of us have been caught up in its wake. Some insight into both the nature and speed of this communications revolution can be gained by imagining an experiment in which a modern home would be stripped of all the communications devices invented or widely used since the turn of the century. The TV set which burns for more than thirty-five hours a week would be the first to go. Then a boxful of radios would be carted away. There would be no movies, telephones, cameras, or phonographs. The family would most likely not own an automobile. Their communications world would be limited to the spoken word and to some books, magazines, and newspapers.

Within this world of limited and controlled information—the real world before the turn of the century—it was possible for the family, church, and school to decide when young people were ready for certain kinds of information. There were few rival communicators to offer contradictory information or to challenge that which was provided by the community. The various agencies within the community tended to reinforce the consensus shared by the adults of the community. That world is pretty much finished. The new media have swept over and around the barriers established by such a static and Maginot Line culture. This is not a value judgment, just a statement of fact. It is in dealing with the fact rather than in lamenting the change that we can measure our concern.

The gravitational pull of threatened groups is to ignore or reject that which threatens them. The movies got this treatment from the churches for long years. The churches acted out Sam Goldwyn's advice for the handling of critics: "Don't pay any attention to them; don't even ignore them." But in the 30s the movies became too big and too brash to be ignored. This was the age when many churchmen used public opinion and political power to exert influence over the film industry. This approach managed to tidy up the moral content of film for a while, but at the same time it made people afraid of the medium. The current rediscovery of film by many church groups is a healthy response to the realities of the electronic age. It is also based more on a respect for film than on a fear of it.

The case for an intelligent and balanced use of film with church groups can be put quite simply without invoking the intercession of a long list of respectable experts. Films deal with man. And great films, like great anything else, communicate insights about man which we should want to share and explore with each other. As one of our twentieth-century liberal arts (or liberating arts), film also speaks in contemporary accents about contemporary themes. This is especially important for church groups whose relevance is measured against their ability to make sense with current problems. Film can provide the human context out of which can arise discussions of human needs and human behavior.

If film can change people, it is also true that people can change film. Expensive media like film and television have to be responsive to their audiences. It follows, therefore, that any improvement of a substantial part of the audience should result in an improvement in the types of programs made available to that audience. It is a supply-and-demand situation. Walt Whitman summed it up when he said: "To have great poets, there must be great audiences."

If Whitman's thesis about the relation of art and audience is true for poems, which can be written on the backs of old envelopes by a production staff of one, it holds with multiplied validity for motion pictures and television, which are wild combinations of art, technology, and commerce. The traditional interplay of artist and patron has to be rethought for each of the new media. Numbers have a great deal to do with what can be communicated through any of the media that involve large financial investments. Both risk and success are measured by increasingly large numbers as one moves from print to stage to film and to television. A hardbound book hits the best-seller lists when it sells 20,000 copies; a Broadway play starts making money after the first 100,000 tickets; a commercial film has to have roughly $2\frac{1}{2}$ patrons for every dollar invested before it breaks even—with the result that a million-dollar movie needs $2\frac{1}{2}$ million patrons; and in television, which is the massest of mass media, a series in prime time needs a continuing audience of approximately 25 million viewers to stay on the air.

East Side/West Side went off the air with a sustaining audience of 14 million regular viewers—an audience that would be astronomical for any of the other media but which is too esoteric to be served by television.

In the commercial media the name of the game is numbers. The one-to-one relationship between Lorenzo de' Medici and Michelangelo has given way to a complicated feedback system between the public and the network or the studio. The public is the patron, and distasteful as this may be to the elitists, this numerical approach to taste is the fact of media life. It has its obvious problems. What most want is not what all should get. And just because people take what they get doesn't necessarily mean that they are getting what they want. The public doesn't know what it wants until it gets it and then may only be accepting what it appears to want. What we need are more choices. Since the quality of films and television depends on the quality of the audience, we should be at pains to improve the quality of that audience.

Because film and television are so important, the development of a tough-minded audience is important. We can ill afford the kind of cliché thinking which writes off the new media as "mere entertainment." William F. Lynch speaks eloquently for a more human and integrated approach to the new media.

What is this "most fundamental part of the problem" of our contemporary cultural life? I wish to propose that it is the abnormally sharp split between two forms of culture and two states of the national imagination, the elite and the popular. There always has been such a division but never as abnormally severe as today. And both cultures are suffering from the size of the gap, because what has happened is a movement on each side toward polarization rather than relationship. There is a tendency on the side of the elite imagination to become private, unintelligible, rarified, and unrelated to the public order, with its own code, initiation and membership. The artists and the intellectuals incline toward having private conversations with themselves in their work. On the other hand, the popular imagination, in its present mass form of films and television, has moved toward the opposite goal of vulgarity and cheapness and a progressive deadening of vision.[1]

It is this danger of a corporate and personal schizophrenia about the new media which urges us to develop a positive rationale for the study of the new media. The mass media are fast replacing the weather as a subject more suited for conversation than for control. Bernard Berelson has suggested a moratorium on much of the party-line rhetoric associated with the new media: "What we do not need is more glib statements of position by the various sides—statements for the record, and little else. What we do need is the responsible joining of issues and the search for devices and mechanisms and ideas that have a chance of improving the situation."

We have not really had time to assimilate the full import of the revolution in communications. As a result, we have had far more reaction to the new media than reflections about them. These reactions span a wide range of emotions and opinions. Unfortunately, these reactions often tend to introduce harmful splits into society: between popular culture and elite culture, between entertainment and education, between industry and the public, between the school and the outside world, between the sacred and the secular.

Such cultural fission and polarization of attitudes unfortunately and unnecessarily suggest that a choice must be made between the two opinions, that one of necessity excludes the other. It results in a tire-

[1] "The Theologian and the Critic," a paper presented at the International Congress on Communications (New York, 1963), p. 1.

some comparison of the best in one area with the worst in another. The gap consequently widens, to the peril of both. This tendency to pose issues in either-or categories is a ditch-digging technique introduced at a time when we need a bridge-building one.

Often, too, the mass media are put under one tent and treated as an "it." This may be the lingering problem of Latin plural in the English language, but more often it reflects a dangerous cultural shorthand. Statements which may be true of one medium have no relevance for another. Each medium has its own language, audience, methods of production, economics, and distribution. Each must be judged within these limits. The print media pose problems far different from the broadcast and image media. Movies differ from TV both in style and distribution. Television and radio operate on channels belonging to the public and therefore have a responsibility to that public different from that of the strictly private-enterprise products of print and film. Better understanding of the media can only result from greater precision in talking about them.

Archimedes claimed he could move the earth if he had a place to apply a lever. The mass media post the same problem of leverage. We need a forum within which qualified and articulate spokesmen can interact with the image industries. I use Gilbert Seldes' phrase "counter-vailing powers" to describe these forces. We must avoid the idealogical trap of referring to such groups as "the opposition" because such a label reflects a questionable bias and because the "pitched battle" techniques will not work.

These countervailing powers include a great variety of institutions freely associated for reasons of politics, economics, culture, religion, and education. They must realize their latent power and choose means to give direction to their activities. Good men doing nothing are still the weak links in any society. As Seldes remarks: "The dangerous situation is that those who could steadily influence the mass media in the right direction are either ignorant of the effects of those media or consider themselves immune to them."

It is easy not to take the new media seriously. They had their origin as vehicles of entertainment. Despite the high talk about their roles as art forms, it is clear that 80 percent of their products are neither art nor worthy objects of study. And there is the lingering human temptation to believe that knowledge marks the end of innocence. To my mind, there will be no intelligent breakthrough into media study until the question is given the stature it deserves.

Most attempts to initiate such study programs are based on the thesis that fear is the beginning of wisdom. The harmful effects, both real and conjectured, of the mass media are described in forceful terms with ample statistics to indicate the amount of a student's time which they consume. The premises seem to be that the mass media are here to stay and that we might as well protect people from the harmful effects. Such an approach is valid, if incomplete, and often does produce a degree of discrimination and taste. My only quarrel is with the somewhat negative attitude which often motivates it—as though we were engaged in a massive campaign to build shelters against the mass media fallout. This is not the way we formulate the goals for our programs in literature and the arts.

If fear is the beginning of wisdom, it is only that—a beginning, a phase which by definition is meant to be transcended. The value of fear as a motive also tends to wane in the course of a long-range enterprise. We must define our goals in positive terms. Being against something is meaningful only in terms of being for something. We need an insight into the new media in terms of the experiences they communicate to man as a consumer and in terms of the new power they place in his hands as a producer and creator.

One positive norm for action suggests that we acquire good taste by tasting good things. This is a true, attractive, but incomplete approach. Such a process undoubtedly improves taste and creates a distaste for junk, but it still falls short of the intelligent understanding we expect of the audience for any art form. It also seems to imply that some elite group establishes the norms for what is good rather than training the individual in making his own judgments. This can produce a new kind of normlessness based on arbitrary authority and presumed consensus. Occasionally we experience its effects in our current romance with any movie bearing subtitles. As educators we are committed to the belief that not only can we make the student good but we can make him smart too.

Making people smart is the job of the schools and the churches. This is where the organized programs of media study belong. One of the reasons we teach literature is to open the student to the world of human experience and values. One man is no man. We want him to grow beyond what Piaget calls the "I, my, me" world of childhood to the freedom of maturity. We want to rescue him from being trapped in the singular, or in himself, so that he can understand the heart of man and the family of man. The print media have no monopoly on

207

these human experiences. We should want people to share these experiences with the same vehemence that we want them to read worthwhile books. And in addition to these more or less literary programs there is the whole range of programs involving history, current events, social questions, science, art, music, and just plain entertainment.

Film has proved to be a privileged medium for communicating with young people. Today's students have a special thing going with the movies. They get turned on when the projector gets turned on. Increasingly, film is becoming the medium in which they both find and express themselves most directly.

It's hard to say whether they are going to the movies more frequently, but the quality of their response has something different about it. They do some thinking both before and after the film. They talk about films—sometimes for days. They do it for all kinds of films: long and short, 35mm and 16mm, those from under the ground and those from over the counter, art films, TV programs, commercials, student-made films. Discussion is very hot on films like *Alfie, Blow-up, A Man and a Woman*. College film programs are often instigated by the students; college film courses are sold out fast; and now the high schools are getting into the act.

Only fools and feature writers are dumb enough to generalize about today's students. Let's use sixteen to twenty-two as the age range. There are at least three generations within those six years. The old biological and chronological measures of generations have been made meaningless in the electronic age when attitude and style of life define the differences. A nineteen-year-old in Watts recently looked at the fifteen-year-olds and said: "I wish I was young again. I just don't dig these kids."

Not digging kids is a fairly popular sport this season. And the reasons for the difficulty frequently plug into walls. Those tiresome people with their tiresome quotes from Socrates about the fact that youth is going to the dogs are just trying to reassure themselves that it's all just a little bit more of the same. It ain't. The moving image, which has served as both a cause and measure of the generation gap, may now have a role to play in some bridge-building.

Much of what is written about students and films has been spun off the specialized experiences gained along the New York-Cambridge-Berkeley college circuit. There are also kids looking at films in Harlem, Idaho, and the Job Corps camps. The quality of student response to film today will be looked at in terms of a few random hunches having to do with history, the students themselves, and the nature of the film medium.

History has something to do with this current romance with the movies. This is the first generation to have grown up with television. The TV set was waiting for them when they got home from the hospital, and they liked it enough to clock 15,000 hours of viewing by high school graduation. Their psychological intake system is programmed for the moving image. The latest in cinematic technique is served up daily in the sophisticated production of the commercials. The "late late show" has much of the history of film waiting for them each evening. And there are films in theaters, in schools, and at Expos. This generation also benefits from a maturing film industry and from the range of choices made possible through specialized theaters, 16mm distribution, film societies, library programs, and independent and foreign films. It all adds up to a lot of images in a lot of students.

The new media are turning out a new kind of student. They are plugged into the "now," and they want to experience it and be involved with it. They are the only people who are the native citizens of the new electronic environment. It is their natural terrain, their turf. They experience it directly as the only world they have ever known; most adults are still translating the present through the criteria of the past. Unfortunately, most of those in charge of the care and feeding of the "now" generation belong to the "then" generation. Traditional mediators of culture, like the family, church, and school, just aren't used to moving at jet-age speeds. They would be well advised to learn because much of the momentum for what is happening and what is judged as relevant has already passed from their hands. Approval or disapproval of what is happening is considerably less important now than the willingness to understand.

We will get back to our feature presentation after one more look at the new student in this hasty, junior-varsity exercise in sociology. The generation gap may not be as important as, or may only be a symptom of, the gap in our culture between intellectual and emotional development. The head and the heart got disconnected somewhere along the line. Mothers start the catastrophe with their speeches to kids on "don't touch, shut up, sit still, stop looking around." The schools keep it alive with the emphasis on book learning, rote, standard exams, college of choice, overwork, remoteness from direct experience.

Others assign some of the blame to Puritanism, literacy, industrialization, and the damp feet of our English forebears. Urbanized, literate Americans just don't show their feelings, you know. Feelings get punished, laughed at, repressed. The result is a stripped-down version of humanity hiding behind a flat, expressionless mask. What we call sentimental is frequently only the first stirring of a little humanity. The comparison between Zorba and his English boss serves nicely.

What gets starved in the official culture now gets fed in the popular culture. Popular music, clothing, films, and dancing underscore this new concern with the person and with the need to envolve all the aural, tactile, visual, and kinetic elements of the individual. If all this sometimes goes too far, it may be because it has had to come from so far; that's the law for pendulums. If the official culture has stressed the outsides of things, today's students want to explore inner space. The LSD thing is just a dramatic instance of the general desire to take the inner trip, to probe personal feelings, to experience as a total human being. Students mistrust formulas or verbalizations; they want experiences.

Words are frequently inadequate to the task. The phenomenon of the silent or stammering student seems to be growing. They would rather look dumb, stupid, or quiet than sound square, phony, or out of it. Their halting manner is frequently a search for a new idiom or style. There are a lot of lovely feelings to express, but we are stuck with some very corny vocabulary to express them. The kids are very sensitive to personal values. They want to learn how to get back and forth to each other—person-to-person, not station-to-station.

Today's young people just don't trust people who don't feel. Motion pictures work well because they are also e-motion pictures. It is something of an anomaly that there has been so little analysis done about the strong feelings films elicit in people. Perhaps this neglect of an almost universally shared experience is in itself a measure of how we are uneasy or distrustful of our own feelings. In a brilliant article in *Psychology Today* Richard Farson discusses this detached attitude which characaterizes so much of American life.

At present, noncognitive and nonverbal skills just aren't considered academically respectable. They have not yet been formulated into a conceptual structure; and they seem imprecise, fuzzy, vague, and even threatening. We feel we must keep the lid tightly closed on Pandora's box, for we fear that it contains the irrational, the potentially explosive elements of human nature.

When emotionality or interpersonal relationships escape from the box, we flinch and take refuge in the dictum that only the qualified professional is capable of dealing with the layers of humanness below the rational. Old-fashioned psychiatry is largely responsible for the prevailing attitude that teachers should avoid tampering with children's psyches. This nonsense has so frightened teachers that they shun almost any engagement with the student as a person.

We treat each other as if we were very fragile, as if any hurt or penetration of our defenses would lead to a crumbling of the entire person; or we regard each other as a tenuously contrived set of social roles which serves to cover what might be the frightening reality—a vicious beast, or at best man's "animal nature."

There is no doubt that educating for humanness will call upon teachers and students to encounter each other in their totality as human beings, with all of the problems and possibilities, the hopes and fears, the angers, and joys, that make up a person. To relate to each other in this way, we will have to learn to be less afraid of what people are like and to recognize that they are not likely to shatter the moment anyone engages them on an emotional level.

This fear of emotionality is in part, I think, responsible for our widespread fear of intimacy. We dare not reveal ourselves, share our feelings. We have developed an elaborate set of social devices which allows us to put distance between ourselves and others, which lubricates our relationships, and which gives us privacy in a crowded and complex society. Even to use such terms as "intimate" or "loving" disturbs most people. Popular belief and much professional opinion hold that the machinery of any social organization, and certainly of a school, will become clogged if people are concerned with each other instead of tending business. Nevertheless, we have a deep need for moments of shared feeling, for they give us a sense of community and remind us of our membership in the human race.[2]

[2] "Emotional Barriers to Education." Reprinted from *Psychology Today* magazine, October, 1967. Copyright © Communications/Research/Machines, Inc.

II.   NOTES ON McLUHAN

"The medium is the message," announced McLuhan a dozen years ago in a cryptic and uncompromising aphorism whose meaning is still being explored. The title of his latest book, an illustrated popular paperback treatment of his theories, playfully proclaims that *The Medium Is the Massage*—a title calculated to drive typesetters and critics to hashish and beyond. The original dictum can be looked at in four ways, the third of which includes a massage of importance.

The first meaning would be better communicated orally—"The *medium* is the message." The *medium* is the thing to study. The *medium* is the thing you're missing. Everybody's hooked on content; pay attention to form, structure, framework, *medium*. The play's the thing. The medium's the thing. McLuhan makes the truth stand on its head to attract attention. Why the medium is worthy of attention derives from its other three meanings.

Meaning number two stresses the relation of the medium to the content. The form of communication not only alters the content, but each form also has preferences for certain kinds of messages. Content always exists in some form and is therefore to some degree governed by the dynamics of that form. If you don't know the medium, you don't know the message. The insight is neatly summed up by Dr. Edmund Carpenter:

> English is a mass medium. All languages are mass media. The new mass media—film, radio, TV—are new languages, their grammars as yet unknown. Each codifies reality differently; each conceals a unique metaphysics. Linguists tell us it's possible to say anything in any language if you use enough words or images, but there's rarely time; the natural course is for a culture to exploit its media biases.[1]

It is always content-in-form which is mediated. In this sense, the medium is co-message.

The third meaning for the M-M formula emphasizes the relation of the medium to the individual psyche. The medium alters the perceptual habits of its users. Independent of the content, the medium itself gets through. Preliterate, literate, and postliterate cultures see the world through different-colored glasses. In the process of delivering content the medium also works over the sensorium of the consumer. To get this subtle insight across, McLuhan punned on message and

John Culkin and Marshall McLuhan

[1] "The New Languages," *Explorations in Communication*, ed. Edmund Carpenter and Marshall McLuhan (Boston: Beacon Press, 1960), p. 162.

213

came up with massage. The switch is intended to draw attention to the fact that a medium is not something neutral—it does something to people. It takes hold of them; it jostles them; it bumps them around; it massages them. It opens and closes windows in their sensorium. Proof? Look out the window at the TV generation. They are rediscovering texture, movement, color, and sound as they retribalize the race.

The fourth meaning underscores the relation of the medium to society. Whitehead said, "The major advances in civilization are processes that all but wreck the societies in which they occur." The media massage the society as well as the individual. The results pass unnoticed for long periods of time because people tend to view the new as just a little bit more of the old. Whitehead again:

> The greatest invention of the nineteenth century was the invention of the method of invention. A new method entered into life. In order to understand our epoch, we can neglect all details of change, such as railways, telegraphs, radios, spinning machines, synthetic dyes. We must concentrate on the method in itself: That is the real novelty which has broken up the foundations of the old civilization.[2]

Understanding the medium or process involved is the key to control.

The media shape both content and consumer and do so practically undetected. We recall the story of the Russian worker whose wheelbarrow was searched every day as he left the factory grounds. He was, of course, stealing wheelbarrows. When your medium is your message and they're only investigating content, you can get away with a lot of things—like wheelbarrows, for instance. It's not the picture but the frame. Not the contents but the box. The blank page is not neutral, nor is the classroom.

McLuhan's writings abound with aphorisms, insights, for-instances, and irrelevances which float loosely around recurring themes. They provide the raw materials of a do-it-yourself kit for tidier types who prefer to do their exploring with clearer charts. What follows is one man's McLuhan served up in barbarously brief form. Five postulates, spanning nearly 4,000 years, will serve as the fingers in this endeavor to grasp McLuhan:

1) 1969 B.C.—*All the senses get into the act.* A conveniently symmetrical year for a thesis which is partially cyclic. It gets us back to man before the Phoenician alphabet. We know from our contemporary

[2] Alfred N. Whitehead, *Science and the Modern World* (New York: Macmillan, 1926), p. 96.

ancestors in the jungles of New Guinea and the wastes of the Arctic that preliterate man lives in an all-at-once sense world. The reality which bombards him from all directions is picked up with the omni-directional antennae of sight, hearing, touch, smell, and taste. Films such as *The Hunters* and *Nanook of the North* depict primitive men tracking game with an across-the-board sensitivity which mystifies Western, literate man. We mystify them too. And it is this cross mystification which makes intercultural abrasions so worthwhile.

Most people presume that their way of perceiving the world is *the* way of perceiving the world. If they hang around with people like themselves, their mode of perception may never be challenged. It is at the poles (literally and figuratively) that the violent contrasts il-lumine our own unarticulated perceptual prejudices. Toward the North Pole, for example, live Eskimos. A typical Eskimo family con-sists of a father, a mother, two children, and an anthropologist. When the anthropologist goes into the igloo to study Eskimos, he learns a lot about himself. Eskimos see pictures and maps equally well from all angles. They can draw equally well on top of a table or under-neath it. They have phenomenal memories. They travel without visual bearings in their white-on-white world and can sketch carto-graphically accurate maps of shifting shorelines. They have forty or fifty words for what we call "snow." They live in a world without linearity, a world of acoustic space. They are Eskimos. Their natural way of perceiving the world is different from our natural way of per-ceiving the world.

Each culture develops its own balance of the senses in response to the demands of its environment. The most generalized formulation of the theory would maintain that the individual's modes of cognition and perception are influenced by the culture he is in, the language he speaks, and the media to which he is exposed. Each culture, as it were, provides its constitutents with a custom-made set of goggles. The differences in perception are a question of degree. Some cultures are close enough to each other in perceptual patterns that the differences pass unnoticed. Other cultural groups, such as the Eskimo and the American teen-ager, are far enough away from us to provide esthetic distance.

2) *Art imitates life.* In *The Silent Language* Edward T. Hall offers the thesis that all art and technology is an extension of some physical or psychic element of man. Today man has developed extensions for practically everything he used to do with his body: stone ax for

215

hand, wheel for foot, glasses for eyes, radio for voice and ears. Money is a way of storing energy. This externalizing of individual, specialized functions is now, by definition, at its most advanced stage. Through the electronic media of telegraph, telephone, radio, and television, man has now equipped his world with a nervous system similar to the one within his own body. President Kennedy is shot and the world instantaneously reels from the impact of the bullets. Space and time dissolve under electronic conditions. Current concern for the United Nations, the Common Market, ecumenism, reflects this organic thrust toward the new convergence and unity which is "blowin' in the wind." Now in the electric age, our extended faculties and senses constitute a single instantaneous and coexistent field of experience. It's all-at-once. It's shared-by-all. McLuhan calls the world "a global village."

3) *Life imitates art.* We shape our tools, and thereafter they shape us. These extensions of our senses begin to interact with our senses. These media become a massage. The new change in the environment creates a new balance among the senses. No sense operates in isolation. The full sensorium seeks fulfillment in almost every sense experience. And since there is a limited quantum of energy available for any sensory experience, the sense ratio will differ for different media.

The nature of the sensory effect will be determined by the medium used. McLuhan divides the media according to the quality or definition of their physical signal. The content is not relevant in this kind of analysis. The same picture from the same camera can appear as a glossy photograph or as a newspaper wirephoto. The photograph is well defined, of excellent pictorial quality, hi-fi within its own medium. McLuhan calls this kind of medium "hot." The newspaper photo is grainy, made up of little dots, low definition. McLuhan calls this kind of medium "cool." Film is hot; television is cool. Radio is hot; telephone is cool. The cool medium or person invites participation and involvement. It leaves room for the response of the consumer. A lecture is hot; all the work is done. A seminar is cool; it gets everyone into the game. Whether all the connections are causal may be debated, but it's interesting that the kids of the cool TV generation want to be so involved and so much a part of what's happening.

4) *We shaped the alphabet and it shaped us.* In keeping with the McLuhan postulate that "the medium is the message," a literate culture should be more than mildly eager to know what books do to people. Everyone is familiar enough with all the enrichment to living mediated through fine books to allow us to pass on to the subtler ef-

fects which might be attributed to the print medium, independent of the content involved. Whether one uses the medium to say that *God is dead* or that *God is love* (— — — — — — — — — —), the structure of the medium itself remains unchanged. Nine little black marks with no intrinsic meaning of their own are strung along a line with spaces left after the third and fifth marks. It is this stripping away of meaning which allows us to x-ray the form itself.

As an example, while lecturing to a large audience in a modern hotel in Chicago, a distinguished professor is bitten on the leg by a cobra. The whole experience takes three seconds. He is affected through the touch of the reptile, the gasp of the crowd, the swimming sights before his eyes. His memory, imagination, and emotions come into emergency action. A lot of things happen in three seconds. Two weeks later he is fully recoverd and wants to write up the experience in a letter to a colleague. To communicate this experience through print means that it must first be broken down into parts and then mediated, eyedropper fashion, one thing at a time, in an abstract, linear, fragmented, sequential way. That is the essential structure of print. And once a culture uses such a medium for a few centuries, it begins to perceive the world in a one-thing-at-a-time, abstract, linear, fragmented, sequential way. And it shapes its organizations and schools according to the same premises. The form of print has become the form of thought. The medium has become the message.

For centuries now, according to McLuhan, the straight line has been the hidden metaphor of literate man. It was unconsciously but inexorably used as the measure of things. It went unnoticed, unquestioned. It was presumed as natural and universal. It is neither. Like everything else it is good for the things it is good for. To say that it is not everything is not to say that it is nothing. The electronic media have broken the monopoly of print; they have altered our sensory profiles by heightening our awareness of aural, tactile, and kinetic values.

5) A.D. 1969—*All the senses want to get into the act.* Print repressed most sense-life in favor of the visual. The end of print's monopoly also marks the end of a visual monopoly. As the early-warning system of art and popular culture indicates, all the senses want to get into the act. Some of the excesses in the current excursions into aural, oral, tactile, and kinetic experience may in fact be directly responsive to the sensory deprivation of the print culture. All the data isn't in on what it means to be a complete human being.

217

III.   SEE THEM AND DISCUSS THEM

The film is the thing. All the discussion and analysis should follow the screening of the film. There are all kinds of films in all kinds of millimeters. The following guidelines underscore some of the choices available for both the content and format of a film study program.

Choice of Films

The selection of specific titles should be determined by the nature of the particular audience with which the moderator is involved. This is why it is essential that the film moderator have seen the films before using them. Some of the record-setting disasters in the film movement have been effected by a neglect of this precept. In general, the experience of others working with similar groups can be of great service. More of this useful material is now being generated as the film movement grows. The appendix to this section contains extensive information on such sources. Choice will also be modified by the nature of the program: whether it is a one-night stand or a continuing series, whether it is a mixed audience, whether the moderator knows his audience. In initiating a film series it is important to open strong, with a well-crafted and relevant film which will lend itself to im-

218

mediate sparks of discussion. At the same time the moderator, who frequently is far ahead of his audience in film sophistication, should resist the temptation to shock the audience by hitting them with a film too far removed from their ordinary movie-going experience. Too many film programs have been torpedoed by such lack of judgment which fails to respect the fact that many film specialists have arrived at their current state of film knowledge and sophistication by passing through a thousand intervening points and that it is unfair to telescope that process into a single evening for someone else. It is also bad politics for the film movement.

This cautionary advice is especially pertinent in film programs for young people. It is not the young people themselves but their parents whose attitudes necessitate this element of good judgment. Parents are often uneasy about the books and films which school or church youth leaders use with their children. That is just a fact. It is a fact with a good many causes, many of which involve their overprotectiveness and lack of knowledge about their own children and about the media. It is a fact, however, which can and should be dealt with in a way that will help everyone in the situation to grow a little.

It has proved very useful to get the parents involved in some way with the film programs for young people. The general purposes and spirit of the project can be communicated to them by letter or at a meeting. It is useful to point out to them that the church and school have a different role to play than the parents in their common concern for the development of the young person. Their hesitancy about the use of specific film titles which they would not send their children to see can often be satisfied by pointing out that the film is being seen within a context in which the young person is with a group who will discuss, analyze, and criticize the film during the postscreening session. It also helps to remind the parent that their children are exposed to much more in their daily life than parents normally like to admit and that the best way of equipping young people for these realities is to train them in the process of making judgments and selections. Parents should also be invited to a film evening of their own when they would see and discuss a film and get some idea of what the whole program is about.

One program got the parents involved with a young people's film program. They were invited to a screening of *The Loneliness of the Long Distance Runner,* a film dealing with the lack of communication between young people and adults. They all saw the film together. The discussion groups were arranged so that adults and young people were represented in all the groups but so that no young person was

Photo courtesy of Continental 16
The Loneliness of the Long Distance Runner

in the same group as one of his parents. After the small groups had discussed the film for an hour, they reconvened, and reports and further discussion went on in the general session. Many young people and parents learned a great deal about one another that evening, most of it positive, but the real communication was the comments which individuals received from others about their own parents or children. Another variation on the same game is to have each of the groups discuss the film independently, to have these discussions recorded on tape and then to swap the tapes. Such a tactic provides a quick lesson in selective perception.

A series built around a common theme has proved to be helpful with many church groups. It affords the advantage of multiple perspectives on a common topic. Chapter V gives a rather full treatment of short films on war and peace.

Use of Commercial Theaters

Theaters and churches have at least one thing in common—they are both empty for most of the hours in the day. Perhaps by cooperating in the filling of some theater seats, the churches can obtain some reciprocal help with church attendance. There are several ways in which church and school groups can work with commercial movie theaters.

1. *Regular Screenings.* The church can plan to base its film discussion on a film currently showing in one of the theaters. The participants are informed of the film and theater, encouraged to see it and then discuss it back at the school or church.

2. *Discussions in the Theater.* Several groups have provided enough interest in particular films that the theater owner has accommodated his schedule to include a few remarks before the film and a brief discussion after it.

3. *Special Screenings.* Most theaters do the bulk of their business on Friday evenings and on the weekend. Several projects have worked out custom-made film programs in the theaters on afternoons, Saturday mornings, and even on weekday evenings. If the organizing group can guarantee enough admissions, they can select film titles of their own choosing and often obtain discount rates.

All these programs have to be worked out with the local theater manager. Such a program is good for him for a number of reasons: it fills empty seats; it gets people back into the habit of seeing films in a theater; it gives him a chance to sell some popcorn; it allows him to perform in the "good citizen" role. Not all the film titles you may want will be available in 35mm since many are out of circulation or sold to television. The advantage of using a theater, of course, is that all the details involved in ordering and screening the films are in the hands of a professional. Several churches have also used commercial theaters to conduct film festivals for young people in a condensed three-day format or over a series of Saturday mornings.

Discuss Them

It is not the film on the screen but the film in the viewer which provides the raw material of film discussions. Everyone is by definition the world expert on what he has experienced. People are rightfully jealous of the insights they develop in response to an experience because these reactions are so personal and so revealing. Discussants are

221

frequently unaware of how much of themselves they reveal in film discussions. These facts suggest that there are some modes of handling film discussions which are derived both from the nature of the medium and the nature of the film experience.

Film is literally an other-directed medium. Both the sequence and pace of the communication are determined by the director. Wrapped in the "narcotic shadow" of the film, viewers are usually swept along by the flow of images. There is no time for critical or analytical reflection. Each new image and sequence stimulates immediate emotional responses. There are no breaks for commercials. Unless the projector breaks down (as it normally does in church or school screenings), you can't call time-out.

The comparison between this experience and the stop-and-go pacing of print can illuminate the impact created by both media. With a book the reader can pace himself. He can begin slowly in order to imbibe the atmosphere of the story and to familiarize himself with the characters and plot. He can check back in his reading. He can pause for minutes or days between chapters. He is in charge of the flow of the story. Not so with a film. There is little opportunity for the viewer to stop and analyze, to refer backward and to project forward, to establish relationships.

This steady stream of images produces an experience which is primarily sensory rather than intellectual. The immediate influence is on the senses and on the emotions, and the pacing of the film precludes any extended analysis of this progression of images. At the end of the film the viewer has accumulated a stack of images which has piled up within him chronologically in the course of the film. This crude psychological description points to the necessity for the viewer to sort out these images, to interpret and relate them, and to impose or rather discover the structure which links them together into a fully human experience.

The total film environment is made of many carefully calculated physical and psychological elements. Seating, lighting, temperature, and all the physical paraphernalia of the theater are programmed to produce a sensory environment in which only sight and sound are allowed to stimulate. In this atmosphere of sense involvement we accept the premises of the film, and during the screening there is a suspension of disbelief. Although we are physically detached from the action of the screen and are only participating vicariously in the drama, psychologically we are frequently quite active in interacting with the emotions expressed on the screen. Movies have a way of getting past our rational and analytic barriers to stir us deeply and in a very personal way. It is one of the few places in our culture where many people experience strong emotional release.

This physical and psychological context explains why the same film can affect different individuals in different ways. In the "generation gap" films, for instance, adult viewers see the dramatic conflict from the point of view of adults, and kids watch it as kids. Fathers identify with fathers and sons with sons. It all seems plain and platitudinous enough until you participate in an emotionally charged discussion in which each of the participatns "knows" that his view is correct and frequently presumes that everybody sees everything pretty much the same way and that they are just being difficult about the whole thing. Three years ago we conducted a group discussion based on *Nobody Waved Goodbye,* a Canadian feature film which leaned

Picture from the National Film Board of Canada production Nobody Waved Goodbye
Nobody Waved Goodbye

223

pretty heavily on the older generation. One parent didn't wait around for the discussion because she knew "they were just going to say how cruel that boy was to his mother." They were about to say nothing of the sort.

A quote from a New York taxi driver might serve as the topic sentence for film discussions and for much more. Tony Schwartz, New York's artist-in-sound, has condensed ten years of conversations with cab drivers into a ten-minute record. The title is taken from the quote of a driver who had given his whole philosophy of life, taken a short breath, and topped it off with: "That is my opinion and it is very true." It is the unarticulated premise of almost all human communication.

Each person sees his own film. This paradox is merely the reaffirmation in a new context of the thesis of individual differences and selective perception. The same film washes over each viewer as an individual with individual past experiences, hopes, loves, fears, needs, and intelligence. The psychological mechanisms of identification and projection come into play. We empathize with some character on the screen. For a while we become who he is, and we fill out the experience by reading our own motivations and emotions back into the film character.

The following practical suggestions attempt to codify some of the pedagogic techniques which seem to work with film discussions:

1. This is not "school." No exams. No failures. No teachers.
2. There is no lecture before showing the film, no what-to-look-for speech.
3. The film should be shown under the best possible standards for viewing and hearing.
4. There should be a break after the film—fifteen hours if possible, fifteen minutes otherwise.
5. The moderator should begin the nondirective discussion, indicate his role as learner, as one in a side-by-side relationship, not face to face.
6. Rules of the game:
    a. Discuss the picture—not ideas in general.
    b. Give for-instances when you discuss.
    c. Be brief and civilized.
    d. Relate each remark to the remark of the previous speaker.
    e. Indicate the way in which the camera conveys ideas.
7. The success of the discussion is not based on whether the discussants agree with the moderator or not. It is good to comment

at the conclusion on the way the discussion progressed without giving "answers" to the film or the discussion. It is ideas that count, not the number of "right answers"—not the quarry but the chase.

8. After the group has seen and discussed several films together, then the moderator can expect cross-reference and comparison of films.

9. The moderator should not look for perfection after the first few screenings.

10. This is not "school." No exams. No failures. No teachers.

IV.   LA STRADA—THE CASE STUDY OF A FILM

As the man once said: "I hate to lapse into autobiography, but I'm all I've got." *La Strada* was *the* breakthrough film for me. It took an avid filmgoer and opened his eyes to the enormous potential latent in the film experience. The screening and discussion of *La Strada* demonstrated the peculiar quality of the medium to get inside people and to help people get back and forth to one another after sharing a common film experience. My dozen years with *La Strada* have been a time of learning how the same film can be open to a rich variety of response by various audiences. The *La Strada* thing has also sensitized me to the situations which emerge from film work and to new uses for films.

On the Road with *La Strada*

Fellini's film *La Strada* was the film which first opened for me the full potential of the medium for communicating with the viewer and for enabling many viewers to communicate with one another. Since my first experience with the film in 1956, I have seen the film more than twenty times and used it more than thirty times with varying kinds of audiences. The analysis of this particular film will be offered here in some detail as a case study of what can be developed with a whole corpus of films once enough films have been used enough times with enough people.

The rather extensive analysis of *La Strada* which follows emerged after many discussions and screenings of the film. It is intended to demonstrate the richness of a great film and to encourage the probing kind of discussion which alone can get at this richness. The analysis itself is the product of this exploratory and communal effort.

Fellini has called *La Strada* his favorite film. Released in 1954, it was the fourth of his corpus of nine and a half films and the one which first brought him world acclaim. It contains a number of themes and treatments to which he returns in later films. And in the judgment of many it is the film in which Fellini seems to be most at home with himself and his subject matter. All the pieces fall into place to form an integral work.

The French love to forage around in what they call *l'univers fellinien*—the ambiance created by Fellini within his films. Some of their minute foraging has scared off others who would like to study films closely and in depth but without destroying their enjoyment in the process. Alfred North Whitehead's rhythm of education serves well here: There should be a stage of romance in which the film is enjoyed for itself, in which as director Sidney Lumet puts it: "You let the film wash over you." The next stage is that of precision or analysis in which all things implicit or hinted at initially are developed. The final stage is that of generalization in which both the intuitive values and the analytical values are coordinated.

A close analysis of beautiful things, however, can kill beautiful things if it gets too far away from the immediate experience of what is under analysis. (The reader will have to pardon this protesting about the task of analysis because the writer has to rationalize for himself a process whose dangers, delights, and repugnance are clearer to him than he would like them to be.) Literature may never recover from its desiccated stage of precision. And analyzing a film in print makes the process even more antiseptic. The real medium for film analysis is a free-flow discussion on the day following the screening of the film. It is the results of some thirty such discussions which will be inadequately cataloged in this investigation of *La Strada*. The groups included all ages and beliefs; they ranged form patients at a mental hospital to graduate students at Harvard; they included high school students, religious retreatants, nuns, Job Corps personnel, and just ordinary citizens. My winters are warmed with the memory of how we talked together about some very basic things.

La Strada evokes this kind of person-to-person communication. Film is a sensory medium. It works around the surfaces of reality to hint at what lies beneath the surface. Much of Fellini's impact derives from the fact that he and his films incarnate a visceral, tactile, and emotional approach to questions which in our culture are treated in a rational style which is uninvolved and antiseptic. Some rainy afternoon Marshall McLuhan can explain why all this came to pass. But for the present, Fellini can help dredge up some of the repressed questions about loneliness, purpose, and love and can treat them with competence, relevance, and humanity while we attempt to develop a vocabulary for handling such hot issues in a cool world.

What follows is a spiral approach to an analysis of *La Strada*. Some data on the characters are followed by a look at the structure of the film and the interaction between the characters. Then there is an analysis of the theological premises of the film. Most of the investi-

Courtesy of Brandon Films
Zampano

228

gation focuses on the film itself, with little reference to Fellini's other films or to biographical data from Fellini's life.

The Characters

La Strada is a people picture. Three people dominate it: Zampano, Gelsomina, and the Fool. A few words about each of them:

Zampano is the man of the road. He lives the homeless, rootless, and lonely life of those on their way but going nowhere. He is tattooed with the sign of the serpent and bound with the links of a chain. He walks in circles repeating formulas. His vocabulary is shot through with references to animals. He is not secure unless he is in complete control. He protests that he doesn't need anybody, yet he constantly uses people. He is the strong man who is not strong. His name means "heavy boot." He is humorless, empty, closed. The film is called *La Strada,* "the road." It is about him.

Gelsomina is the girl of the sea. She lives by the sea; she loves the sea; she dies by the sea. In her own naïve and innocent fashion she is attuned to the primal and enduring elements of life. In the film she

Courtesy of Brandon Films
Gelsomina

229

is often surrounded by children. She responds to nature in her dialogue with the fire, her imitation of the tree, her planting of the tomatoes. She has no defense against music. She intuitively empathizes with the suffering of Oswaldo, the macrocephalic child. She has an at-homeness with things religious in the procession and in her encounter with the nun. She is open and responsive to reality, just as Zampano is closed to it. Her name means "little flower" or "jasmine." She has the spirit of St. Francis about her.

The Fool (*Il Matto*) is the man of the sky. He wears wings, and we first discover him on the high wire. He is constantly surrounded by the signs of the spirit—fire and wind. He is a man of humor, of music, of intelligence, of vitality. And like all the fools in literary and dramatic tradition, he is no fool.

But there is something more to *Il Matto*. A close look at his death starts a new line of thought. When he is killed by Zampano, he is dragged away with his arms outstretched, cruciform. His body is placed in a stone culvert. This clue invites a closer look at how he died. He was struck three times. His watch stopped. He died clutching the earth in front of three trees. In fact he died in front of the middle one. An interesting death. A death which—by the way—he predicted.

Courtesy of Brandon Films
The Fool

Courtesy of Brandon Films
Zampano kills the Fool

His death leads the investigation back into his life. He first appears at the religious festival. Gelsomina has been led to him by the three musicians. The camera follows the procession into the church and then sweeps upward from the altar to the tightrope. The winged Fool stands above the crowd outside on a wire stretched between the church and the bar. He informs the crowd that he has two appetites, and he invites the people to join him for supper. Gelsomina is in awe of him. The first glance they exchange is almost a recognition scene.

They next meet in Rome where Gelsomina is awakened by a donkey, an animal used in the Fool's circus act. The Fool appears in the billowing tent playing the song which Gelsomina already knows. He taunts Zampano, and the battle is on. Or better, the battle continues—the perduring tension between two styles of life: the open and thou-oriented life of the spirit versus the closed and egocentric existence of

231

the brute. It will lead to the death of the Fool and the birth of Zampano.

The Fool is also the revealer. It is his discussion with Gelsomina which gives her insight into the meaning and purpose of her life with Zampano. The choice of a pebble as the reminder of this new understanding has an interesting parallel in the Book of the Apocalypse or Revelation. "I will give him a white stone, with a new name written on the stone which no one knows except him who receives it." (2:17.) Zampano describes the Fool as "the bastard son of a gypsy." The Fool describes himself as one alone and "without a roof over my head." Fellini describes him as "the most intelligent of the three, but with an intelligence that is not merely rational. . . . He is an adventurous spirit, a vagabond; he loves to move about and to travel." In commenting on the Fool's teasing of Zampano, Fellini says: "He is amused by the brutishness of Zampano. He understands things more quickly than Zampano, but he doesn't act out of malice. The mentality of a man like Zampano seems too closed and immobile to him."

In the last meeting between the Fool and Gelsomina outside the jail, he sings her name and places his locket around her neck as "a souvenir." Her whole attitude is that of a communicant. The name of the Fool, incidentally, is Nazzareno—"the Nazarene."

The Structure

La Strada begins and ends by the sea. Fellini has said that for him the sea is "a comforting mystery, conveying the idea of permanence, of eternity, of the primal element." The sea appears in all his films except *Il Bidone*. The sea in both psychology and literature also connotes openness, life, cleansing. Gelsomina is the girl of the sea, and all these values of the sea are part of her world. Zampano is the man of the road, and he understands none of these values. Midway through the film both Gelsomina and Zampano stop by the seashore. She runs to the sea like a liberated bird. He uses it as a washroom. Zampano finally abandons Gelsomina by a seawall, and we are told later that she eventually dies by the sea. And the road on which Zampano travels begins and eventually ends by the sea.

The ending of *La Strada* is the place to begin the discussion of the film. After learning of the death of Gelsomina, Zampano returns to the circus and once more goes through the dull routine of his act. That night he gets drunk and in the ensuing fight keeps repeating that he wants to be alone, that he doesn't need anybody. He walks to the sea, and there is a moment at which it appears that he may be considering killing himself. Instead, he throws water on his face and returns to shore. On the beach he looks at the water, the sky, the stars, the earth. He begins to weep. He now knows what it means to

Courtesy of Brandon Films
Zampano learns of the death of Gelsomina

to be alone, but he also knows what it is to be human. Fellini calls them "sobs of desperation, but also of liberation." Zampano clutches the earth with the same gesture used by the Fool as he died. The film ends with the music of the song associated with Gelsomina and the Fool. The road has led back to where it started.

The ending of the film and the change in Zampano are the result of a process begun with the appearance of the Fool and precipitated by his death. The Fool is the catalytic agent in the film. The Fool's incessant and very incisive teasing is the first thing to start breaking through Zampano's defenses. The Fool's death sends Gelsomina into the whining depression which annoys, infuriates, and haunts Zampano.

233

"The Fool is hurt. The Fool is hurt." Zampano finally abandons her by the seawall ten days after the death of the Fool. But something new has been set in motion. Zampano feeds Gelsomina. He sleeps outside the motorcycle. He responds, rationalizes, notices. And in the very act of leaving her, he is already showing signs of humanity. He covers her with blankets, he gives her some money, and in a gesture both tender and unexpected, he leaves the trumpet with her. It is the instrument the Fool had taught her to play with a delicacy in strong contrast to Zampano's cruelty in teaching her to play the drum. It is the instrument on which she played the song identified with her and the Fool, the spiritual theme of the film. Before she goes to sleep her last words are: "The Fool is dead. Everything is all right." As Zampano leaves along the road, the music of the theme song accompanies him for the first time in the film.

Gelsomina's role in the humanization of Zampano was shaped through her encounter with the Fool. He put some meaning into what she was doing. "If you don't stay with him, who will?" He could have

Courtesy of Brandon Films
The circus act of Zampano and Gelsomina

talked her into coming with him, but he understood Zampano's need and Gelsomina's unique role. "Poor fellow. He's like a dog who wants to talk, but he can only bark." The message of the Fool is reinforced by the nun at the convent who told her that Gelsomina's vocation was to follow Zampano just as she herself followed Christ. And in a scene cut from the final version of the film, the parallel between the nun and Gelsomina is underscored when the nun tells how she thought of running away from the convent until a voice said to her: "Leave, if you wish, but where will you go?" The Fool converts her innocence and naïveté into an aware and active goodness.

The Theology

There is more to the theology of the film than the uncovering of an apparent Christ-figure or the presence of a religious procession. There is a way of looking at the world which suffuses the whole picture. It is a vision which runs through all Fellini's work and which can most completely be analyzed with material from all his films. The theology of *La Strada* is manifest in the character of the Fool, the attitude of the film toward organized religion, and the basic view of man presented in the film.

The Fool. The data on the Fool has already been elaborated. The interpretation of the data is left to the individual. Any one of the items which touch on his role as a Christ-symbol seems casual in itself, but the cumulative effect seems strong in support of such an interpretation. Film-making is a highly selective process, and all the things in the film were thus selected. Whether it was a conscious or unconscious process of selection is another question. They are *in* the film. We discover them there; we do not put them there. Literary scholars label these two opposite approaches with the fancy titles of exegesis and eisegesis.

It is true of course that each person sees his own film and that selective perception based on background, belief, and bias will incline each person to see or not see certain things which are in the film. In addition, repeated screenings and discussions of the film will reveal many things which no one could be expected to arrive at after one screening. The best test of any such theorizing about the meaning of a film is the film itself. The film can obviously be seen and understood without the interpretation of the Fool as a Christ-figure, but once discovered, the interpretation is both a useful insight and a generous cinematic lagniappe or bonus.

235

Organized Religion. Formal religion gets its comeuppance in all Fellini's films. The main encounter in *La Strada* occurs in the religious procession. The film records an actual procession. The Bishop is a rather hard-bitten, cold man who dispenses tired and mechanical blessings to people who seem to have more faith and warmth than he does. The music is heavy and lugubrious in contrast to the bouncy version of the same melody played by the three musicians who led Gelsomina to the festival. There is a stress on external trappings with strong elements of superstition. Gessomina is both fascinated and awed by the whole thing. The later episode in the convent conveys a feeling of simplicity and innocence, but there is an undertone of naïveté and repression.

Fellini is hardly an antireligious man. His films reveal a strong intuitive faith. They also manifest a love-hate relationship with the church. His attitude might be described as religious rather than ecclesiastical. But at the same time he is completely enamored of Pope John, who also saw beyond the ecclesiastical to the religious.

Because he is both religious and a critic of religion, Fellini has been caught in a critical crossfire. He is frequently too religious for the secularists and too secular for the religionists. The secular mind stands by cheering when he takes on the clerical establishment, but it hardly relishes his basic theological premises. The churchmen, on the other hand, can do without the criticism and occasional eroticism. What both would do well to understand is that Fellini is probing, in a very personal way, tensions which he finds in his own life and in his own culture. He is not propounding a package theory. He, like his characters, is with a circus traveling along a road.

View of Man. Fellini might be described as an idealistic realist. He says: "I am not a pessimist. I believe there is a slow conquest toward the divine state of man." His films document his own tortuous journey along that route. He is working toward the state of innocence after knowledge. Three basic attitudes toward man emerge from his films:

1. *Worth of the Individual.* People are important to Fellini. He delights in finding them in their own environment just being themselves. He accepts them for what they are. All the characters in *La Strada* footnote this thesis beautifully—the three protagonists, Giraffa and the circus family, the nuns, the children, the prostitute, the members of the wedding. Because of this basic respect for the love of people, Fellini is desperately concerned with the need for communication between people. The theme recurs in all his films, as indeed it does

in most serious films today. He tells us that *"La Strada* is the history of a closed person who would like to communicate with others, of a woman who would like to speak to a man who doesn't want to understand."

2. *Redeemability of Man.* Fellini's films always end on a note of hope. It's not the fraudulent, giddy optimism of the naïve. It's the hope that blooms on the brink of despair, the hope that has lived through and understands the alternatives to itself. To be alive is to have a chance. The world of Fellini abounds in grace—people, places, actions calculated to remind the individual of his worth. The setting and tone are thoroughly Christian. God is the silent protagonist in the world of Fellini.

3. *Unity with the Universe.* The print-oriented man delights in his antiseptic categories. Neither Fellini nor his films lend themselves to such easy division and compartmentalization. All the elements of reality are intertwined in a marvelous and mysterious skein. Each man is closely connected with every other man in a great family which is frequently pictured as a traveling circus. Man is closely tied to nature—to the enduring qualities of the sea, to the cycles of days and seasons which reflect his moods, to the trees, flowers, and animals which always delight and remind. And man's past and present are always with him in his own culture whose history and beliefs are the air he breathes. This is why Fellini will never make a film outside Italy. He would be out of communication with "the spirits of the place." Since he is a "man of the provinces," it may also explain why he is still not quite at home in dealing with the city. This incarnational view of the universe which sees the connectedness of things and which sees all of reality as charged with meaning is almost unique with Fellini among contemporary film-makers. Alienation from man, nature, religion, and oneself are the order of the day. Fellini also probes these themes but within a basic framework which promises some redeeming insight and hope. His films could have been made only by a man working within and reacting to a Christian tradition, more specifically, that of Italian Catholicism.

La Strada is but one of the nine and a half films made by Fellini. Any definitive judgment on his theology would have to include an analysis of all his films. Of his three most recent films, *La Dolce Vita* seems to offer the richest material for future investigation. Everyone has to be his own final arbiter in deciding on the aptness or appropriateness of such attempts to interpret films.

V. PERSPECTIVES ON WAR: A TEACHING UNIT OF FILMS

One of the most pressing problems facing the contemporary world is the problem of war. Teachers can explore this problem with their students in a challenging way calculated to evoke thoughtful, critical response through the use of contemporary films. The films described in this chapter offer a practical, stimulating body of material for the creative teacher.

Short films on war have several advantages. Although feature-length films can offer more detail and depth, the short films have the virtues of brevity and relevancy. These give a class manageable experiences that lead to involving discussion and active thinking.

The teacher can be more selective with short films. He can combat the subtle way in which war is often glorified on television. *Hogan's Heroes,* for example, makes Nazi prisoner-of-war camps seem like extensions of the Howard Johnson chain, full of chuckles and merri-

This chapter is the first in a series of such units being prepared by Fordham's National Film Study Project, directed by *Media and Methods* Advisory Board member John M. Culkin, S.J. "Perspectives on War" is the work of David A. Sohn (Director of Curriculum Research), Henry E. Putsch (Director of Teacher Training), and A. Schillaci, O.P. (Director of Special Projects).

ment. Supposedly realistic combat series on television contain much of the challenge and excitement of war but little of the sickness, suffering, and death.

Many short films, on the other hand, question war as a solution to human problems. The best of such films avoid rhetoric but make strong comments through allegory and example. Some use history for perspective. For example, *Chickamauga, An Occurrence at Owl Creek Bridge,* and *A Time out of War* use a rear view of the Civil War to comment on the present.

The films dealt with in this chapter are some of the best short films, experimental and conventional, animated and traditionally photographed, documentary and feature. They seem to fall into overlapping groups according to their preoccupations and approaches to war. Nuclear warfare and its moral implications are the concern of *The War Game, The Hole, A Short Vision, The Big Fair,* and *Very Nice, Very Nice.* The inhumanity of war and its desensitizing effect are presented vividly in *Toys, A Time out of War, An Occurrence at Owl Creek Bridge, Munro,* and *The Magician.*

The value of human life is considered through the toll of senseless suffering and death upon individuals in *The Soldier, An Occurrence at Owl Creek Bridge,* and *Neighbors,* or upon the society in *Vivre (To Live), Memorandum, The Battle of Culloden, Night and Fog, The War Game, A Short Vision, Chickamauga,* and *The Warsaw Ghetto.*

The sticky topic of the causes of war is treated through indirection in *The Hat, Neighbors, The Hole,* and others.

Films afford a way to portray war realistically. It is one thing to talk in the abstract about the Nazi slaughter of six million Jews and other prisoners under Hitler, but *The Warsaw Ghetto, Memorandum,* and *Night and Fog* are vivid and almost overpowering in their ability to re-create these atrocities. One can talk about the horrors of the battlefield and of nuclear war, but *Vivre, The War Game,* and *The Battle of Culloden* make their points by the direct experience of the horrors.

From thinking, talking, and writing about the experience of these films, teachers and students can become aware of the nature of war. The question of individual responsibility will arise in considering war as a social inevitability or an avoidable evil. When war is perceived as a choice, peace becomes an alternative.

239

I. WAR: THE IMMEDIATE THREAT

The War Game (England, 1966), feature documentary: b/w, 50 minutes. A film by Peter Watkins, produced by the BBC. Distributor: Contemporary Films. Rental: $100.

Although this film was commissioned by the BBC, it was never broadcast by the network because of the fear that a repetition of the public hysteria that resulted from Orson Welles's broadcast of *The War of the Worlds* might occur. It was, however, released for theatrical distribution. *The War Game* won an Academy Award as the best feature documentary of 1966.

Courtesy of Contemporary Films/McGraw-Hill
The War Game

The War Game is a staged documentary account of the nightmare that might occur if nuclear war should break out in the near future. It postulates the entry of Chinese troops into South Vietnam, America's threat to use nuclear weapons against them, Russia's decision to take over West Berlin unless the threat is withdrawn, rioting at Checkpoint Charlie, the decision to move NATO divisions to relieve the city, and the moment when "the American president is *forced*" to order the use

240

of tactical nuclear weapons. The holocaust that follows is shown with chilling, precise details. Such problems as devastating fire storms, identification of victims through wedding rings, the necessity to execute victims burned beyond all help, the psychoses caused by the attack, are documented by actual historical incidents during World War II. They raise the question: Will the living envy the dead?

The horrors of the bomb are realistically revealed throughout the film. The issues are deeper, however, than those of panic, grief, suffering, and protest. Actual statements by certain churchmen—for example, "The church must tell the faithful to live with, though they need not love, the bomb"—the opinions of men and women interviewed in the street who hardly hesitate before deciding that retaliation in kind would be necessary, and the accusation that there is, in fact, "a conspiracy of silence" surrounding the issue of nuclear weapons in both the press and politics, offer grounds for thoughtful, analytical discussion. Watkins, the film's maker, has in fact stated that what the BBC really feared was that the truth about nuclear weapons would result in a massive outcry to ban the bomb if the film were shown on television. The BBC has forbidden its release up to this time to any television service anywhere in the world.

The War Game is a work of art. Kenneth Tynan of *The London Observer* pointed out: "I cannot think that it is diminished as art because its vision of disaster corresponds with the facts. Like Michelangelo's *Last Judgment,* it proposes itself as an authentic documentary image of the wrath to come." He later commented: "I suspect that it may be the most important film ever made."

DISCUSSION QUESTIONS

1. This film was obviously shot with a hand-held camera. How, and why, did the film-maker make it look like a documentary?

2. Why did the film-maker spend so much time interviewing people? What was the effect of the interviews on the audience? On you? Do you know about carbon 14? Should we retaliate with nuclear weapons if we are attacked with nuclear missiles?

3. The film projected some lines that looked like a song, a folk ballad:

> . . . with weapons so deadly
> The World must grow older.

241

And die in its tracks
If it does not
Turn kind.

Assuming it is a song, why did the film-maker decide to render the song in silence? Would music have made it a more or less effective verse?

4. Did you find the behavior of the police, the doctors, and the townspeople believable? What special problems of human behavior did you notice?

5. What did the film suggest about "a conspiracy of silence" among the press and the politicians concerning nuclear weaponry?

6. The film-maker seems careful to show that the President would, in fact, be *forced* to order the use of tactical nuclear weapons. He also suggests that the Russians too would be *forced*. Forced by whom? By what? If political leaders are forced to such actions, who or what is in control?

7. If you agree that these nightmarish, theoretical events seem real, what devices and techniques does the film-maker use to make them seem real?

8. Did you notice any events or occurrences in the film that you did not realize might happen during a nuclear attack? If so, what were some of them?

Other Short Films to Use with *The War Game*

Vivre (*To Live*) (France, 1959), documentary: b/w, 8 minutes. A film by Carlos Vilardebo. Distributor: Contemporary Films. Rental: $7.50. Sale: $75.

This is a film without dialogue that shows the effects of war through the use of newsreel clips that were photographed in many countries over several decades. A haunting cello accompanies the scenes that illustrate that suffering and despair are universal wherever there is war.

A Short Vision (United States), animated: color, 10 minutes. A film by George K. Arthur. Distributor: Encyclopaedia Britannica Films. Rental: $13.50. Sale: $120.

Here is a fantasy about a mysterious thing that flies over the city and destroys not only the city but the world. It is closely related to *The War Game* in its theme although it treats the subject allegorically.

There are striking scenes of total destruction, and the story is told as a parable with narration.

The Big Fair (France), drama: b/w, 10 minutes. A film by George K. Arthur. Rental: $10.50. Sale: $100.

Using an amusement park as a symbol, the film develops the idea that "playthings of youth can become the weapons of maturity." It contrasts roller coasters, toy planes, and other amusements with actual destructive weapons. With comparison shots, dodge-'em cars become actual race cars that crash, airplane rides become actual dive bombers, skaters become boxers, falling blocks become bombed buildings, and at the end, all is silent as a nuclear warhead destroys everybody. The big fair is empty, deserted.

A Trip down Memory Lane (National Film Board of Canada, 1966), documentary: b/w, 13 minutes. A film by Arthur Lipsett. Rental and sale: apply to Contemporary Films.

Assembling old newsreel clips that cover the past sixty years, Lipsett shows us how ridiculous we appear in a satirical, visual review of our own past. There are some incisive comments on war presented here.

Vice Nice, Very Nice (National Film Board of Canada, 1961), experimental documentary: b/w, 7 minutes. A film by Arthur Lipsett. Distributor: Contemporary Films. Rental: $10.

Through a rapid visual bombardment of still photographs, Lipsett implies a need for social awareness and a sense of responsibility. The detonation of an atomic bomb and the rise of a rocket from its launching pad are the only two motion picture clips in the picture, and they are germane to its theme. One statement—"People seem to live in a kind of dissolving phantasmagoria of the world"—is illustrated by the film. Demonstrations against the bomb are shown, and the vast rush of humanity is examined from many viewpoints with ingenious cutting techniques. This is a film which will certainly provoke discussion. Will students agree that "warmth and brightness will return and renewal of the hopes of men"?

The Magician (Poland), drama: b/w, 13 minutes, 1963. Distributor: Sterling Films. Sale: $75.

At the beginning of this allegory a magician, through innocent tricks, lures a group of children at the beach to an amusement stand.

He gradually leads them to play with guns in a shooting gallery, then little by little causes them to shoot at toys they cherish. The film ends with the children desensitized and converted to a military viewpoint. They march over the hill, and a volley of shots is heard. The magician then prepares to lure the next group of children to see his tricks.

A comment on totalitarian devices and indoctrination, this film has obvious parallels to many dictatorships of the past.

Toys (National Film Board of Canada, 1967), color, 7 minutes. Distributor: Contemporary Films.

Picture from the National Film Board of Canada production Toys

Toys

A store window full of toys, possibly the Christmas season, a sound track pulsing contemporary music, and a group of delighted children open what appears to be an exuberant and beautifully photographed scene of childhood fascination and wonderment. Then the war toys, playthings of childhood innocence, come alive and fight a full-scale battle in a most imaginative and spectacular battle sequence. Possibly

244

our constant awareness that the toys are, after all, toys makes their actions—bombing, strafing, the burning "alive" of one soldier, for example—even more horrifying than would be real-life newsreel of the same events. A new film, *Toys* employs vivid color and brilliant sound. It is certain to win prizes the world over.

DISCUSSION QUESTIONS

1. When the toys began to move, how did the children begin to move? Why?

2. What was the attitude of the children toward the war they witnessed?

3. What kind of toys other than war toys do small children play with that are of questionable, possibly even destructive, value? What kinds of toys do you play with? What kinds do adults play with?

4. Were there techniques in the visualization and sound of this film which could not have been achieved by any other kind of communication? In words, for example?

The Battle of Culloden (England), a production of BBC-TV: b/w, 72 minutes. Directed by Peter Watkins. Distributor: Peter M. Robeck & Co. Rental: $50. Sale: $400.

The Battle of Culloden is another staged documentary, a treatment of the famous Battle of Culloden, which was fought in 1746 between Bonnie Prince Charlie, pretender to the British throne, and the army of British regulars sent to Scotland to put down the rebellion. The overwhelming power of the film derives from its documentary technique, in which members of opposite sides are interviewed and motives and loyalties are exposed as are the horrors of modern war—in this case "modern" because this battle is one of the earliest in which artillery was proved devastating in its use against infantry. Watkins has successfully re-created history in a vivid and experiential way. Some critics have compared this film to Bergman's *The Seventh Seal* in its effective re-creation of historical atmosphere and realism.

Watkins used *The Battle of Culloden* to explore the reasons why wars have occurred in history and thus to explore the reasons why men fight wars in any time. The usual glamor which is associated with men of history and their wars is here exposed as fraud. The battle was a hideous disaster for the Scotch, who lost over a thousand men while the British lost only fifty. The pacification of the Scotch Highlanders

245

by the marauding British troops is one of the most harrowing experiences yet created on film.

Other Films Worth Noting in Conjunction with *The War Game*

23 Skidoo (National Film Board of Canada). Distributor: Contemporary Films.

Actua-Tilt (National Film Board of Canada). Distributor: Janus Films, New Cinema.

La Jetee (National Film Board of Canada). Distributor: Janus Films, New Cinema.

23 Skidoo shows the feeling of desolation in a typical city scene where there is no living soul. At the end one discovers that a neutron bomb has destroyed all living cells. *Actua-Tilt*, like *The Big Fair*, uses comparisons between games and war scenes to depict the violence of wars, while *La Jette* is a look into the future after the third world war ends.

II. WAR: THE HISTORICAL PERSPECTIVE

An Occurrence at Owl Creek Bridge (France, 1961), drama: b/w, 27 minutes. Directed by Robert Enrico. Adapted from the short story by Ambrose Bierce. Distributor: Contemporary Films. Rental: $17.50. Sale: $200.

An Occurrence at Owl Creek Bridge is an exceptionally powerful adaptation of the Bierce classic story to the screen. A Confederate soldier (or spy?) is about to be hanged by a Union platoon. As the preliminaries are extended, we see his fear and the futility of his gaze at possible avenues of escape. But when he drops, his bound body falls into the river, where we see the severed rope. He frees himself and rises to the surface where he enjoys a few vivid impressions before he is the target of the entire platoon. Swimming violently, above and below water, he leaves the bridge and is swept over a dangerous waterfall, where he narrowly escapes drowning and has just enough strength to drag himself on the shore. Even there a shell is lobbed at him, and he runs wildly until, by evening, he stumbles exhausted down a lane of trees. Suddenly he recognizes his surroundings and races joyfully forward to discover his own plantation with his wife hastening to meet him. He makes an agonizing effort to reach her, but when he does, as her hands caress his neck, he throws his head back, and we see his body dangling at the end of the rope stretched from the bridge. The escape was a condemned man's fantasy, and the camera slowly winds its way back along the river for a last view of the body hanging from the bridge.

This film creates a more complete and moving drama than many feature films, largely through the use of a superb set of film techniques. In the film we move constantly from actual time to the psychological time of the condemned man. The preparations, for example, seem endless, and exaggerated sound adds menace to them. The same is true of the underwater escape, and it is a rare viewer who does not hold his breath in sympathy. Time stops, and overwhelming beauty indicates again the heightened sensations of the man's love for life, only to have this idyll broken by his discovery and the renewed threat of being shot, all of this shown in ugly silhouette, with slowed-down motion and sound contributing to the menace. The series of hazards which he overcomes become the gauge of his love for life, and we are emotionally spent as he dodges bullets, poisonous snakes, a waterfall, shellbursts, and fatigue in his fantasy escape. These are exaggerated by the director to indicate their basic unreality, but our desire for his escape continually raises hopes where there is no hope. At the beginning of the film we wonder who he is and whether he is guilty, but soon we wish but one thing, his safety and reunion with his wife. No scene is more effective than the last futile race toward his wife, made more nightmarish than ever by the use of a head-on telephoto-lens shot and a threefold repetition of his run. The film is seasoned with many ironies, but none more exquisitely cruel than the translation, in return from fantasy to reality, of his wife's touch into the killing jolt of the hanging rope. Throughout, the film is paced beautifully, and the acting of Roger Jacquet remains completely convincing in a most difficult role.

DISCUSSION QUESTIONS

1. How do the details of the story, such as the Civil War period, the civilian clothing of the condemned man, and the attitudes of his executioners contribute to the themes of the film?

2. Why does the film execute such an elaborate fantasy of the moments before a man's death, especially when we are not easily aware that we are witnessing a fantasy?

3. Is the surprise ending merely a gimmick, or does it accomplish something in this film which could not have been achieved by other means?

4. What are some of the visual indications throughout the film that we are participating in a fantasy and not reality? Do they lessen the suspense and participation or enhance them?

5. Is the film depressing in the finality of its ending, or does it give us reason for hope in what it tells us, either of the man hanged, or of life itself?

A Time out of War (United States, 1954), drama: b/w, 22 minutes. Directed and written by Denis Sanders. Distributor: Contemporary Films. Rental: $10. Sale: $120.

A Time out of War presents an interesting exchange between two Union soldiers and a Confederate separated by the battle line of a river. On a dull, hot day they call a truce until evening, step out into clear

Courtesy of Contemporary Films/McGraw-Hill
A Time out of War

sight, and exchange news, food, and tobacco while one of the Union men does a little fishing. Gradually the sunny day and sparkling river give way to evening shadows. But when the soldier fishing shouts that he has a big one, his catch proves to be the body of a Union comrade killed in a previous battle. The relationship subtly changes as the two bury their man and the Confederate soldier joins in the rifle salute in his honor. The truce is broken, and the men return to the business of war.

This film develops its mood slowly and deliberately, with great attention to photographic composition and visual beauty during the truce. The remarks shouted across the stream carry a certain dignity and grace that was lacking in battle, and each is eager to outdo the other in generosity. Subtle differences in personality are part of the rich texture of the drama, and we feel that just as we are coming to know the men, the harsh reality of war separates them. Subjective camera plays an important role in developing the individual point of view and also in assisting the viewer to identify with both parties. The degree of this identification is evident when the body is found and the truce has ended.

DISCUSSION QUESTIONS

1. Is this film about other concerns than simply that of war? If so, what are they? How are they affected by its setting in a civil war situation?

2. What does "civil war" really mean? How does it differ from other forms of war? Are there civil wars going on in our society at present? Do they go on in all times and places?

3. What are some of the indications of the changing relationships between the two sides as shown in the visual techniques?

4. Do the men return to war changed by this respite from battle, or does the resumption of hostilities leave them the same as they were before the film began?

Chickamauga (France, 1961), drama: b/w, 33 minutes. Directed by Robert Enrico. Distributor: Contemporary Films. Rental: $22.50. Sale: $225.

Chickamauga is one of two films based on the Civil War stories of Ambrose Bierce. Unlike *An Occurrence at Owl Creek Bridge,* this story takes a battle incident as its subject, allowing a young boy enchanted with the glory of war to encounter a band of retreating soldiers. The ironies build as the boy's fantasies clash with the harsh realities of the soldiers' fear and suffering.

249

Documentaries

There are many documentaries that relate to problems of war. Mc-Graw-Hill has a large list of useful war documentaries. One of the best is *The Twisted Cross* (b/w, 55 minutes. McGraw-Hill. Distributor: Alden Films. Rental: $15. Sale: $275). This film, originally a NBC *Project 20* television production, traces the rise and fall of Adolf Hitler and the Nazi movement using captured German films.

Over There, 1914-1918 (France, 1963), b/w. Distributor: McGraw-Hill. Rental: $32.50, minimum for classroom showing. Sale: $300.

The film consists of newsreels and army films from World War I.

The Spanish Turmoil (England), b/w, 64 minutes. Distributor: Peter M. Robeck & Co. Rental: $50. Sale: $275.

The Spanish Turmoil is a documentary about the Spanish Civil War and Franco's rise to power. It was originally a BBC-TV production.

Documentaries often add a dimension of realism to the study of a subject. They are especially useful when one studies the nature of war. The teacher has many other documentaries to choose from if he examines distributors' catalogs.

The War Years, an anthology of more than sixty-five films commemorating the twenty-fifth anniversary of World War II, has been prepared by Association Instructional Materials for 16mm distribution. The half hour and hour-long films, selected from the award-winning CBS News *Twentieth Century,* are comprised of wartime documentary footage, special interviews with military leaders, correspondents and personalities of the period, contemporary footage of battle sites and former theaters of war. Many of the films in the project have won awards for excellence. Included are: *From Kaiser to Fuehrer* (the rise and fall of the Weimer Republic), *FDR: Third Term to Pearl Harbor* (the last months of isolation and neutrality in the U.S.), *D-Day* (a two-part documentary on allied strategy: and landings), *Hiroshima* (the dropping of the first A-bomb), *Who Killed Anne Frank?* and sixty others.

A brochure on the films is available through Association Instructional Materials, 600 Madison Avenue, New York, New York 10022.

III. WHAT CAUSES WAR?

The Hat: Is This War Necessary? (United States, 1965), a cartoon by John and Faith Hubley: color, 18 minutes. Distributor: McGraw-Hill. Rental: available through Florida State University, Indiana University, and Syracuse University film libraries, rates vary. Sale: $220.

The bright, spontaneous quality of this lively cartoon is the result of the improvisational achievement of jazz trumpeter Dizzy Gillespie and pianist Dudley Moore (of *Beyond the Fringe*), who improvised both the music and the dialogue for the film. The simple concern and bewilderment of the two soldiers as they debate very complicated issues translate its formidable subject into a very approachable one. The striking animation, the brilliant work of John Hubley, was done in response to the taped improvisations.

Two zany soldiers patrol a border line. Animals seem to cross the line freely, but the two men seem caged by it. Then one trips and his hat falls over the line, and the fun begins. What to do about the hat? The opposing soldier is unable to find a military regulation which will solve the dilemma, and the two men spend days, even weeks and months, debating the larger issues of national honor, international relationships, the reality of boundary lines and the possibility of disarmament in very human, simple, down-to-earth terms. Sirens in the background at the close suggest that time for debate is running out.

The Hole (United States, 1963), a cartoon by John and Faith Hubley: color, 15 minutes. Distributor: Brandon Films. Rental: $10. Sale: $195.

The Hole is a serio-comic debate on the dangers of nuclear destruction by two construction workers as they labor on an underground sewer. The white worker is extremely anxious about accidents, whether they be on the job or accidental nuclear explosions. The Negro proposes the theory that accidents are psychologically willed and therefore controllable. As they discuss the topic vigorously, the cartoon pictures a hypothetical situation in which a burrowing mole sets off a massive alert and the United States and Russia prepare for attack. At the same time, a crane working on the same construction site drops a large piece of machinery. The coincidence is too great, and when the workers rush to the surface, they imagine the scene that would confront them had the bomb been dropped. As they come back to reality and the work resumes, they realize that there is still time, but how much?

John Hubley's cartoon technique is a very free watercolor type of wash method, in which the figures freely change shapes as the emotional mood or conversational emphasis demands. A sense of three-dimensional reality is created through use of transparent overlays in which foreground and background change relationships as the camera ranges over the formidable array of underground missiles, nuclear submarines, and other weapons. The improvised dialogue has a ring of truth to it and is skillfully made to bear several meanings ranging from job safety to political survival. Both the cartooning and the dialogue may be somewhat obscure to unexperienced audiences, who may have to see the film twice in order to understand it.

DISCUSSION QUESTIONS

1. Does the cartoon resolve the debate on accidents which happen by chance and those that are willed? Into which category do the fallen machinery and the nuclear bomb scare fall?

2. What is the significance of staging this debate in a hole, which provides the title for the cartoon?

3. Would the theme of the film have been more effectively presented in clear photography with a carefully articulated script?

Neighbors (National Film Board of Canada, 1952), animated film by Norman McLaren. Color, 8 minutes. Distributor: Contemporary Films. Rental: $6. Rental and Sale: International Film Bureau.

The distinctive stylistic feature of *Neighbors* is called pixilation animation, a process in which live actors are submitted to the principles normally used to animate drawings. The effect of this technique with its look of people-puppets is both disturbing and hilarious to watch. With no dialogue or narration, the film uses a sound track of synthetic music and experimental sound effects.

The story of *Neighbors*, told entirely through visuals, is a simple parable of two fellows who live next to each other in respect and harmony until a flower grows on the dividing line of their properties. What begins as exuberant comedy quickly becomes a horrible tale of destruction as they fight to the grueling death over possession of the flower.

DISCUSSION QUESTIONS

1. Some students have suggested that the technique of this film

damages its power to communicate. Is its simple story made more or less effective by animation?

2. Is this an adeqpate statement about why men fight? Does it try to be? Is such a statement relevant to the complexities of a world in which countries seem unable not to fight one another?

3. Norman McLaren made *Neighbors* his response to the Korean War. Assuming your experience of the film is your only source of information, what do you suspect are his attitudes about that and other wars?

IV. THE EFFECTS OF WAR

Memorandum (Canada, 1966), documentary: b/w, 58 minutes. Directed and written by Donald Brittain. Produced by the National Film Board of Canada. Distributor: Contemporary Films. Rental: $25. Sale: $250.

Memorandum takes its title from the July 21, 1941, communication sent by Hermann Goering to SS Chief Reinhard Heydrich, implementing what Adolf Hitler called "the final solution to the Jewish question." The film presents a pilgrimage to Bergen-Belsen by a group of survivors who were freed by the British in 1944. Concentrating on one member of the party, Bernard Laufer, a Canadian glass cutter, the film takes us for a series of contrasting scenes ranging from cultured, affluent Germany of today to the Germany of the past shown in German and British newsreel and documentary footage. Although the pilgrims were not certain themselves what they were seeking, it is difficult to avoid a sense of frustration upon returning to the scene of past horrors to find them so distant. There are ironic touches of obsequiousness shown the "tourists" by contemporary Germans, and many other ironies due to the passage of time (e.g., the lord mayor of Hamburg is a Jew). The scale of the crime remains unimaginable, defying any attempt to assess it even by those who only narrowly escaped extermination. But in the contrasts between past and present there lies the stark revelation that we have perhaps not learned our lesson.

The film has a technical competence which conceals itself in its concentration upon providing the audience with insights and revelations. The cinema-*vérité* technique used to record Bernard Laufer's journey to a horrible past makes transitions to visual records of that past easy. The taped, spontaneous dialogue reveals meaning under banalities, while the searching faces of the survivors, looking for a reality which is both unendingly vivid and increasingly dim, have a powerful emotional effect on the objective viewer. The treatment of documentary footage and the use of stills transport the viewer into the appalling era of genocide more effectively than even the memories of the surviving inmates. What is seen there challenges because the contrasts and comparisons with our own age and condition are clearly felt.

DISCUSSION QUESTIONS

1. What does the pilgrimage of Bernard Laufer and the others add to our understanding and experience of the Nazis' scientific genocide operation known as "the solution"?

2. What are some of the more striking contrasts and comparisons between past and present revealed by switching back and forth from the pilgrimage to documentary footage of the camps?

3. In asking, "If it could happen in the fairyland of Hansel and Gretel, and the Pied Piper of Hamelin, could it not happen anywhere?" does the film become too explicit in its challenge?

4. Is it possible in this, and in other films on the destruction of the Jews by Hitler, that by suggesting we are all guilty, we are in effect saying that no one is guilty?

5. At the end of the film we hear a survivor boast of having tracked down and revealed hundreds of Bergen-Belsen officials who had escaped the war crimes trials. Does the film end by leaving us with this note of a relentless justice, or does it create another emotional climate in its audiences?

Night and Fog (France, 1955), documentary: b/w, 31 minutes. Directed by Alain Resnais. Distributor: Contemporary Films. Rental: $30. Sale: $250.

Night and Fog is probably one of the most effective documentaries ever produced. The film alternates between past and present, taking the viewer through Buchenwald, Treblinka, Auschwitz, and other extermination camps. The major effect is created by scanning carefully selected newsreel and documentary footage of the camps in construction and operation, then cutting from this black-and-white scene to the relative unreality of the present-day camps shown in color, with grass and wild flowers erasing their horrors. The development is roughly chronological, beginning with the building of the camps, their early uses, and then the coming of the "final solution to the Jewish problem." Before our eyes we see deportations, work details, emaciated bodies standing nude in lines, then the succession of horrors associated with the ovens and gas chambers. In a sense the disease and death are not as moving as the despair recorded in the eyes of inmates peering through barbed wire. The final scene, in which the camera dollies over mountains of clothing, hair, human skin, and then bodies, gives way to the final irony of the trials, shown only briefly, in which three men involved in running the camps repeat the statement, "I am not responsible." The narration, which throughout has been restrained and factual, now challenges with the final question directed to "those of us who pretend to believe that this all happened only once, at a certain time and in a certain place, and those who refuse to see, who do not hear the cry to the end of time."

The film fulfills one of the highest functions of the documentary, which is to invite the audience to "live" through the human situation which is its concern. This ability to re-create the event is all the more remarkable since it is accomplished through still photographs, left by the meticulous German officials, which come alive through camera scanning of artistic excellence. The device of switching from the color present to the harsh, grainy black and white of the past is used subtly to underline the theme of forgetfulness, as if to point out that men cannot afford to forget, even if the grass, the wild flowers, and nature seem able to do so. The camera is constantly in motion, probing the interiors of the camps, rooting out their secrets, and evoking the memory of those who suffered and died there. Restraint and understatement are the appropriate notes of the narrative of an event too horrifying to treat in any other manner. At the end, the viewer is left numb by the suffering he has witnessed.

DISCUSSION QUESTIONS

1. What are some of the devices the director uses to gain a deep involvement by the viewer in the situation of the film?

2. Does the film present a historical event, seeking to fix the blame and guilt for it, or does its tone of irony place it in a much different context?

3. What can a documentary film such as *Night and Fog* accomplish in terms of challenge to the individual which a dramatization of the same event could not hope to do?

4. Would the images of the film accuse the audience without the narration, or do we need the closing statement to remind us of our common guilt?

5. Although the film does not make parallels, do we find ourselves comparing its situations and events with those of contemporary life?

The Soldier (United States, 1965), drama: b/w, 4 minutes. Produced by Family Theater. Distributor: Family Theater. No rental. Sale: $25.

The Soldier presents a frightened and weary G.I. on the beach in combat. Distracted by gulls' cries, he relaxes, walks into the water to bathe his face, and returns to feed one of the birds on the shore. As the bird flies off, he tosses up a piece of chocolate, and as the morsel leaves his hand, a shot rings out, killing him. His fall to the ground is delayed by slow motion, and we see him turn in midair, his rifle and helmet flying off as his body hits the sand. The scene closes as night is falling and the tide washes his body. As he falls, Psalm 42 is narrated in part: "As the deer longs for running waters, so does my soul long for you, O my God. . . . Why are you sad, my soul, as your enemies mock you saying, 'Where is your God?' . . . Trust in God, who saves me from shame, my own God."

Superb photography and tight editing give this film the impact and compression of a television commercial. Extreme close-ups and details create a mood of anticipation and then shock as a fragmentation lens holds the moment of the bullet's impact in a freeze shot. The dying fall is made graceful and strangely beautiful by slow motion, a factor which fits the psalm narrated, not as an illustration but as a visual drama related obliquely to the words. Nightfall and the setting on the shore give the film a significance far beyond its modest dimensions.

DISCUSSION QUESTIONS

1. Why was the moment of death shown in a freeze shot and then the dying fall caught in slow motion? Do these devices reverse the mood of the film for dramatic reasons?

2. Do the words of the psalm narrated represent the dying thoughts of the soldier, a comment by an observer, or some other element?

3. Is this a film about war, about death, or is it concerned with more basic and elemental ideas?

APPENDIX I—AN ANNOTATED LIST OF FILMS

Availability of Films

Films of all varieties are available in all kinds of millimeters. Standard church and school showings are built around 16mm films. The appendix contains a list of sources for purchase or rental of 16mm films. The feature-length films are available only for rental or occasionally for extended lease, but not for sale. The shorter films are normally available for either rental or purchase.

Feature films usually become available in 16mm within two ′years after their initial theatrical release. Sometimes a specific title will not be available because of contracts with the original producers or because of sale to television. The catalogs of the maor 16mm distributors are an essential part of any film moderator's equipage.

The short films are available from the usual commercial sources, but there

257

are also possibilities for obtaining them from public libraries, school and college audiovisual libraries, embassies, and private collections. Many schools and churches find it useful to band together in small regional film cooperatives to purchase titles which are in frequent use.

After working through the philosophical and psychological dimensions of the use of films, any moderator will tell you that the single biggest obstacle to having people see films is faulty projection. There are some who say that no film of more than thirty minutes length has ever been projected in a church or school without interruption. It is enough to send one back to making shadow pictures manually on the wall.

The ideal, of course, is what we normally experience in a good theater. Most auditoriums in the real world are at a level somewhat short of this ideal.

Feature Length Films
That Open Up Moderns

Ingmar Bergman: There are two paradoxes in this Swedish screenwriter-director's career: how his intensely nationalistic works are so universal and why a man who has formally disregarded organized religion has, more than any other director, returned to the theme of man seeking God.

The Seventh Seal: The Devil pursues a medieval knight and his traveling companions across a plague-stricken land. A crosssection of humanity reveals itself in facing death. (J* 96 min.)

Courtesy of Janus Films
Wild Strawberries

* See the Key to Feature Film Distributors, p. 272.

258

Wild Strawberries: A contemporary drama of an elderly doctor reviewing the impact of his life through flashback and fantasy as he drives across the country to receive a final honor. The film is the equivalent of a human last judgment. (J 90 min.)

The Virgin Spring: A stark, naturalistic medieval fable of a lord who dedicates a chapel over the death site of his raped and murdered only child, a fable of human revenge interwoven with pagan and primitive Christian motifs. (J 88 min.)

Through a Glass Darkly: The first of a trilogy on the frustrating contemporary search for God's presence. An intimate family unit on a secluded island vacation is torn apart as the wife loses touch with reality. She sees God as a preying spider. (J 91 min.)

Winter Light: The second film in the trilogy, a doubting minister is tortured by the demands of his parishioners and relatives. (J 80 min.)

The Silence: The silence of God amid the silence of men. (J 105 min.)

The Magician: The scientific mind confronted by the spiritual element. (J 102 min.)

Courtesy of Janus Films
Winter Light

Michelangelo Antonioni: While Bergman probes the psyche of Swedish man across the centuries, Antonioni accurately reflects the surface of modern man. Bergman's work evidences a mastery of all the theatrical elements of film-making, Antonioni imposes a singular cinematic pace and composition to his works.

The Night: A settled married couple attempts to find a basis for relationship amid higher social and cultural groups. (UA 120 min.)

Eclipse: A stock agent from the Bourse begins an affair with the daughter of one of his clients. Monica Vitti, the Antonioni heroine, is seeking some meaning in her social encounters. (Au 123 min.)

Red Desert: A young wife and mother finds her grasp on life and her family relationships slipping from her in a sterile, mechanized environment. (Au 116 min.)

Blow-Up: A youthful fashion photographer in a frenetic mod world is touched by an ambiguous murder that his camera may or may not have caught. (FI 110 min.)

Federico Fellini: Fellini makes an affirmation of life and the dignity of man in a carnival, pastiche style miles apart from the cool, detached amoral observations of Antonioni. Both began with realistic, documentary-like dramas and progressed to creating worlds of their own choice.

La Strada: Fellini's heroine, the vulnerable, volatile Giulietta Massina, akin to Chaplin in her expressive pantomining, is a child-woman bonded into the service of the crude, animalistic Great Zampano (Anthony Quinn). Richard Basehart is the angelic Fool who finds meaning in the existence of a pebble. (Br 107 min.)

The Nights of Cabiria: A prostitute of transparent emotions survives a series of crass abuses of her personal dignity. Massina is especially effective in planting her heart on her sleeves in an emotional pilgrimage. (Br 116 min.)

La Dolce Vita: An epic-sized cross section of Rome's high society as viewed by a disengaged reporter. Marcello Mastroianni finds the sweet life turn to ashes. (Au 180 min.)

The Screenwriter-Directors

Richard Brooks: A tough-minded novelist with a dramatic flair.

The Blackboard Jungle: Reformation in a ghetto school. (FI 101 min.)

Something of Value: Reconciliation among African nationalists and white colonists. (FI, 113 min.)

The Brothers Karamazov: The surface electricity of Dostoyevsky's probing. (FI 146 min.)

Cat on a Hot Tin Roof: In 1968 America's most-viewed film via TV, another in a series of first-class, posh, intelligent adaptations of Tennessee Williams' compassionate gallery of warped humanity. Brick the disillusioned, Maggie the voracious, Big Daddy the passing czar, and Big Momma the hopeless, portray the hang-ups of a Southern family. (FI 108 min.

Elmer Gantry: A gutsy, sprawling tale of a cynical gospel preacher in the Midwest Bible Belt from the novel by Sinclair Lewis. Burt Lancaster's whoring salesman, Jean Simmons' saintly preacher, Arthur Kennedy's jaundiced reporter, Harry Andrews' mendicant Babbitt, and the Midwest preachers make you want to take sides. (UA 146 min.)

Sweet Bird of Youth: A slightly up-beat version of Tennessee Williams' drama of a fading movie star and her opportunist lover in a politically corrupt Southern (where else?) town. (FI 125 min.)

Billy Wilder: A cynical observer of America's headlines, Wilder's one idealistic film, *The Spirit of St. Louis,* was a boxoffice flop. Otherwise, his black-tipped pen has found a responsive chord in the nation.

The Lost Weekend: Don Birnam's alcoholic odyssey from barroom expansiveness to delirium tremens. The film has a New York griminess that adds to the realistic experience. (UEVA 101 min.)

The Big Carnival (Ace in the Hole) : Wilder's most forthright condemnation of a mercenary society which fests over a man trapped in a cave-in. An overeager news media comes in for a drubbing as well. (FI 112 min.)

The Apartment: Wilder exults in detailing the extracurricular mores of American businessman but salvages the story with an affirmation of human dignity. (UA 125 min.)

A Foreign Affair and *One, Two, Three:* These two interject humor with the crasser facts of life in gutted Berlin. (UEVA 116 min.) (UA 108 min.)

Double Indemnity: James Agee described this film as the holy trinity of sex, money, and the readiness to murder. (UEVA 107 min.)

The Fortune Cookie: Describes the maneuvers of an insurance fraud. (UA 125 min.)

Orson Welles: A big man in talent and bulk whose presence dominates every second of his electrifying cinematics.

Citizen Kane: A facsimile of William Randolph Hearst inherits the earth but loses his human heritage (AU–Br, FI, J 119 min.)

The Trial: A cinematic evocation of Joseph Kafka's little man in the Temple of the Law. (Br 118 min.)

Touch of Evil: A tour de force portrayal of the corruption of the law in a seedy border town. (UEVA 95 min.)

The Legacy of New York Television

The Golden Age of Television in the 50s was liberal, humanitarian, and based in New York. The craftsmen who winged their first solos on *Playhouse 90, Studio One*, and the *US Steel Hour* often pursued similar themes after being lured to Hollywood.

Fielder Cook:

Patterns: A trenchant investigation of the machinations behind executive jockeying for top posts. (Au–Br 83 min.)

Sidney Lumet: The most successful American adapter of dramas, telescripts, and novels.

Twelve Angry Men: A hymn to the American jury system and how it can overcome personal prejudice, indifference, and psychological hang-ups. (UA 95 min.)

Courtesy of UA Sixteen
Twelve Angry Men

A View from the Bridge: Arthur Miller's modern tragedy of the lethal flaw in a Brooklyn stevedore. (Col6 114 min.)

Long Day's Journey into Night: Eugene O'Neill's magnificent introspective drama of a miserly father, an addicted mother, an alcoholic, whoring elder son, and a consumptive youngster. (Au 136 min.)

Fail-Safe: A realistic answer to *Dr. Strangelove's* atomic stalemate. (Au–Br. 111 min.)

The Hill: Military prisoners fighting for their identities. (FI 122 min.)

The Group: A caustic delineation of female Ivy League graduates through a decade of social changes. (UA 150 min.)
(Lumet also directed *The Pawnbroker,* but it is not available.)

John Frankenheimer: Frankenheimer has not consistently pursued serious dramatic themes along the line of Lumet, but he has always nurtured personal statements, even in his action flicks. He is also the most audacious and cinematic of the old TV school.

Birdman of Alcatraz: The biography of Robert Stroud, a social outcast in lifetime solitary imprisonment, an international expert on aviary diseases, and a critic of the penal system. (UA 146 min.)

Seconds: A contemporary scientific fable on an organization that gives businessmen fulfillment of their Faustian desires for a youthful second life. (FI 106 min.)

The Young Stranger: Frankenheimer's first film from a TV teleplay about the generation gap in a California family. (Au 100 min.)

The Young Savages: A district attorney saves a member of New York's ghetto gangs in the 50s. (UA 103 min.)

Manchurian Candidate: A wild black comedy with potshots at momism, the right wing, and Communist brainwashing. (UA 126 min.)

Seven Days in May: A tense contemporary drama of a right-wing military attempt at a political coup in the U.S. (FI 120 min.)

Martin Ritt: Ritt has latched on to Paul Newman as Frankenheimer has latched on to Burt Lancaster. He has stayed with the contemporary American social scene more than any other Hollywood director until his recent films.

No Down Payment: Four suburban families, shingle to shingle, work out their problems with booze, the credit system, and racial integration. (FI 105 min.)

Hud: In a contemporary western setting the moral malaise spread by an opportunistic predator is offset by a trio of honest characters. (FI 85 min.)

Edge of the City: In Ritt's first film a draft dodger learns from a Negro friend how to stand up for himself. (FI 85 min.)

Delbert Mann: Mann showed the most promise among the TV directors until he concerned himself with preserving Doris Day's virginity. The best of Mann's films are from Paddy Chayefsky teleplays.

Bachelor Party: The boys at the office—the playboy, the young husband, the old man, the faithful one—take an aspirant to the altar out on an all-night stag party. (UA 93 min.)

Middle of the Night: A middle-aged widower in the garment district has to decide if he can find happiness in marriage with a confused young divorcée. (Au–Br 118 min.)

The Outsider: Ira Hayes, the Indian survivor of the Iwo Jima flag-raising, succumbs to alcoholism under the pressures of national adulation. (UEVA 108 min.)

263

Courtesy of UA Sixteen
Marty

Marty: In an outstanding drama of ordinary life a Bronx butcher chooses a meaningful relationship over the opposition of friends and family. (UA 91 min.)

Separate Tables: A quartet of residents at an English inn opt for individual dignity against the illusion of social reputation. (UA 98 min.)

Robert Mulligan: Mulligan floundered in the Hollywood dream factories until he found himself in a brief return to TV in the late 50s.

To Kill a Mockingbird: Two young children view their understanding father fight Southern racial hatred. (UEVA 129 min.)

Love with the Proper Stranger: A Macy's shopgirl and a musician, who conceive a child in a brief affair, face life together and reject an abortion. (FI 100 min.)

Fear Strikes Out: An extraordinarily candid account of Jimmy Piersall's encounters with mental breakdowns. (FI 100 min.)

264

The Dominant Directors

Many directors who are not able to originate their own material still consistently choose humanistic themes that appeal to their creative talents as film-makers.

Fred Zinnemann: Zinnemann's best pictures over the last two decades have concerned themselves with individuals who make a critical choice of conscience in trying circumstances.

The Men: A paraplegic is goaded out of self-pity into personal responsibility. (Au–Br 85 min.)

A Hatful of Rain: The long-suffering family of a New York dope addict band together in his attempt to kick the habit. (FI 107 min.)

The Nun's Story: A religious Sister in the early part of the twentieth century leaves her order when she finds its rules crippling her humanitarian efforts. (Au–Br 149 min.)

A Man for All Seasons: Thomas More stands by his conscience against his king, his family, and his associates. Robert Bolt's screenplay is especially literate in presenting the issues. (Col 120 min.)

Theresa: A veteran with an Italian war bride shakes off momism. (FI 105 min.)

The Seventh Cross: A fugitive from the Nazi regime receives help from the people of Germany. (FI 112 min.)

High Noon: Sheriff Will Kane stands alone to face his past. (Au–Br 87 min.)

From Here to Eternity: Human dignity takes a stand in a brutal military compound. (Au–Br 118 min.)

The Search: A young Jewish refugee finds some adults who care in the wreckage of Germany. (FI 112 min.)

Member of the Wedding: A young tomboy puzzles out her existence in an adaptation of Carson McCullers' poignant play. (Au–Br 91 min.)

Behold a Pale Horse: The Zinnemann hero, this time styled around an exiled Loyalist revolutionary, fights off old age and the corruption of ideals to make his final stand. (Au–Br 112 min.)

William Wyler: Wyler has been successful in his dramatic adaptations longer and more often than any other American director. He shows excellent taste in his choice of vehicles and an uncanny knack at getting to the psychological essence of a scene.

The Little Foxes: Willian Hellman's acidic dissection of the mercenary motivations of a Machiavellian Southern belle. (FI 116 min.)

The Best Years of Our Lives: The closest thing we have to an epic of the common man. Three veterans—a Naval amputee, an ex–bank president, and a boy from the other side of the tracks—attempt to readjust to civilian life. (FI 170 min.)

Friendly Persuasion: A warm-hearted Quaker in Pennsylvania finds the encroaching Civil War tearing his family apart. Each member of the family finds his pacifist ideals challenged. (Au 137 min.)

Dead End: Sidney Kingsley's dramatic treatise on corrupting slum life. (FI 92 min.)

The Heiress: A homely young woman finds herself in an adaptation of Henry James's sophisticated novel. (UEVA 115 min.)

Detective Story: An idealistic law enforcer in a cross section of a New York precinct sets his standards too high for human performance. (FI 103 min.)

Desperate Hours: The head of a family finds his home invaded by sadistic convicts. (FI 112 min.)

The Children's Hour: Two female founders of a school have their lives wrecked by malicious allegations to their personal relations. (UA 107 min.)

The Collector: A neurotic young man seals off a student in his basement. (Col 119 min.)

Elia Kazan: Kazan has brought the turbulance and power of his Broadway productions to the American screen. In his own intense way he is as successful as Wyler in drawing the best from his actors.

Gentleman's Agreement: A crusading reporter in the 40s investigates the gentleman's agreement that bans Jews from social clubs and organizations. (FI 118 min.)

On the Waterfront: An ex-pugilist on the New York docks crosses from animal to human existence. A militant priest helps him find his soul in a conflict with a corrupt, dehumanizing labor union. (Au–Br 108 min.)

East of Eden: John Steinbeck's modern biblical allegory of a domineering father who rips apart his family by his puritanical laws. (Au–Br 115 min.)

A Tree Grows in Brooklyn: Betty Smith's novel of a young adolescent evolving into womanhood in the Brooklyn slums. (FI 128 min.)

Pinky: A Negro woman with white characteristics chooses her heritage in the face of racial prejudice. (FI 102 min.)

Wild River: An individualistic matriarch holds out on her Tennessee River island against TVA. (FI 105 min.)

Man on a Tightrope: A circus owner in Communist-occupied Czechoslovakia leads his troupe over the Austrian border. (FI 105 min.)

Tony Richardson: With an early success in *Look Back in Anger,* Richardson has been at his best in portraying social rebels in a naturalistic, "kitchen sink" environment.

The Loneliness of the Long Distance Runner: Colin, a misfit in society and in a reform school, resists the blandishments of an establishment he finds disgusting. (Col6 103 min.)

A Taste of Honey: Shelagh Delaney's touching drama of a teen-age mother's attempt to keep her bearings in a restless social environment. (Col6 100 min.)

Tom Jones: An introduction to a lustier time and a cruder society in particularly contemporary cinematic terms. Albert Finney's Tom Jones is larger than life and just has to be taken on his own terms. (UA 127 min.)

Stanley Kramer: A producer and director of a long string of critical favorites, Kramer tends to tattoo his message on the brain case but has good taste and a flair for casting.

A Child Is Waiting: A candid dramatization of the plight of a retarded child in a family environment and a government institution. Mongoloid children share casting with Burt Lancaster and Judy Garland in a nonexploitive manner. (UA 104 min.)

The Defiant Ones: A Southern red-neck and a Negro prisoner are chained together as they make a break for freedom. The magazine *America* has described the film as a powerful working out of the theme of the common brotherhood of men without acknowledging the common fathership of God. (UA 97 min.)

Judgment at Nuremberg: A long but remarkably tense courtroom enactment of the aftermath of nazism. Kramer works in the context of the post-war city of Nuremberg as an American judge affixes personal guilt on German judges for Nazi war crimes. (UA 186 min.)

Inherit the Wind: Another strong courtroom drama, this time in the context of a fundamentalist Southern town hosting the circus that was the Scopes monkey trial. (UA 127 min.)

The Wild One: An early production of Kramer's, this is a brutal depiction of the motorcycle gang phenomenon. (Au–Br 78 min.)

Vittorio de Sica: The warmest of the talented Italian directors, de Sica has directed under the guise of neo-realism, but in reality he uses the traditional melodramatic devices to tap the wellspring of human vitality.

The Bicycle Thief: Nonprofessional actors in a near-documentary style re-enact the pathos of a poor man deprived of his single means of livelihood. (Br 89 min.)

Umberto D: A stark drama of old age trying to maintain a dignified status of living on a government pension. (Br 89 min.)

Two Women: A mother attempts to mend the psychic wounds of her teen-age daughter after a gang rape by soldiers in wartime Italy. (Au 105 min.)

Miracle in Milan: A gay modern fable of shantytown residents enlisting the supernatural help of an angel of mercy. (Au 95 min.)

Marriage Italian Style: A lusty melodrama in which a mistress of many years finally traps her man. (Au 102 min.)

Joseph Losey: One of the best of modern stylists. He often hovers on the sordid edges of morality but occasionally takes a direct swipe at moral evils.

The Servant: A hypnotic depiction of the slithering corruption of a rich weakling by a malicious manservant. (Au 115 min.)

King and Country: A hidebound military court tries and condemns a simplistic deserter. The execution is unforgettably obscene. (Au 86 min.)

Films from Individual Sources

Alfie: A confirmed lady-killer shares his musing with the audience in a series of unsatisfying affairs. An illegal abortion performed on a married conquest turns his stomach but leaves him unreformed. (FI 114 min.)

All Quiet on the Western Front: Millions of people around the globe have responded to this powerful pacifist statement against the cruel injustice of war on the enlisted fighting man. (UEVA 103 min.)

The Angry Silence: An angry social drama about the physical and mental harms perpetrated on the sole worker who opposes a wildcat strike. The brief inclusion of a Communist fellow traveler slightly confuses the theme of the common man's inhumanity to his fellow worker. (Au 95 min.)

Becket: Richard Burton reins in his screen presence as Thomas à Becket, and Peter O'Toole lets loose as Henry II in a freewheeling, opulent adaptation of the historical issues of church and state in Norman England. (FI 148 min.)

Before the Revolution: The lyrical, bemused story of a young man crossing the bar from revolutionist to member of the establishment. Filmed in Parma by a twenty-two-year-old cinematic poet, Bernardo Bertolucci. (Au 115 min.)

The Best Man: Gore Vidal's searing portrayal of political necessities canceling out liberal ideals in the back rooms of a national convention. (UA 102 min.)

Billy Budd: Herman Melville's allegory on the mutual extinction of the extremes of good and evil within the microcosm of a British warship. Robert Ryan's Claggart and Terence Stamp's Budd reincarnate the moral opposites under Peter Ustinov's direction. (Au 123 min.)

Brief Encounter: David Lean and Noel Coward teamed up for a fourth time to create this "vanity-sized *Anna Karenina*" in which two thoroughly ordinary people, separately married, are lured into a doomed affair by chance encounters and vagrant emotions. (UEVA 99 min.)

Darling: A mushy, pulp-magazine commentary supplies the ironic counterpoint for an exciting visual essay of a beautiful model using people and being used among the hip set. (Au 122 min.)

Death of a Salesman: Another Stanley Kramer production, this visualization of the Arthur Miller tragedy stresses realism over lyrical evocation but delivers the goods through Fredric March's rendition of the crumbling of the great American materialistic dream. (Au–Br 115 min.)

Diary of a Country Priest: Robert Bresson's extremely austere struggle of a frail vessel of grace against the inbred evils of a country parish. (Br 95 min.)

Dr. Strangelove: The reigning black comedy classic of the American screen, Strangelove plays around on the surface of plausibilities with the harrowing implications of nuclear armament. (Col 93 min.)

The Easy Life: In this ebullient tragicomedy, a gregarious, shallow salesman indoctrinates a retiring student lawyer into the easy life of sports cars, games, and women-hopping. (Au 105 min.)

Forbidden Games: René Clément adroitly mocks peasant morality and religious customs by comparing their selfish coarseness to the innocent inclinations of children. The theme of a child orphaned by an inane adult war is beautifully worked in. (Au 90 min.)

David and Lisa: A successful small-budget film in the *Marty* tradition, *David and Lisa* is an intimate drama of neurotic teen-agers reaching out to each other for help. (Co16 94 min.)

The Four Hundred Blows: François Truffaut's story of an evolving delinquent in a bitter family unit is a hundred-in-one shot. Truffaut lets loose a barrage of effective cinema techniques, but the boy's plight remains front and center. (J 98 min.)

Photo Courtesy of Continental 16
David and Lisa

Freud: The tasteful period atmosphere and effective acting of the principals do not disguise the fact that *Freud* is a rare treatise of ideas. The film covers Freud's transition from hypnosis to psychoanalysis and his adoption of the theory of eroticism in children. (UEVA 140 min.)

The Gospel According to St. Matthew: An Italian Marxist conceived this faithful dramatization of the good news of the Jewish evangelist. Using bleak Italian locales and non-actors, Pier Paolo Pasolini maintains a rapid pace in recounting Jesus Christ's extraordinary apostolate. (Br 135 min.)

The Grapes of Wrath: In this cross-country odyssey of Dust Bowl refugees, John Ford merges his highly emotional brand of film narrative within the framework of John Steinbeck's indictment of an affluent society. (FI 115 min.)

Hiroshima, Mon Amour: Alain Resnais interweaves the enduring memory of two tragedies, that of a French woman who fell in love with a German soldier and that of a city blasted from life by the atom bomb. The cinematic style compels involvement. (Au 88 min.)

The Hoodlum Priest: Father Dismas, founder of a midway house, decries capital punishment and personalizes the heartbreak of readjusting the few ex-cons who can make a go of it in civilian life. (UA 101 min.)

The Hustler: A brutally, thrusting drama of moral resurrection in the nether world of pool-hall gamesmanship. George C. Scott's incarnation of a gambling agent reeks of the ubiquitous corruption of evil (FI 135 min.)

Ikiru: In this film by the masterful Japanese director, Akira Kurosawa, a cog in the machinery of a vast society frantically attempts to find a dimension to life when his physician assesses him a few more months of existence. The theme is "to live is to love." (Br 140 min.)

Lillies of the Field: With a few humorous twists a Negro veteran is challenged to full manhood by the frustrating demands of a community of immigrant nuns in the Southwest. (Au 97 min.)

Miss Lonelyhearts: Dore Schary's adaptation of Nathanael West's puzzling novel brings out most of the dramatic power of the original. A cub reporter is bullied into the lonelyhearts column by a sardonic editor. He finds himself taking on the burdens of mankind. (UA 101 min.)

Mafioso: Alberto Lattuada reached his maturity as a film-maker in this tragicomedy. The first part, about the return of a successful businessman to Sicily, is hilarious. In the second, he is horrified to find himself crated to a New Jersey barbershop for an assassination of honor. (Au 100 min.)

A Man Called Peter: Thanks mainly to the personable sincerity of Richard Todd, *A Man Called Peter* is one of the few reputable biographies of men of the cloth. Peter Marshall was a Scotsman who trained for the ministry at Columbia Theological School and later became chaplain of the United States Senate. (FI 119 min.)

Marat/Sade: A motion picture without a definition. In a play within a play, the Marquis de Sade stages an inventive recitative dramatization of the issues of the French Revolution—crushing human wrongs, implacable revolutionaries without heart, opportunistic politics—performed by the groveling inmates of his asylum. (UA 115 min.)

270

The Miracle Worker: Anne Bancroft and Patty Duke in a vibrant interplay evoke the freeing of Helen Keller's spirit from its corporal bondage. Gibson's play is a beautiful tribute to a unique American sage. (UA 107 min.)

Courtesy of UA Sixteen
The Miracle Worker

Night of the Iguana: Tennessee Williams' cauldron this time around is a Mexican hothouse in which a defrocked minister and a repressed spinster come to some degree of peace with themselves. Williams' poetic message is melded to the tour de force acting his films customarily warrant. (FI 125 min.)

Nobody Waved Goodbye: Along the pattern of *Four Hundred Blows*, this film achieves audience identification and an atmosphere of spontaneous reality by improvising the script and lensing. A Canadian teen-ager rejects his parents but does not have the necessary skills or personal integrity to make a go of it on his own. (Br 80 min.)

Nothing but a Man: The plight of the Negro male emasculated by a dominant white society. (Br 92 min.)

Odd Man Out: Everybody wants a piece of Johnny McQueen, a dying IRS fugitive: his leadership, his neck, his soul, his love. In a powerful cinematic style, Carol Reed progresses from documentary to dramatic fantasy. (UEVA 117 min.)

The Organizer: With a particularly Italian brand of earthiness, Mario

271

Monicelli finds sprigs of idealism in the coarse efforts of Italian workers to alleviate a fourteen-hour day. (Col6 126 min.)

Paths of Glory: In several instances *Paths of Glory* is the most explosive condemnation of an unfeeling military establishment in wartime conditions. Three men are executed for alleged cowardice as an example to their confreres. (UA 87 min.)

The Pumpkin Eater: With a dazzling virtuosity, Jack Clayton ticks off the many pressures on the mother of a large family. The screenplay by Harold Pinter is candid, sophisticated, and elliptic. (Au 110 min.)

Question 7: Worshipers of different age levels have their personal commitments to religion challenged by the hostility of a Communist regime in eastern Europe. The accent is on the crisis among the young. (Au–Br 107 min.)

A Raisin in the Sun: An insurance check provides a Negro family with a series of options. They accept the hardships that will go along with maintaining personal dignity in a decent middle-class neighborhood. (Au–Br 127 min.)

Rebel Without a Cause: Nicholas Ray's visual pyrotechnics keep pace with the dramatics of James Dean in this touching tragedy of three teen-agers betrayed by parental strictness, mushiness, and indifference. (Au–Br 111 min.)

Shop on Main Street: The Czechs have been prolific with innovations in cinema styles, but their focus has been on the wealth of drama in ordinary living. *Shop on Main Street* presents the dilemma of a Czech collaborator under German occupation after he has personalized his relationship with an old Jewish shopkeeper. (Au 128 min.)

The Slender Thread: The drama of a suicide squad maintaining around-the-clock telephone help and advice to people contemplating self-destruction. (FI 100 min.)

Suddenly Last Summer: Joseph Mankiewicz expands and melodramatizes Tennessee Williams' allegory in which all the world, including mankind, is a perpetual cycle of the preying and the preyed upon. (Au–Br 114 min.)

This Sporting Life: In a crushing film experience an inarticulate brute of a man succeeds on the soccer field but fails to relate as a man to a withdrawn widow. (UVEA 129 min.)

Whisperers: Dame Edith Evans projects the alienation of old age as a lady brightening her drab, pensioned life with fragile fantasies. The film treatment is more conventional and warmer than that of *Umberto D.* (UA 105 min.)

Zorba the Greek: A Greek hymn to living life to its fullest. A crafty old live wire thaws out a young English stiff. (FI 142 min.)

Key to Feature Film Distributors

Au Audio Film Center
   34 MacQuesten Parkway South, Mount Vernon, New York 10550

Br Brandon Films
    221 West 57th Street, New York, New York 10019

Au–Br Indicates Audio and Brandon and most of the hundreds of local
       dealers across the country with autonomous names

Col Columbia Pictures Corporation
     711 Fifth Avenue, New York, New York 10022

Co16 Continental 16
      Walter Reade Organization
      241 East 34th Street, New York, New York 10016

FI Films Incorporated
    38 West 32nd Street, New York, New York 10001

J Janus Films
   24 West 58th Street, New York, New York 10019

UA United Artists
    729 Seventh Avenue, New York, New York 10019

UEVA Universal Educational and Visual Arts
      221 Park Avenue South, New York, New York 10019

Note: Audio, Brandon, Films Incorporated, and Universal Educational and Visual Arts have other distribution exchanges across the country. A letter to the above addresses will secure a catalog with these locations, all prints available, and rental and exhibition terms listed.

Short Features That Open Up Moderns

Time Piece: (Co* 8 min.) A touchstone of modern short films, visually hilarious, and trenchantly symbolic of the plight of the 9-to-5 modern.
Arthur Lipsett tapes together bits and pieces from the Canadian Film Board's disposal units and comes up with chilling, disjointed collages of the face of modern society: *Very Nice, Very Nice* (NFBC 7 min), *21-87* (NFBC 9 min.), and *Free Fall* (NFBC 9 min.).
The Drag: A stylish color cartoon, *The Drag* tweaks the love-hate relationship of cigarette smokers. (NFBC 9 min.)
Flatland: Geometrical allusions are used to dramatize the plight of the believer of the supernatural. (Co 10 min.)
The Hand: An ambiguous fable by the puppeteer Jiri Trnka, elevates the struggle of the nonconformist common man to epic heights. (Co 19 min.)

* See the Key to Short Feature Distributors, p. 279.

Help, My Snowman's Burning Down: Presents an emotionally aloof playboy guarding his preserve on a way-out wharf in New York's harbor. Several interpretations are possible. (Co 10 min.)

The House: Luis van Gesteren rents the fabric of time in depicting the habitation of a house by three generations. (Co 30 min.)

The Little Island: Employs sophisticated symbols in depicting the eternal struggle of the good (religion), the true (science), and the beautiful (art). (Co 30 min.)

Plain Man's Guide to Advertising: Parodies modern advertising's all-out assault on the weaknesses of humanity. (Co 14 min.)

Seven Authors in Search of a Reader: A lyrically cinematic treatise that reflects the ubiquitous influence of the printed media in a microcosm of humanity. (Co 21 min.)

That's Me: Written and acted by Alan Arkin, *That's Me* disarms the viewer with its park-bench encounter of a smug Puerto Rican and an overeager social worker. (Co 12 min.)

The Top: Visualizes in cartoon form the eternal struggle of the opportunist for a materialistic heaven. (Co 8 min.)

Super-Up: A confused Negro boy is chased through a kaleidoscope of advertising lures. (Br 12 min.)

Universe: The viewer is awed by this meticulously re-created journey from the sun to the outer galaxies. Like most National Film Board products, it is science with a heart. (NFBC 28 min.)

The Violinist: Amuses itself with the demands of art and humanity on the individual. (Br 7 min.)

The Underprivileged in America

The Poor Pay More and *Harvest of Shame:* Conventionally filmed TV documentaries with powerful visual and factual messages. Edward R. Murrow showed the latter to the country on Thanksgiving, but the plight of the harvesters has improved little. (NET 58 min.) (McH 54 min.)

On the Bowery: Shot entirely among the derelicts of New York's bowery. The volunteer actors from the streets lend it a frightening reality. (Co 65 min.)

The Exiles: Shot on the West Coast, *The Exile* captures the pathetic disorientation of the American Indian in metropolitan locales. (Co 72 min.)

Who Do You Kill? An *East Side, West Side* segment that dramatizes the frustration of a ghetto family after their child is killed by a rat. (CF 51 min.)

Children Without and *Christmas in Appalachia:* Emotional documentaries of the white poor with their educational drawbacks and dearth of adequate living standards. (MMM 30 min.) (MMM 29 min.)

I Wonder Why: A single-concept film of a Negro girl's plaintive hopes to experience the simple joys in life. (Co 6 min.)

Blind Gary Davis: Allows a balladeer of the slums to express his views on life and contains a chilling succession of hollow black faces on the sidewalks of a ghetto. (Co 12 min.)

The Inheritance: One of the great propaganda films, allowing the union movement to claim credit for all the great social changes in America. But the narartive is a stirring account of the rise of white immigrants from the slums. (Co 60 min.)

A Chance for Change: Records the progress of an optimistic Head Start program in the deep South. (Co 40 min.)

Uptown: A Portrait of the South Bronx: A rich aural and visual tapestry of the face of a New York ghetto area. (Co 27 min.)

Good Night, Socrates: Dramatizes the demise of a Greek ghetto area. (Co 34 min.)

The Quiet One: Traces the reclamation of a disturbed black youth in a a special school. Commentary by James Agee. (Co 67 min.)

Flavio: Allows Gordon Parks the opportunity to expand on film his photographic record of a South American slum family. (Co 12 min.)

The Handicapped

Four sensitive documentaries provide participation in the family dilemma of caring for a handicapped member. The parents who accept their burden with great courage are the heroes of these films. *Stress—Parents with a Handicapped Child* (Co 30 min.), four case histories, sums up the individual problems of *Eternal Children* (NFBC 30 min.), the retarded child; *Thursday's Children* (Co 22 min.), the deaf child; and *One of Them Is Brett* (Co 30 min.), the thalidomide child.

Racial Prejudice

No Hiding Place: Another *East Side, West Side* segment, this time dramatizing the hostile reaction of a middle class neighborhood to the arrival of a black family. (CF 51 min.)

Night and Fog and *St. Matthew's Passion:* Shattering masterworks on the treatment of Jews in Nazi concentration camps. The latter uses only Bach's oratorio for commentary. (Co 31 min.) (Co 21 min.)

Memorandum: Reprises the same theme in retrospect by detailing the pilgrimage of a Jewish-Canadian glass cutter in the 60s to the sites of his internment during World War II. (NFBC 58 min.)

The Streets of Greenwood and *Sit-in:* Capture two stirring segments of the civil rights movement. (Br 20 min.) (McH 54 min.)

The Ku Klux Klan: The Invisible Empire: Presents the opposition in action and in historical perspective. (CF 47 min.)

A Time for Burning: One of the most important documentaries of our times. A team of photographers hired by the Lutheran Church tells it like it was when Pastor Youngdahl of Augustana Church in Omaha, Nebraska, was ousted from his congregation for suggesting that white and Negro families meet in dialogue. (Co 58 min.)

These Four Cozy Walls: Filmed of Casa View United Methodist Church, Dallas. A documentation of six weeks of this church's life. (MMM 58 min.)

Courtesy of TRAFCO
These Four Cozy Walls

Willie Catches On: Dramatizes the osmosis of prejudices from careless parents. (NFBC 25 min.)

Hangman: An allegory on a Hitler-like campaign for the extinction of hated races. (Co 12 min.)

Problems of Life in a Mechanized Society

Of Time, Work, and Leisure: Looks to the future difficulties of man emancipated from the forty-hour week. (MMM 30 min.)

Nice Time: Sardonically groups the empty pleasures of revelers in Piccadilly Circus. (Co 19 min.)

Detached Americans and *Conformity:* (From a great local TV tradition, these films intelligently probe two sicknesses of our society. (CF 30 min.) (CF 55 min.)

The Great American Funeral: Borrows its theme from Jessica Mitford's challenging book, *The American Way of Death*. (McH 54 min.)

Superfluous People: Interviews ghetto residents and older people displaced by building projects. (CF 54 min.)

Crime in the Streets: Seeks through interviews the causes of another contemporary ill. (NET 60 min.)

Day After Day: Records the drab existence of a factory town. (NFBC 25 min.)

Caroline: In the style of modern foreign films dramatizes the internal pressures of a working mother. (NFBC 28 min.)

The Living Machine: In two segments intelligently questions what type of society is being formed in a cybernetic age. (NFBC 56 min.)

Assembly Line: Recaps the theme of *Day After Day*. (Br. 35 min.)

Have I Told You Lately That I Love You?: A visual witticism of a family that communicates only through machines. (MMM 16 min.)

Religious and Eschatological Themes

Parable: The most popular short feature on the essence of the good news, *Parable* allegorizes the phoenix-like succession of Christian apostles. (MMM 22 min.)

An Occurrence at Owl Creek Bridge: From the short story by Ambrose Bierce, Eulogizes life through the fantasies of a condemned man's final moments. (Co 27 min.)

It's About This Carpenter: An amusing university film of a carpenter who resembles Christ carrying a finished crucifix across New York. (MMM 14 min.)

The Red Kite: Effectively dramatizes faith in God through physical manifestations. (NFBC 17 min.)

Run: An exciting allegory of man racing to his grave pursued by symbols of social pressure. (Br 16 min.)

The Smile: Visualizes the Buddhist affirmation of God in nature. (Co 18 min.)

The National Film Board of Canada has done several sensitive documentaries on organized religion. Among the best of them are *The Hutterites* (28 min.) ; *Blood and Fire* (27 min.), the Salvation Army; *The Little Sisters* (30 min.), a cloistered order of nuns; and *Pilgrimage* (30 min.), Catholic worship at St. Joseph's Oratory in Montreal.

Sex Education

From Generation to Generation: A standard with educators, this film places the details of reproduction in a warm family setting. (McH 25 min.)

Human Reproduction and *Biography of the Unborn:* Devoid of social context, these are two reliable text films. (McH 20 min.) (EBF 16 min.)

Boy to Man and *Girl to Woman:* Successfully relate the changes in the adolescent body. (Ch 16 min.) (Ch 16 min.)

Overture/Nyitany: Rhythmically unfolds the wonders of chicken embryology with the help of still-motion photography and the emotional up-lift of Beethoven's *Egmont Overture.* (Co 9 min.)

The National Film Board of Canada has a frank trio of dramatizations on teen-age encounters with sex. *Phoebe* (25 min.) uses Fellini methods to explore the mind of a pregnant, unwed teen-ager. *The Game* (28 min.) switches to the Antonioni style in presenting a boy virgin-hunter. *Merry Go Round* (23 min.) offers an intimate boy-meets-girl story interwoven with the conflicting advice of adult "experts."

Teen-age Dilemmas

No Reason to Stay: With great vitality and witty cinematics exaggerates the hang-ups of an intelligent dropout. (NFBC 28 min.)

The Dropout: Documents the case of the ordinary slow student. (Co 28 min.)

The Young Americans: Interviews college students across the country on the relevant issues of the day. (NET 60 min.)

Sixteen in Webster Groves: Frustratingly allows the middleclass, conservative, Midwest, stand-pat student his say. (CF 47 min.)

The End of Summer: Dwells on the musings of adolescent boys and girls about each other, religion, and responsibilities. (NFBC 27 min.)

You're No Good: By George Kaczender, the director of *Phoebe* and *The Game.* An eclectic visualization on the dilemma of a semidelinquent. NFBC 28 min.)

Lonely Boy: Intimately films a daily album on a teen-age entertainment phenomenon, Paul Anka. (NFBC 27 min.)

Notes on a Film About Donna and Gail: Traces two older girls who are out of school attempting to make it on their own (NFBC 60 min.)

War

The War Game: Re-creates in a harrowing manner the holocaust of a nuclear conflagration in a surburban setting. (Co 50 min.)

Battle of Culloden: An earlier documentary by Peter Watkins, *Battle of Culloden* uses the same cinema-*vérité* simulation as in *The War Game* to re-create the total slaughter of a conventional war, the last battle fought on British soil. (PR 72 min.)

The Magician: A fable about an insidious military recruiter of young children. (SF 13 min.)

Chickamauga: Traces a young deaf-mute through the carnage of a backwater Civil War battlefield, (Co 33 min.)

The Anderson Platoon: Documents with intimacy the face of the Vietnam War. (Co 75 min.)

Toys: Vivifies a windowful of military toys through the eyes of young onlookers. (NFBC 7 min.)

Key to Short Feature Distributors

CF   Carousel Films
1501 Broadway, New York, New York   10036

CMC   Center for Mass Communication
440 West 110th Street, New York, New York   10026

Ch   Churchill Films
662 Torth Robertson Boulevard, Los Angeles, California   90069

Co   Contemporary Films/McGraw Hill
330 West 42nd Street, New York, New York   10036

EBF   Encyclopaedia Britannica Films
4420 Oakton Street, Skokie, Illinois   60076

McH   McGraw-Hill Films
330 West 42nd Street, New York, New York   10036

MMM   Mass Media Ministries
2116 North Charles Street, Baltimore, Maryland   21218

NET   National Education Television
Indiana University
Audio. Visual Center, Bloomington, Indiana   47401

NFBC   National Film Board of Canada
680 Fifth Avenue, New York, New York   10019
    The Film Board's catalog indicates which companies have sales rights to their titles in the U.S. Contemporary has rental rights on practically all NFBC titles.

PR   Peter M. Robeck & Co.
230 Park Avenue, New York, New York   10017

SF   Sterling Educational Films
Walter Reade Organization
241 East 34th Street, New York, New York   10016

APPENDIX II

A. Selected Films for Children

TITLE	THEME SUGGESTIONS *	TIME	DISTRIBUTOR
BARBARA	awareness of self	7 min.	Interlude
THE BIRD HUNT	God's creatures sanctity of life	11	University of California
BLACK PATCH (U.S.S.R.)	God's creatures	18	Brandon
BOSWELLE'S BON VOYAGE	God's creatures	9	Sterling

* Theme suggestions are based upon the reaction of children to the films. Nationality based on the settings may prove valuable for "family of man" theme.

TITLE	THEME SUGGESTIONS*	TIME	DISTRIBUTOR
THE CHICKEN	family life	15	Contemporary
CHRISTMAS CRACKER	materialism love	9	Contemporary
CHUK AND GEK (U.S.S.R.)	family life	48	Brandon
FADILA (Algeria)	friendship love	27	Brandon
FAMILY OF N'GUMBA	sanctity of life family life	11	Sterling
THE GOLDEN FISH	love of nature goodness in simple living	20	Contemporary Columbia
HEIDI (Switzerland)	simple pleasures family life	98	Brandon
HEIDI AND PETER	simple pleasures friendship family life	89	Brandon
JUGGLER OF OUR LADY	use of talents	9	Carousel
THE KING AND THE LION	human dignity kindness	13	Contemporary
THE LITTLEST ANGEL	love kindness sacrifice	6	Sterling
THE MAGIC HORSE	God's creatures wonder	57	Brandon
MARVELS OF THE HIVE	love of nature	20	Contemporary
NEIGHBORS	love of others	8	International Contemporary
PADDLE TO THE SEA	love of others sacrifice	28	Contemporary
THE RED BALLOON	loneliness understanding kindness	34	Brandon
A SCRAP OF PAPER AND A PIECE OF STRING	friendship importance of little things	6	Contemporary

TITLE	THEME SUGGESTIONS*	TIME	DISTRIBUTOR
THE SECRET WAY (Germany)	sympathy care	6	Brandon
SMALLEST ELEPHANT IN THE WORLD	dignity of individual	6	Sterling
STEADFAST TIN SOLDIER (Denmark)	love integrity	14	Brandon

STEFAN ON SUNDAY	beauty and wonder
	  of God's world
		14	Encyclopaedia
			  Britannica

TREASURE OF OSTEND (Belgium)	God's creatures	14	Brandon
WHITE MANE	family life understanding patience	40	Contemporary
THE WHITE POODLE (U.S.S.R.)	family poor but happy	70	Brandon
WILLIE CATCHES ON	prejudice	24	Contemporary McGraw-Hill
WONDER	dignity of man	5	Family Theater

B. Films Which Assist in a Thematic Study of Man and His World

THEME	SHORT FILMS	TIME	SOURCE	FEATURE FILMS
AWARENESS				
IDENTIFICATION	CLAY	6	MMM*	THE LONELINESS OF THE LONG DISTANCE RUNNER— Richardson
	ADVENTURES OF AN ASTERISK	10	Co	THE PUMPKIN EATER—Clayton
	ACT YOUR AGE	14	MMM	THE HEART IS A LONELY HUNTER— Robert E. Miller
	THE LEAST OF MY BROTHERS	27	PP	RACHEL, RACHEL— Newman
	THE BALLAD OF ALMA GERLAYNE	27	MMM	
	THE TRUTH ABOUT TIME	27	PP	
	GOOD NIGHT, SOCRATES	34	MMM	
	CONFORMITY	49	CF	
	THE INDIVIDUAL	60	MMM	
COMMUNICATION	CHAIRY TALE	10	Co	LA STRADA—Fellini
	THE TOYMAKER	15	Co	FOUR HUNDRED BLOWS— Truffaut
	GENERATION WITHOUT CAUSE	26	CF	THROUGH A GLASS DARKLY— Bergman
	END OF SUMMER	27	Co	
	PHOEBE	28	Co	
EMPATHY	HANGMAN	12	Co	JUDGMENT AT NUREMBERG—Kramer
	RUN	16	Co	THE OX BOW INCIDENT—Wellman
	CHILDREN ADRIFT	26	Co	MONSIEUR VINCENT—Cloche
	THE RED BALLOON	34	Br	
	THE DETACHED AMERICANS	35	CF	

* See the Key to Sources, p.288.

THEME	SHORT FILMS	TIME	SOURCE	FEATURE FILMS
FAMILY	FLAVIO	12	Co	THE PUMPKIN EATER—Clayton
	HE LIVED WITH US, HE ATE WITH US, WHAT ELSE, DEAR?	27	PP	THE BICYCLE THIEF—de Sica
				RAISIN IN THE SUN—Petrie
	MUMMY	27	PP	FOUR HUNDRED BLOWS—Truffaut
	AND WHO HAS EVER SEEN XANADU?	27	PP	
	FROM GENERATION TO GENERA-TION	30	MMM	
	THE PARENTS	60	MMM	
FULFILLMENT	BARBARA	7	Int	A MAN FOR ALL SEASONS—Zinnemann
	TWO MEN AND A WARDROBE	15	Co	THE TRIAL OF JOAN OF ARC—Bressen
	OF TIME, WORK, AND LEISURE	29	IU	SUMMER INTERLUDE—Bergman
	HELEN KELLER IN HER STORY	45	LR	DIARY OF A COUNTRY PRIEST—Bressen
FRIENDSHIP	ALF, BILL, AND FRED	10	MMM	SUNDAYS AND CYBELE—Bourguignon
	THE CHICKEN	15	MMM	ZORBA THE GREEK—Cacoyannis
	FADILA	27	Br	
	ALMOST NEIGHBORS	34	MMM	
	THE END OF SUMMER	27	MMM	
LOVE LTD.	HATE SYNDROME	27	PP	ALFIE—Gilbert
	KINDS OF LOVE	30	MMM	DARLING—Schlesinger
	THE PLAYBOY AND THE CHRISTIAN	54	MMM	ECLIPSE—Antonioni
				THE SILENCE—Bergman
				MORGAN—Reisz
				GEORGY GIRL—Narazzino

THEME	SHORT FILMS	TIME	SOURCE	FEATURE FILMS
LOVE AND MARRIAGE	HAVE I TOLD YOU LATELY THAT I LOVE YOU	16	UC	THE LAST BRIDGE—Kautner
	LOOK BACK TO THE GARDEN	27	PP	LUCK OF GINGER COFFEE—Hershner
	THE OLEANDER YEARS	27	PP	WHO'S AFRAID OF VIRGINIA WOOLF—Nichols
	A FUNNY THING HAPPENED ON THE WAY	27	PP	
	PROMETHEUS BOUND	27	PP	
YOUNG LOVE	THE TENDER GAME	7	Co	NOBODY WAVED GOODBYE—Owens
	THE LOVERS	27	PP	DAVID AND LISA—Perry
	PHOEBE	28	Co	TOM JONES—Richardson
	THE MEANING OF LOVE	27	PP	
	THE HANG-UP	27	PP	
YOUTH	I NEVER WENT BACK (dropout)	16	MMM	SATURDAY NIGHT AND SUNDAY MORNING—Reisz
	MEANING OF ADOLESCENCE	16	MMM	LORD OF THE FLIES—Brook
	CRIME IN THE STREETS	60	MMM	THE FIANCES—Olmi
	THE COFFEE HOUSE	27	PP	THE COOL WORLD—Clarke
				111th STREET—Federbush
				FOUR HUNDRED BLOWS—Truffaut
DRINK-DOPE	BENNIES AND GOOF BALLS	23	MMM	
	SNOW IN SUMMER	27	PP	
	THE SANDALMAKER	27	MMM	
	THE DOG THAT BIT YOU	27	PP	
	THE HOUSE ON THE BEACH	60	MMM	

THEME	SHORT FILMS	TIME	SOURCE	FEATURE FILMS
FRUSTRATION	SHOP TOWN (unemployment)	6	Br	IKIRU—Kurosawa
	THE NEW LOOK IS THE ANXIOUS LOOK	11	Br	
	AN OCCURRENCE AT OWL CREEK BRIDGE	27	Co	
	A PLACE TO LIVE (aged)	30	Br	
	LET MY PEOPLE GO	54	W	
LONELINESS	LONELY BOY	17	Co	TRILOGY—Perry
	STRING BEAN (old age)	17	Co	THE HEART IS A LONELY HUNTER— Robert E. Miller
	THE GOLDEN FISH	20	Col	
	MINT TEA	20	MMM	
	THE QUIET ONE	67	MMM	
POVERTY	A VALPARAISO	30	Co	GRAPES OF WRATH—Ford
	HARVEST OF SHAME	60	McH	
	THE HARD WAY	60	MMM	
REJECTION AND ACCEPTANCE	BROTHERHOOD OF MAN	11	Br	NOTHING BUT A MAN— Young and Roemer
	THE GOLDEN DOOR (immigration)	15	Br	RAISIN IN THE SUN—Petrie
	AN AMERICAN GIRL	28	Br	STRANGE VICTORY—Hurwitz
	JIMMY	30	MMM	A TIME FOR BURNING— Jersey and Connell
	ALL THE WAY HOME (housing)	30	Br	
	CRISIS IN LEVITTOWN	30	Br	
	A DREAM DEFERRED	37	Br	
	CHILDREN OF REVOLUTION	60	MMM	

THEME	SHORT FILMS	TIME	SOURCE	FEATURE FILMS
MAN'S INHUMANITY TO MAN—WAR	VIVRE	8	Co	FORBIDDEN GAMES—Clement
	THE TOYMAKER	15	Co	THE WAR GAME—Watkins
	THE HOLE	15	Br	THE LAST BRIDGE—Kautner
	TOYS ON A FIELD OF BLUE	20	Br	
	TIME OUT OF WAR	22	Co	
	THE THREE-CORNERED FLAG (draft)	27	MMM	
	NIGHT AND FOG	31	Co	
MAN AND MACHINE	AUTOMANIA	10	Co	MY UNCLE—Tati
	DON'T ELBOW ME OFF THE EARTH	27	PP	MAN OF ARAN—Flaherty
	AUTOMATION: THE NEXT GENERATION	30	MMM	LOUISIANA STORY—Flaherty
	DAY AFTER DAY	27	Co	
	ASSEMBLY LINE	35	Br	
MAN AND SOCIETY— THE SYSTEM	EYE OF THE BEHOLDER	26	MMM	THE BICYCLE THIEF—de Sica
	THE OLD GLORY	111	MMM	CITIZEN KANE—Welles
	THE INHERITANCE	60	MMM	THE INFORMER—Ford
				LA DOLCE VITA—Fellini
				NIGHTS OF CABIRIA—Lopert
				ON THE WATERFRONT—Kazan
				ROOM AT THE TOP—Clayton
				SOUND OF TRUMPETS—de Sica
				IKIRU—Kurosawa

Key to Sources

Br Brandon Films
221 West 57th Street, New York, New York   10019

CF Carousel Films
1501 Broadway, New York, New York   10036

Col Columbia Pictures Corporation
711 Fifth Avenue, New York, New York   10022

Co Contemporary Films
330 West 42nd Street, New York, New York   10036

IU Indiana University
Audio-Visual Center, Bloomington, Indiana   47401

Int Interlude Films
524-C East Glenoaks Boulevard, Glendale, California   91207

McH McGraw-Hill Films
330 West 42nd Street, New York, New York   10036

MMM Mass Media Ministries
2116 North Charles Street, Baltimore, Maryland   21218

PP Paulist Productions
17575 Pacific Coast Highway, Pacific Palisades, California   90272

LR Louis de Rochemont Associates
18 East 48th Street, New York, New York   10017

UC University of California Extension Media Center
2223 Fulton Street, Berkeley, California   94720

W David L. Wolper, Inc.
8544 Sunset Boulevard, Hollywood, California   90069

APPENDIX III

A. Bibliography

Books About Film*

Agree, James. *Five Film Scripts*. Boston: Beacon Press, 1964.
_____. *Reviews and Comments*. Beacon Press, 1964.
Alpert, Hollis. *The Dreams and the Dreamers*. New York: Macmillan, 1962.
Arnheim, Rudolf. *Film as Art*. Berkeley: University of California Press, 1957.
Bazin, André. *What Is Cinema?* Ed. and trans. Hugh Gray. Berkeley: University of California Press, 1967.
Bluestone, George. *Novels into Film*. Berkeley: University of California Press, 1957.

* Specially recommended.

Bobker, Lee. *Elements of Film.* New York: Harcourt, Brace & World, 1969.

Cornwell-Clyne, Adrian, ed. *Colour Films.* 2nd ed. London: Focal Press, 1963.

Durgnat, Raymond. *Eros in the Cinema.* London: Calder & Boyars, 1966.

Eisenstein, Sergei. *Film Form and Film Sense.* Meridian Books; Cleveland: World, 1960.

Fulton, A. R. *Motion Pictures: The Development of an Art from Silent Films to the Age of Television.* Norman: University of Oklahoma Press, 1960.

Gessner, Robert. *The Moving Image: A Guide to Cinematic Literacy.* New York: Dutton, 1968.

Grierson, John. *Grierson on Documentary.* Ed. Forsyth Hardy. Rev. ed. Berkeley: University of California Press, 1966.

Haas, William Paul. "The Contemporary Arts." Washington: Thomist Press, 1965.

Hall, Stuart and Whannell, Paddy. *The Popular Arts.* Boston: Beacon Press, 1968.

Houston, Penelope. *The Contemporary Cinema.* Baltimore: Penguin Books, 1963.

Jacobs, Norman, ed. *Culture for the Millions: Mass Media in Modern Society.* Boston: Beacon Press, 1964.

Kael, Pauline. *I Lost It at the Movies.* Boston: Little, Brown, 1965.

————. *Kiss Kiss Bang Bang.* Boston: Little, Brown, 1968.

Kauffmann, Stanley. *A World on Film.* New York: Harper, 1966.

Kepes, Gyorgy. *The Nature and Art of Motion.* New York: Braziller, 1964.

*Knight, Arthur. *The Liveliest Art.* Mentor Books; New York: New American Library, 1959.

Koenigil, Mark. *Movies in Society.* New York: Robert Speller & Sons, 1962.

Kracauer, Siegfried. *Theory of Film.* Galaxy Books; New York: Oxford University Press, 1960.

*Lindgren, Ernest. *The Art of the Film.* Rev. ed. New York: Macmillan, 1952.

MacCann, Richard Dyer. *Film and Society.* New York: Scribner's, 1964.

————, ed. *Film: A Montage of Theories.* New York: Dutton, 1966.

MacGowan, Kenneth. *Behind the Screen.* New York: Delacorte Press, 1965.

Montagu, Ivor. *Film World.* Pelican Books; Baltimore: Penguin Books, 1964.

Rhode, Eric. *Tower of Babel: Speculations on the Cinema.* Philadelphia: Chilton Book Co., 1967.

Rotha, Paul, and Griffith, Richard. *The Film Till Now.* 3rd ed. New York: Twayne Publishers, 1968.

Stephenson, Ralph, and Debrix, J. R. *The Cinema as Art.* Pelican Books; Baltimore: Penguin Books, 1965.

Taylor, John Russell. *Cinema Eye, Cinema Ear.* New York: Hill & Wang, 1964.

Thompson, Denys, ed. *Discrimination and Popular Culture.* Baltimore: Penguin Books, 1964.

Warshow, Robert. *The Immediate Experience.* Garden City, N.Y.: Doubleday, 1964.

White, David M., and Averson, Richard. *Sight, Sound, and Society.* Boston: Beacon Press, 1968.

Selected Film Books for Teachers

Boutwell, William D., ed. *Using Mass Media in the Schools.* New York: Appleton-Century-Crofts, 1962.

Culkin, John M. *Film Study in the High School.* Bronx: Fordham University Press, 1965.

Fischer, Edward. *Screen Arts.* New York: Sheed & Ward, 1960.

Gardiner, Harold C., and Walsh, Moira. "Tenets for Movie Viewers." New York: America Press.

Harcourt, Peter, and Theobalk, Peter, eds. *Film Making in Schools and Colleges.* London: Shenval Press.

Haselden, Kyle. *Morality and the Mass Media.* Nashville: Broadman Press, 1968.

Hodgkinson, A. W. *Screen Education.* New York: UNESCO, 1965.

Hubbard, Celia T. *Let's See: The Use and Misuse of the Visual Arts in Religious Education.* Glen Rock, N. J.: Paulist Press, 1966.

*Jackson, B. F., Jr., ed. *Communication—Learning for Churchmen.* Nashville: Abingdon Press, 1968.

*Jones, G. William. *Sunday Night at the Movies.* Richmond: John Knox Press, 1967.

Keisman, Michael E., and Sheratsky, Rodney E. *The Creative Arts: Four Represenative Types.* New York: Globe Book Co., 1968.

Kitses, Jim, and Mercer, Ann. *Talking About the Cinema: Film Studies for Young People.* London: British Film Institute, 1966.

*Kuhns, William. *Short Films in Religious Education.* Dayton, Ohio: George A. Pflaum Publisher, 1967.

Kuhns, William, and Stanley, Robert. *Exploring the Film.* Dayton, Ohio: George A. Pflaum Publisher, 1968.

Larson, Rodger, Jr. *A Guide for Film Teachers: Film-Making by Teenagers.* New York: Cultural Affairs Foundation, 1968.

Lewis, Jacobs. *Introduction to the Art of the Movies.* New York: Noonday Press, 1964.

*McAnany, Emile, and Williams, Robert. *The Filmviewers' Handbook.* New York: Paulist Press, 1965.

*McCaffrey, Patrick J. *Films for Religious Education.* 2 vols. Notre Dame, Ind.: Fides Publishers, 1968.

McLuhan, Marshall. *Understanding Media: The Extensions of Man.* New York: New American Library, 1966.

McLuhan, Marshall, and Fiore, Quentin. *The Medium Is the Massage.* New York: Bantam Book, 1967.

McLuhan, Marshall, and Carpenter, Edmund S., eds. *Explorations in Communication.* Boston: Beacon Press, 1960.

*Mallery, David. *Film in the Life of the School.* Boston: National Association of Independent Schools, 1968.

_____. *The School and the Art of Motion Pictures.* Rev. ed. Boston: National Association of Independent Schools, 1966.

Parrington, Ruth. "An Educator's Guide to the Use of Film." Chicago: Argus Communications.

Peters, J. L. M. *Teaching About the Film*. New York: UNESCO, 1961.

Rosenthal, Raymond, ed. *McLuhan: Pro & Con*. New York: Funk & Wagnalls, 1968.

Sarris, Andrew. *The Film*. Indianapolis: Bobbs-Merrill, 1968.

*Schillaci, Anthony. *Movies and Morals*. Notre Dame, Ind.: Fides Publishers, 1968.

Schumach, Murry. *The Face on the Cutting Room Floor: The Story of Movie and Television Censorship*. New York: Morrow, 1964.

Sohn, David A. *Films in the Schools*. New York: Citation Press.

Stearn, G. E., ed. *McLuhan: Hot and Cool*. New York: Dial Press, 1968.

Stewart, David C., ed. *Film Study in Higher Education*. Washington: American Council on Education, 1966.

Sullivan, Sr. Bede. *Movies: Universal Language*. Notre Dame, Ind.: Fides Publishers.

Selected Bibliography for Media Approach

Choose Life Series 1969
Argus Communications
3505 North Ashland Avenue, Chicago, Illinois   60657
• multimedia approach to the study of revelation in the student's life through twelve nontext texts

Dialogue with the World 1965
Films Incorporated
1114 Wilmette Avenue, Wilmette, Illinois   60091
• program of seventy films in ten significant categories selected by Protestant and Catholic religious education consultants under the leadership of G. William Jones, then minister of education at Casa View Methodist Church, Dallas; study guide for discussion of theatrical films

The Eye of the Beholder
Stuart Reynolds Productions
9465 Wilshire Boulevard, Beverly Hills, California   90210
• film and study guide dramatizing twelve hours in the life of an artist
• stresses importance of caution in judging people and the wide spread of difference between judgments
• recommended for adult groups, counselors, teachers, junior and senior high school students.

Film Appreciation: How to See a Motion Picture
OFM Film Productions
1229 Santee Street, Los Angeles, California   90015
• includes *4-Part Film Appreciation Series, War on Gobbledygook,* and *Film Appreciation* with study guide

Films 1967
National Catholic Office for Motion Pictures
453 Madison Avenue, New York, New York   10022
• reviews, commentary, ratings of current films

A Guide to Short Films for Religious Education 1968
Two volumes by Patrick J. McCaffrey
Fides Publishers
Box F, Notre Dame, Indiana   46556
- film listings and evaluations, recommendations on use of films, samplings of experiences with various types of audiences

Insight Series 1968
Paulist Productions
17575 Pacific Coast Highway, Pacific Palisades, California   90272
- fiifty film series dramatizing the essential link between human dignity and spiritual faith, categorized in themes of spiritual conflict in the twentieth century

Short Films in Religious Education   1968
By William Kuhns
George A. Pflaum, Publisher
38 West Fifth Street, Dayton, Ohio   54502
- film listings and guides with valuable thematic index—loose-leaf book

Sources for Information and Materials for Screen Education

Academy of Motion Picture Arts and Sciences
9036 Melrose Avenue, Los Angeles, California   90069
- film archives with complete collection of technical and historical information about films
- special screenings for use of students of film

*Center for Film Study
21 West Superior Street, Chicago, Illinois   60610
- service established in 1962: publishes *Catholic Film Newsletter,* which reviews current quality films, gives information on directors, current issues in film study, supplies guides for feature and short films with suggestions for discussion

*Christian Communications Service
223 Main Street, Ottawa 1, Ontario, Canada
- publishes *Christian Communications* magazine and *Media Education,* a mass media handbook for educators

George Eastman House
900 East Avenue, Rochester, New York   14650
- collects and exhibits photographs, motion pictures, photographic equipment
- conducts special studies and seminars for membership of Associates of George Eastman House affiliate organization

* Sources of particular value to teachers of religion.

Larry Edmunds Cinema and Theater Bookshop
6658 Hollywood Boulevard, Hollywood, California   90028
- publishes annual catalog of film books, directors, and other sources in *Cinema List*

Library of Congress
Motion Picture Section, Washington, D.C.
- cataloged films since 1952; record of copyright entries of films and film-strips since 1894

Mass Media Ministries
2116 North Charles Street, Baltimore, Maryland   21218
- a church ministry–oriented group which sponsors a 16mm film rental service and publishes a biweekly newsletter of current short and feature films, television programs, recordings, books

Museum of Modern Art Film Library
11 West 53rd Street, New York, New York   10019
- sponsors film festivals, special showings of films, photography, "light shows"
- issues supplementary lists of films and activities in monthly newsletter

National Council of Catholic Men Film Center
50 East 42nd Street, New York, New York   10017
- publishes lists of selected films with comments

National Council of Churches of Christ in U.S.A.
475 Riverside Drive, New York, New York   10027
- information center for films, reviews, group-study information

National Film Study Project
Center for Communications
Fordham University, New York, New York   10458
- established under grant from National Endowment for the Arts to encourage and develop the study of film and television for schools and study groups
- activities include: research and consultant service for screen education and film production, conferences and workshops, film festivals, distribution of brochures and guides

Religion in American Life, Inc.
184 Fifth Avenue, New York, New York   10010
- interfaith agency of nation's major church and synagogue organizations
- services: preparation, distribution, and promotion of national mass media religious advertising and community materials

St. Clement's Film Association
423 West 46th Street, New York, New York   10036
- concerned with arts as they influence the church—focus on film

- services: film-booking information, discussion guides, regional workshops, monthly bulletin "Eye on the Arts"

Teaching Film Custodians, Inc.
25 West 43rd Street, New York, New York   10036

- activities directed toward use of film in education
- rental service of film excerpts with guides

Handbooks

Dialogue with the World
Encyclopaedia Britannica Films
General Offices
425 North Michigan Avenue, Chicago, Illinois   60611

- church-group discussion handbook for theatrical films with an introduction by G. William Jones

Film and Television in Education for Teaching
British Film Institute
81 Dean Street, London W. 1, England

- result of a joint working party of the Association of Teachers in Colleges and Departments of Education and the British Film Institute

Film Making in Schools and Colleges
By Peter Harcourt and Peter Theobold
British Film Institute
81 Dean Street, London W. 1, England

- valuable for bibliography of basic books for those beginning film-making; specifics on film use from preschool through college

Film Society Primer
American Federation of Film Societies
110-42 69th Avenue, Forest Hills, New York   11375

- compilation of articles about and for film societies

Film Teaching 1964
British Film Institute
Education Department
81 Dean Street, London W. 1, England

- studies in teaching film in formal education; four courses described

A Handbook for Screen Education
By Alex Richardson, R. C. Cannoey, Don Waters
Society for Education in Film and Television
7 Cumberland Close, Twickenham, Middlesex, England

Handbook of Educational Programming for Newman Clubs
National Newman Club Federation
Cleveland, Ohio

295

Media Education
National Catholic Centre for Radio, Television, Film, and Press
830 Bathurst Street, Toronto 4, Canada
- the role of parents and teachers in the communications apostolate

Using Films 1967
Edited by James L. Limbacher
Educational Film Library Association
250 West 57th Street, New York, New York   10019
- contains information for religious groups

Film Periodicals

American Cinematographer (monthly)
American Society of Cinematographers
1782 North Orange Drive, Hollywood, California   90028
- international journal of motion picture photograph and production techniques
- current reports on products, services, and literary
- analyses of new films from a cinematic point of view

Cahiers du Cinema (in English) (monthly)
635 Madison Avenue, New York, New York   10025
- in-depth articles, reviews, and interviews about recent films treated analytically and in terms of production
- shows influence of French New Wave directors

Educational Screen and Audio-Visual Guide Magazine (monthly)
Educational Press Association of America
434 South Wabash Avenue, Chicago, Illinois   60605
- standard guide for educators
- published under auspices of Federation of Film Societies
- reviews and articles about documentaries, features and shorts, film-makers, actors

*Film Comment (quarterly)
11 St. Luke's Place, New York, New York   10014
- contains provocative reviews and articles
- journal of fact and opinion on film art as it relates to contemporary social issues
- contains legal and ethical problems of films, censorship, blacklisting "sexploitation" films, Nazi films, American government film propaganda, avant-garde film, etc.

Film Culture (quarterly)
Box 1499, G.P.O., New York, New York   10001
- America's independent motion picture magazine

- organ of Jonas Mekas and other underground film-makers
- articles and reviews on contemporary culture, reviews of film conferences and festivals, news on experimental film-making

Film Heritage (bimonthly)
University of Dayton
Box 42, Dayton, Ohio   45409

- comments on current films, important directors
- new concepts in film criticism

Film Library Quarterly
Film Library Information Council
101 West Putnam Avenue, Greenwich, Connecticut   06830

- aims to promote wider and more effective use of materials
- develops criteria, standards, procedures in new technology, especially film

Film News (bimonthly)
250 West 57th Street, New York, New York   10019

- film reviews on short and feature 16mm films
- special information on festivals, features, showings

Film Quarterly
University of California Press, Berkeley, California   94720

- highly rated American film magazine which concentrates on style and structure of films, recent and older

Film Reports (The Green Sheet) (monthly)
522 Fifth Avenue, New York, New York   10036

- sponsored by film boards of national organizations
- guide to current entertainment films which gives consideration to a wide range of tastes
- foreign and American films

Film Society Review (eight issues a year)
American Federation of Film Societies
144 Bleecker Street, New York, New York   10012

- organ of American Federation of Film Societies
- contains up-to-minute happenings in film societies
- listing of available films in 16mm
- includes student film-making sources and activities

Filmboard
25 Steadman Street, Chelmsford, Massachusetts   01824

- service of National Screen Education Committee
- by consultants in screen education

Filmfacts (biweekly)
P. O. Box 213
Village Station, New York, New York   10014

- source on domestic and foreign films released in the United States: costs, credits, synopses, major critical reactions, awards

Filmis
The International Catholic Cinema Office
117 via Quattro Fontane, Rome, Italy
- center for information, study, stimulus for film apostolate in the world today
- film reviews
- catalog of 16mm films

Films in Review
National Board of Review of Motion Pictures
31 Union Square, New York, New York   10003
- timely reviews of recent films with articles about actors and directors

Journal of the University Film Producers Association (quarterly)
Ohio State University
Motion Picture Division of the Department of Photography
1885 Neil Avenue, Columbus, Ohio   43210
- practical yet sophisticated journal of articles pertaining to curriculum for film, production, student film analyses
- lists film dissertations

Landers Film Reviews (monthly)
P.O. Box 69760
1545 North Kings Road, Los Angeles, California   90069
- handy loose-leaf sets of film evaluations—16mm

*Media and Methods (formerly *School Paperback Journal*)   (monthly)
Media and Methods Institute
405 Lexington Avenue, New York, New York   10017
- *the* magazine for high school and youth-group teachers of film
- practical presentation of new techniques and approaches; in-depth analyses for use in discussion; film listings for workshop study

Monthly Film Bulletin
British Film Institute
81 Dean Street, London W. 1, England
- comments, evaluations, news of current films—extensive and in-depth

Motion Picture Herald (biweekly)
Quigley Publishing Company
1270 Avenue of the Americas, New York, New York   10020
- up-to-the-minute articles and reviews of films

New Book Review (quarterly)
Herder & Herder
232 Madison Avenue, New York, New York   10016
- publication began in 1966 as *Herder Book Supplement*

- critical reviews of all important religious-oriented books, reviews with authors, periodic reports of educational developments
- media studies and resources for religion teaching
- covers thirty-three publishers

The Newsletter (monthly)
Ohio State University
College of Education, Columbus, Ohio   43210
- film, press, and broadcasting information for teachers

Newsreel (bimonthly)
McGraw-Hill Films
330 West 42nd Street, New York, New York   10036
- for librarians and educators
- considers film as an art form as well as a teaching tool

Saturday Night (monthly)
Saturday Night Publications
55 York Street, Toronto 1, Ontario, Canada
- film editor: Marshall Delaney
- religion editor: William Nicholls
- cultural magazine with emphasis on the arts

Sight and Sound (quarterly)
155 West 15th Street, New York, New York   10011
- in-depth articles on films, directors, stars, genres, trends in film and society

Take One (bimonthly)
P.O. Box 1778
Station B, Montreal 2, Quebec, Canada
- new and exciting ideas that appeal to students of film

Tempo (biweekly)
National Council of Churches
Department of Information
475 Riverside Drive, New York, New York   10027
- news and opinion of the life of the church in society
- film comment and film reviews

Variety (weekly)
154 West 46th Street, New York, New York   10036
- the Bible of show business—covers theatrical films, radio, television, vaudeville, legitimate theater, and film reviews of national and foreign releases—uses lingo of show business

Periodicals for Students of Film—By Students

Cineaste (quarterly)
27 West 11th Street, New York, New York   10011

- magazine for the film student founded in 1967
- multilithed magazine with student articles, reviews, columns, creative ideas, reviews of other film magazines

Filmagazine (irregular intervals)
Associated Students of San Francisco State College
1600 Holloway Avenue, San Francisco, California 94132

- first issue May, 1968
- for students by students; represents avant-garde film-makers; abounds in pop art layouts, montages, poetry, film ideas

General Periodicals with Film Sections—Film Editors Listed

Argosy
205 East 42nd Street, New York, 10017
  WARD KENNEDY

Cosmopolitan
1775 Broadway, New York, New York 10019
  LIZ SMITH

Esquire
488 Madison Avenue, New York, New York 10022
  WILFRED SHEED

Family Circle
488 Madison Avenue, New York, New York 10022
  HARRY EVANS

Glamour
420 Lexington Avenue, New York, New York 10017
  MARGUERITE LAMKIN

Good Housekeeping
959 Eighth Avenue, New York, New York 10019
  RUTH HARBERT

Holiday
641 Lexington Avenue, New York, New York 10022

Life
Time and Life Building
Rockefeller Center, New York, New York 10020
  TOMMY THOMPSON

McCalls Magazine
230 Park Avenue, New York, New York 10017

Mademoiselle
420 Lexington Aevnue, New York, New York 10017
  LEO LERMAN

New Republic
1244 19th Street, N.W., Washington, D.C. 20036
  STANLEY KAUFFMAN

New York Times
229 West 43rd Street, New York, New York 10036

New Yorker
25 West 43rd Street, New York, New York 10036
  JUDITH CRIST

Newsweek
444 Madison Avenue, New York, New York 10022
  JOE MORGENSSEN

Parade
733 Third Avenue, New York, New
York 10017
LLOYD SHEARER

Parents' Magazine
52 Vanderbilt Avenue, New York,
New York 10017
CATHERINE EDWARDS

Redbook
230 Park Avenue, New York, New
York 10017
FLORENCE SOMERS

Saturday Review
380 Madison Avenue, New York,
New York 10017
ARTHUR KNIGHT AND HOLLIS AL-
PERT

*Scholastic Teacher
50 West 44th Street, New York,
New York 10036
MARGARET RONAN

Seventeen
320 Park Avenue, New York, New
York 10022
EDWIN MILLER

This Week Magazine
United Newspapers Magazine Corp.

485 Lexington Avenue, New York,
New York 10017
BOBSY ASHLEY

Time
Time and Life Building
Rockefeller Center, New York, New
York 10020
BRUCE WILLIAMSON

The Torch
Educational Communication Association
1346 F Street, N.W., Washington,
D.C. 20004

Vision (in Spanish)
Vision Building
635 Madison Avenue, New York,
New York 10022
HESTOR PHELPS

Vogue
420 Lexington Avenue, New York,
New York 10017
ALLENE TALMAY

Woman's Day
67 West 44th Street, New York,
New York 10036
HOLLIS ALPERT

Religious Periodicals with Film Sections

America (weekly)
106 West 56th Street, New York,
New York 10019
MOIRA WALSH

Ave Maria (weekly)
Notre Dame, Indiana 46556
EDWARD FISCHER

Catholic World (monthly)
304 West 58th Street, New York,
New York 10019

Christian Advocate (bimonthly)
P.O. Box 423, Park Ridge, Illinois
60068

Christian Heritage (monthly)
Christ's Mission
275 State Street, Hackensack, New
Jersey 07602

Encounter
Christian Theological Seminary
P.O. Box 88267, Indianapolis, In-
diana 46208

* Offers weekly study guide for films recommended for classroom study.

Home Magazine (monthly)
Society of St. Paul, Canfield, Ohio
44406

Lutheran Teacher (monthly)
American Lutheran Church
426 South Fifth Street, Minneapolis,
Minnesota 55415

Mission (monthly)
American Baptist Convention, Valley Forge, Pennsylvania 19481

motive (monthly)
P.O. Box 871, Nashville, Tennessee
37202

National Catholic Reporter (weekly)
300 East 36th Street, Kansas City,
Missouri 64111

Social Justice Review
Catholic Central Union of America
3835 Westminster Place, St. Louis,
Missouri 63108

Tempo (biweekly)
National Council of Churches
Department of Information
475 Riverside Drive, New York,
New York 10027

Today (monthly)
Ave Maria Press
Notre Dame, Indiana 46556

U. S. Catholic (monthly)
Claretian Publications
221 West Madison Street, Chicago,
Illinois 60606

Humanities and Arts Periodicals with Significant Film References for Religious Programming

Cultural Affairs (quarterly)
Associated Councils of the Arts
1564 Broadway, New York, New
York 10036
  • organ of the Associated Councils of the Arts; concerned with arts and their implications for a pluralistic society

The Humanist (bimonthly)
Humanist House
125 El Camino del Mar, San Francisco, California 94121
  • organ of the American Humanist Association
  • journal of contemporary ethical concerns: personal, interpersonal, social

The Humanities Horizon (quarterly)
Educational Services Division
Encyclopaedia Britannica Educational Corporation
425 North Michigan Avenue, Chicago, Illinois 60611

Objectives (quarterly)
Eastman Kodak Company
200 Park Avenue, New York, New
York 10017

Pace (bimonthly)
Pace Publications Moral Re-Armament, Inc.
835 South Flower Street, Los Angeles, California 90017

Selected Catalogs

Guide to Films for Catholic Schools
Contemporary Films
330 West 42nd Street, New York,
New York 10036

828 Custer Avenue, Evanston, Illinois 60202
1211 Polk Street, San Francisco,
California 94109

A Half Century of the American Film
16mm film resource guide
Films Incorporated
435 North Michigan Avenue, Chicago, Illinois 60611

Mass Media Ministries
2116 North Charles Street, Baltimore, Maryland 21218

Office for Audio Visuals 1967-68
Catalog and guide on Audiovisuals

Stewardship Council
United Church of Christ
1501 Race Street, Philadelphia, Pennsylvania 19102
1720 Chouteau Avenue, St. Louis, Missouri 63103

Twyman Films
Annual catalog of religious films
329 Salem Avenue, Dayton, Ohio 45406

Almanacs and Yearbooks

Educational Film Guide
H. W. Wilson Company
950 University Avenue, New York, New York 10452
- cumulative revision issued annually

The Film Index: A Bibliography
H. W. Wilson Company
950 University Avenue, New York, New York 10452
- considered a major bibliography for film

Index to 16mm Education Films 1967
National Information Center for Educational Media
University of Southern California, University Park
3551 University Avenue, Los Angeles, California 9007
McGraw-Hill Book Company
330 West 42nd Street, New York, New York 10036

International Motion Picture Almanac (annual)
Quigley Publishing Company
Rockefeller Center
1270 Avenue of the Americas, New York, New York 10020

- complete index of people, films, and organizations in feature and short

Screen Education (annual)
National Screen Education Committee
15 Trowbridge Street, Cambridge, Massachusetts 02138
- organ of the National Screen Education Committee
- facts and reviews valuable to screen education

Screen Education Yearbook
Society for Education in Film and Television
34 Second Avenue, London E. 17, England

Screen Educators Exchange
1307 South Wabash Avenue, Chicago, Illinois 60605
- publication of Screen Educators Society

Screen World (annual)
Crown Publishers
419 Park Avenue South, New York, New York 10016
- complete and statistical record of current movie season, replete with photographs

303

B. Selected Film Distributors, Libraries, and Organizations

Film Distributors

Academy Film Service
2110 Payne Avenue, Cleveland, Ohio 44114

American Craftsmen's Council
29 West 53rd Street, New York, New York 10019

American Film Registry
831 South Wabash Avenue, Chicago, Illinois 60605

American Friends Service Committee
160 North 15th Street, Philadelphia, Pennsylvania 19102

Anti-Defamation League of B'nai B'rith
222 West Adams Street, Chicago, Illinois 60603
315 Lexington Avenue, New York, New York 10016

Association Films
600 Grand Avenue, New York, New York 10002

Audio Film Center
34 MacQuesten Parkway South, Mt. Vernon, New York 10550
2138 East 75th Street, Chicago, Illinois 60649
406 Clement Street, San Francisco, California 94118

Brandon Films
211 West 57th Street, New York, New York 10019

20 East Huron Street, Chicago, Illinois 60611
244 Kearny, San Francisco, California 94108

Charard Motion Pictures
2110 East 24th Street, Brooklyn, New York 11229

Cinema 16 Film Library
80 University Place, New York, New York 10003

Consort-Orion Films
116 East 60th Street, New York, New York 10022

Contemporary Films/McGraw-Hill
330 West 42nd Street, New York, New York 10036
828 Custer Avenue, Evanston, Illinois 60202

Continental 16
Walter Reade Organization
241 East 34th Street, New York, New York 10016

Economy Film Library
4328 West Sunset Boulevard, Los Angeles, California 90029

Embassy Pictures
1301 Avenue of the Americas, New York, New York 10019

William M. Dennis Film Library
2506½ West Seventh Street, Los Angeles, California 90057

304

Encyclopaedia Britannica Films
4420 Oakton Street, Skokie, Illinois 60076
38 West 32nd Street, New York, New York 10001
3034 Canon Street, San Diego, California 92106

The Film Center of Washington D.C.
915 Twelfth Street N.W., Washington, D.C. 20005

Film Classic Exchange
1926 South Vermont Avenue, Los Angeles, California 90007

Film-Makers Cooperative
175 Lexington Avenue, New York, New York 10016

Films Incorporated
38 West 32nd Street, New York, New York 10001
4420 Oakton Street, Skokie, Illinois 60076
2639 Grand River, Detroit, Michigan 48201
161 Massachusetts Avenue, Boston, Massachusetts 02115
277 Pharr Road N.E., Atlanta, Georgia 30305
1414 Dragon Street, Dallas, Texas 75207
5625 Hollywood Boulevard, Hollywood, California 90028
44 East South Temple, Salt Lake City, Utah 84111
2129 N.E. Broadway, Portland, Oregon 97212

Harrison Pictures
1501 Broadway, New York, New York 10036

Hartley Productions
279 East 44th Street, New York, New York 10017

Ideal Pictures
1010 Church Street, Evanston, Illinois 60201

Institutional Cinema Service
29 East Tenth Street, New York, New York 1003
203 North Wabash Avenue, Chicago, Illinois 60601
2323 Van Ness Avenue, San Francisco, California 94109

International Film Bureau
332 South Michigan Avenue, Chicago, Illinois 60604

International Film Foundation
475 Fifth Avenue, New York, New York 10017

Irving Lesser Enterprises
527 Madison Avenue, New York, New York 10002

Janus Film Library
24 West 58th Street, New York, New York 10019

McGraw-Hill Films
330 West 42nd Street, New York, New York 10036

Mass Media Ministries
2116 North Charles Street, Baltimore, Maryland 21218

Modern Sound Pictures
1410 Howard Street, Omaha, Nebraska 68102

Mogull's Camera and Film Exchange
112 West 48th Street, New York, New York 10019

Museum of Modern Art Film Library
11 West 53rd Street, New York, New York 10019

National Film Board of Canada
680 Fifth Avenue, New York, New York 10019

Roa Films
1696 North Astor Street, Milwaukee, Wisconsin 53202

Royal 16 International
711 Fifth Avenue, New York, New York 10022

Swank Motion Pictures
201 South Jefferson Street, St. Louis, Missouri 63103

Trans-World Films
332 South Michigan Avenue, Chicago, Illinois 60604

Twyman Films
329 Salem Avenue, Dayton, Ohio 45406

United Artists
729 Seventh Avenue, New York, New York 10019

United World Films
221 Park Avenue South, New York, New York 10003

287 Techwood Drive, N.W., Atlanta, Georgia 30313

425 North Michigan Avenue, Chicago, Illinois 60611

2227 Bryant Street, Dallas, Texas 75201

1025 North Highland Avenue, Los Angeles, California 90038

5023 N.E. Sandy Boulevard, Portland, Oregon 97213

David L. Wolper, Inc.
8544 Sunset Boulevard, Hollywood, California 90069

Major University Film Libraries

Brigham Young University
Provo, Utah 84601
Columbia University Press

Center for Mass Communication
440 West 110th Street, New York, New York 10025

Indiana University
Audio-Visual Center, Bloomington, Indiana 47401

Iowa State University
Visual Instruction Service, Ames, Iowa 50010

Kent State University
Audio-Visual Center, Kent, Ohio 44240

New York University Film Library
26 Washington Square, New York, New York 10001

Northern Illinois University
De Kalb, Illinois 60115

Southern Illinois University
Audio-Visual Aids Service, Carbondale, Illinois 62901

Syracuse University Film Library
1455 East Colvin Street, Syracuse, New York 13210

University of California Extension Media Center
2223 Fulton Street, Berkeley, California 94720

University of Illinois
Visual Aids Service
704 South Sixth Street, Champaign, Illinois 61820

University of Michigan
Audio-Visual Center
A-3 South Campus, Ann Arbor, Michigan 48104

University of Southern California
Cinema, Film Distribution Division
University Park, Los Angeles, California 90007

University of Wisconsin
Bureau of Audio-Visual Instruction
P. O. Box 2093, Madison, Wisconsin 53701

Wayne State University
Audio-Visual Utilization Center
5448 Cass Avenue, Detroit, Michigan 48208

Yeshiva University Film Library
526 West 187th Street, New York, New York 10033

Film Organizations

American Federation of Film Societies

144 Bleecker Street, New York, New York 10012

- serves and represents several hundred film societies, especially those on college campuses
- services include: program notes, current trends, publication of *Film Society Review* and *Film Society Newsletter*

American Film Institute

1707 H Street, N.W., Washington, D.C. 20006

- founded June 5, 1967, "to bring cinema to its fullest stature in the country of its birth; to preserve, stimulate, enrich, and nurture the art of film in America"
- activity areas: preservation and cataloging of oustanding American films, education of film audiences, training of film-makers, production, publications

British Film Institute

81 Dean Street, London W. 1, England

- exists to encourage the development of cinema and television, to promote their use as a record of contemporary life, and to foster the serious study of all aspects of both media
- services include: consultants to teachers, lectures, publication of pamphlets on films and film-makers, source of extracts from films and study units
- publishers of *Sight and Sound, Screen Education,* and *Screen Education Yearbook*

International Cinema Association

7101 West 80th Street, Los Angeles, California 90028

- project of Communications Institute of America to promote better motion pictures, establish policy programming, etc.

Motion Picture Association of America
522 Fifth Avenue, New York, New York 10036
- a public relations association source for information on specifics of film

National Screen Education Committee (NSEC—formerly SEFTUS)
15 Trowbridge Street, Cambridge, Massachusetts 02138
- membership advantages include the NSEC News (monthly), *Screen Education,* and the annual meeting
- offers assistance to teachers of youth groups

Television Information Office
745 Fifth Avenue, New York, New York 10022
- services sponsored by television networks to provide information about the medium to educators, students, government agencies, press, clergy, librarians, etc.

INDEX OF FILMS

INDEX OF SUBJECTS